About the author

Don Milligan was an activist in the early days of gay liberation and has written widely on sexuality and politics for many years. He is a journalist and teacher, and is presently writing a book on the emergence of the modern individual.

Sex-life

Sex-life

A Critical Commentary on
the History of Sexuality

Don Milligan

Pluto  Press

LONDON · BOULDER, COLORADO

First published 1993 by Pluto Press
345 Archway Road, London N6 5AA
and 5500 Central Avenue,
Boulder, Colorado 80301, USA

British Library Cataloguing in Publication Data
A catalogue record for this book is available
from the British Library

ISBN 0 7453 0611 X hb
ISBN 0 7453 0612 8 pb

Library of Congress Cataloging in Publication Data
Milligan, Don.
    Sex-life : a critical commentary on the history of sexuality / Don
Milligan.
        p.   cm.
    Includes bibliographical references and index.
    ISBN 0-7453-0611-X. – ISBN 0-7453-0612-8 (pbk.)
    1. Sex. 2. Sex customs. I. Title.
HQ21.M645   1993
306.7–dc20   92-36245
                                                         CIP

Designed and produced for Pluto Press by
Chase Production Services, Chipping Norton
Typeset from author's disks by
Stanford Desktop Publishing Services, Milton Keynes
Printed in Finland by WSOY

Contents

Preface

Books on sexuality generally fall into three categories: theory, practice, and entertainment. This book is about theory. It is an advanced introduction to the discussion of sexuality. However, because there is no broad agreement about what constitutes the theory of sexuality – the vital questions or the principal problems – I have had to avoid the studied neutrality evoked by the authors of many introductory books. Over the last hundred years bespoke theoretical approaches, tailored for particular purposes, have arisen. They cannot easily be employed for different purposes or applied to opposing ideas. Consequently, they must be understood before the nature of the disagreements *between* the different schools of thought can be grasped. It is not a task that can be accomplished by a chronological narrative because of the commerce between opposing ideas, and the way in which they have modified each other throughout the course of the century. However, this book remains a history in the sense that it attempts to derive our current concerns and perplexities from the preceding development. It reaches conclusions that present the reader with more questions, and establishes yet another point of departure for further work. It does not break the log-jam. But in critically surveying the confusion I hope it will make a contribution to our understanding.

My thanks go to all the staff at the Bodleian and the John Radcliffe Science Library at Oxford; the Kean Street Science Reading Room and the British Library at Bloomsbury; and at the Marx Memorial Library at Clerkenwell. I should also like to thank all at Pluto Press for their labours in making the book ready for publication and in presenting it to the public. For their criticism, insight and assistance I must thank Anne Beech, Sarah Ellis, Frank Füredi, Gilly Hoskins, Kate Ingrams, Dave Lee, Sean Mortimer and Roger Pearson. Finally, my thanks go to Gary Banham for his patient support, his editorial assistance, and his ruthless criticism. The conclusions, mistakes and infelicities are all my own.

Don Milligan
August 1992

1 Sexuality

The Nature of the Problem

Sexuality promises oblivion, pleasure beyond endurance. The scientifically minded call this orgasm, the more prosaic prefer to come. Sexuality has many layers, masks, disguises, rituals, but momentary dissolution is always sought; the dissolution of the 'I' into the 'we', or, as Shakespeare might have put it: 'into the double-backed beast'. The dissolution of the frail, singular, mortal into the timeless moment where life goes on forever. Absolution from consciousness is applied for; the demise of all thought is the outcome. Oblivion is the motive of sexuality. It is its purpose. Love can be its obstacle or its catalyst, even its vehicle, but the *petit mort* is sexuality's reason. Without oblivion sexuality is a poor and useless thing. Doctors are consulted and psychiatrists are informed. Sex therapists massage the sagging imagination and flaccid muscles. A grave problem is dealt with. The choked spring, the source of happiness, warmth and security, is bubbling free. Sexuality is sparkling and flowing again. The *possibility* of oblivion has restored sex-life to the patient because *promise* is all that is needed for health. It is competence, not conquests, that admit the personality to sexuality's *Legion of Honour*.[1]

Once admitted to the Order the hold on sex-life must be maintained at all costs because loss of sex-life will result in nasty suspicions, suspicions that concern your capacity for oblivion, and consequently, your fitness for life. So, come alone, come together, come apart. Do whatever you like, but do come. If you do not come you must publicly suffer. You must make known your anxiety and frustration. Such signs are emblems of your normality. You must allude to your capacity, you must talk, joke, dress, move sexually. You must exude your promise like musk. Even when uninterested you must pretend: 'I fake orgasms on occasion when I'm bored with what is happening ... I do it the same way a woman does it, dramatically and with feeling.'[2]

You must fuck as if your life depended on it. Apparently, it does. The desire for sex-appeal and sex-promise is self-evident. The general atmosphere of desire conjured by sexuality has conferred upon us all a

1

full range of *official* and *unofficial* desires. These desires are *natural* and arise within our memories and our imaginations in the manner decreed by our genitals and our gendered infancy, childhood and adolescence. They have made us all (as small-proprietors of sex-life), dependent upon the imperious demands of sexuality. They are desires that can be assumed, anticipated, budgeted for. They concentrate around the desire for an infinitely repeatable series of orgasms; they are desires that centre upon those serial moments of oblivion whose absence condemns us to an existence without happiness, warmth or security. Insatiable but uncomplicated; the desire to do sex and have it done must not be questioned or suspected. Even if the desire remains *unengaged* it must never be denied. If it is, health, mental stability, morality, and even public order, may suffer.

There is a sense in which we understand all this to be true and untrue simultaneously. This phallocentric sexuality has more than an element of truth in it. It is true at the same time that we know it to be false. We know it is all contrivance and artifice. We know, too, sex's ancient human root in our animal constitution; its root in death and predation; its origin in the struggle to survive the violence of bestial competitors, human rivals, and the hostility of climate, seasons and terrain. This sexuality is both given to us by God *and* created by man. This is generally not understood as contradiction but as ambiguity. The two different ideas sit together in a mutually sustaining tension. The philosopher of the British 'moral majority', Roger Scruton, expresses this tension well in his book *Sexual Desire*:

> A tree grows in the soil, from which it takes its nourishment, and without which it would be nothing. And it would be almost nothing *to us* if it did not also spread itself in foliage, flower and fruit. In a similar way, human sexuality grows from the soil of the reproductive urge, from which it takes its life, and without which it would be nothing.[3]

However,

> Sexual desire is a social artefact. Like language, and like morality, it is born from the social relations between human beings, and adds to those relations a structure and firmness of its own. It does not follow from this, however, that sexual desire is 'merely conventional', or not a part of human 'nature'. For some artefacts are natural to human beings: in particular, all those which stem directly from social existence and which form the basis for the construction of personality.[4]

Here, common prejudices are deployed with subtle sophistry and dignified with theoretical status. However, in expressing the tension, and interplay, between natural forces and social forces Scruton is reflecting a central constitutive theme of the debate about sexuality. Throughout the twentieth century sexuality as an object of discussion, and focus of struggle, has been situated in the midst of this conflict. The dichotomy between biological impulses and social impulses; between nurture and nature; between the structural imperatives of society, and the morphology, drives and disposition of the organism have determined the manner in which theorists, moralists and political activists have approached the 'sex question'.

It is a dichotomy that could not have arisen until society had itself become a discrete object of theoretical and empirical investigation. On the basis of the work of Montesquieu (1689–1755), Condorcet (1743–94) and Comte (1798–1857) a modern discussion of the relationship between biology and human culture became possible. Ancient concern with the mythic 'social fabric' underwent a scientific metamorphosis to become the project of analysing and interrogating the *système social*.[5]

Domestic interest in population and social structure in Europe grew in response to these intellectual innovations. However, by the last quarter of the nineteenth century colonisation proved to be the decisive catalyst to the development of work on cultural variety. Anthropology picked its way through the process of cultural disintegration and the annihilation of peoples.[6] Through the veil of conceptions of 'higher' and 'lower' races evolutionary ideas concerning the development of society began to provide empirical support to the idea that human disposition was as much the product of society and the 'level' of social organisation as it was of biological or organic disposition. In 1871 Edward Burnet Tylor published his book *Primitive Culture*. In it he suggested that:

> The condition of culture among the various societies of mankind, in so far as it is capable of being investigated on general principles, is a subject apt for the study of laws of human thought and action. On the one hand, the uniformity which so largely pervades civilisation may be ascribed, in great measure, to the uniform action of uniform causes: while on the other hand its various grades may be regarded as stages of development or evolution, each the outcome of previous history, and about to do its proper part in shaping the history of the future.[7]

Disregarding the assumption that all human societies were but rungs on the ladder of civilisation ascending from *dark* ignorance to the

European *light*, Tylor's book marks an important step forward in the understanding of society. It became possible to 'describe and analyse kinship terminologies and systems, household structures, familial economic functions, sex roles and legal and religious norms as part of the total social fabric'.[8] Lewis Henry Morgan (1819–92), Friedrich Engels (1820–95) and others started to analyse intimate relationships between individuals and the manner in which those relationships con- stituted, layer by layer, the institutions and outlook of a particular society.[9] The struggle to understand what anthropologist Evans- Pritchard called the 'web of belief' ensued. As he explained: 'The web is not an external structure in which he is enclosed. It is the texture of his thought and he cannot think that his thought is wrong.'[10]

However, anthropology could not make real headway in its attempts to comprehend the manifestly familiar (yet different) 'structures of feeling' it encountered at 'the ends of the earth' until the invention of psychoanalysis took the consideration of mental processes beyond the physiological limits established in the nineteenth century. Sigmund Freud's (1856–1939) work in the 1890s culminating in the publication of the *Interpretation of Dreams* in 1899/1900, indicated a profoundly different way of thinking about feelings and perceptions of reality.[11] His elaboration of the unconscious was prefigured in the work of Eduard von Hartmann (1842–1906) and Friedrich Nietzsche (1844–1900).[12] However, Freud's new science took a sharply different direction from his predecessors and from his immediate contemporaries. Whereas Sir James George Frazer (1854-1941), author of *The Golden Bough*, traced and described the common origins of religion in a common human capacity for irrationality, and in our universal entanglement in myth, Freud attempted to develop a science of thought and emotion.[13] In his work can be seen, for the first time, the distinctively modern conception of the existence of a definite and discoverable relationship between psychic life and society; indeed Freud's work arouses interest in the social manifestations of psychic life.

By the outbreak of the First World War it was understood that the social fabric could assume an infinitely variable form. The categories of human thought were not fixed. For Emile Durkheim (1858–1917) they were made, unmade and remade incessantly; they changed places and times.[14] Following Durkheim's death his nephew, Marcel Mauss, continued to do work on this kind of observation. He investigated the 'notion of person; the notion of self', and attempted to show 'the succession of forms that this concept has taken on in the life of men in different societies, according to their systems of law, religion, customs, social structures and mentality'.[15] In accordance with the spirit of the age the most fundamental elements of social thought, the smallest particles of the social fabric, the most sacred assumptions, were laid open to question.

In the early 1930s anthropologist Margaret Mead (1901–78) published the striking observation that societies constructed personalities for themselves. She noted the myriad ways in which societies may elevate, deny, suppress or corral the different dispositions and personalities to hand:

> Now as each culture creates distinctively the social fabric in which the human spirit can wrap itself safely and intelligibly, sorting, reweaving, and discarding threads in the historical tradition that it shares with many neighbouring peoples, it may bend every individual born within it to one type of behaviour, recognising neither age, sex, nor special disposition as points of differential elaboration. Or a culture may seize upon the very obvious facts of difference in age, in sex, in strength, in beauty, or the unusual variations, such as a native propensity to see visions or dream dreams, and make these dominant cultural themes.[16]

At the same time as these developments in anthropology *Annales,* the influential journal of the social sciences, was established. Founded by Lucien Febvre (1878–1956) and Marc Bloch (1886–1944) in 1929, the journal stimulated activities that greatly strengthened interest in the scientific study of the social fabric. *Annales* indicated the possibility of a form of historical scholarship in which the texture and nuance of vanished lives might be reconstituted; studies in which the kinds of connections (or social sinews) in times past might be better understood.[17] For the first time in historical work extensive use was made of police reports, oral testimony and folklore. New subjects like popular culture were opened up and new specialist fields of work like cultural anthropology began to take shape.[18] The foundations of social history were being laid.

In opposition to this view some theorists cite Karl Marx's (1818–83) *The Eighteenth Brumaire of Louis Bonaparte* (published in 1852) as evidence of an older tradition of social history. Some are even tempted to argue that social history 'dates from Herodotus'.[19] However, it is not really possible to sustain much of a case for the existence of social history before the activity of the *Annales* school. And, social history with its contemporary institutional presence and intellectual range does not take shape until the 1950s.[20] After 1960 the idea that history could legitimately concern cultural texture: manners, private spaces, companionship, popular beliefs, pastimes and sexual conduct started to take root. Within the next 10 to 15 years it was firmly established.[21] In the field of sexuality the long process of scholarly maturation met up with the urgent demands of the women's movement and gay liberation.

The academy had not been entirely insulated from the perennial pressure for women's equality, nor even from the emerging struggles of lesbians and homosexual men from the 1940s onwards. However, the developments in the outlook of social scientists and theorists do have a different pace and morphology from that of the popular struggles that came to prominence around 1970. Developments in the academy may be understood as thousands of parallel, crossed and knotted strands, from philosophy, history, anthropology, being twisted together in a shaggy rope. This rope itself is cabled together with ideas, experiences and imperatives drawn from the battles waged by women, by lesbians, by homosexuals and other 'misfits' against sexuality and against the sex-life it confers.

Sexuality has made enemies. Women activists, writers and theorists have challenged the 'eternal' and 'self-evident' verities of sexuality. As Gayle Rubin put it in 1975:

> Men and women are, of course, different. But they are not as different as day and night, earth and sky, yin and yang, life and death. In fact, from the standpoint of nature, men and women are closer to each other than either is to anything else – for instance, mountains, kangaroos, or coconut palms … Far from being an expression of natural differences, exclusive gender identity is the suppression of natural similarities. It requires repression: in men, of whatever is the local version of 'feminine' traits; in women, of the local definition of 'masculine' traits.[22]

This effect of subordination to difference in sexuality and sex-life has provoked a long struggle that has resulted in what Michel Foucault (1926–84) called 'a veritable movement of de-sexualisation'. It has been a liberation movement where women have formulated demands that have gone far beyond the rigid forms of culture and resistance assigned to them by sexuality.[23] In their wake – through the breaches barged open in the edifice of sexuality – have poured the male homosexuals, the transsexuals and a host of other malcontents. The enemies of sexuality have multiplied in direct proportion to the growth of knowledge about it. As more has become known of sexuality the chorus of its enemies has swollen, growing louder, more caustic and corrosive all the time.

This effect is more than popularity born of success. On the contrary, it is the *strange* effect *produced by the knowledge itself*. It is the effect of developments in critical theory that have elaborated an idea of 'constitutive discourse' in which the phenomenon – sexuality – has been produced by the manner in which people have written, talked, legislated, known, and worried about it. In this sense sexuality is understood to have been socially constructed during the elaboration and articulation of the discourse: sexuality. As Monique Wittig expresses it: 'There is no sex. There is but sex that is oppressed and sex that oppresses. It is oppression that creates sex and not the contrary.'[24] In this way many modern theorists seek to articulate the manner in which all the fixed categories of sexuality (e.g., man, woman, lesbian, heterosexual, homosexual) have been brought into existence artificially by the exercise of power. The reality of these categories is not decreed by *essential, ahistorical* or *natural* 'facts', but rather by constantly shifting cultural imperatives. When discussing men and women Gisela Bock recently made the point that:

> Gender or the sexes refer neither to an object, nor to various objects; rather, they refer to a complex set of relations and processes. 'Thinking in relations' is needed in order to understand gender as an analytical category as well as a cultural reality, in the past as well as in the present. Such a vision of gender has implications for all forms of history as they are now practised.[25]

It is important to grasp the nature and extent of the challenge being made to the common ways of approaching or understanding these problems. Old certainties become fraught with new confusions and novel possibilities. Surprises abound. As Wittig explains: 'It would be incorrect to say that lesbians associate, make love, live with women, for "women" has meaning only in heterosexual systems of thought and heterosexual economic systems. Lesbians are not women.'[26]

The logic of this argument is that women have no existence outside of the definite system of knowledge, power and relationships that give rise to sexuality. In the aptly named essay, 'One is not Born a Woman' Wittig insists that 'what makes a woman is a specific social relation to a man, a relation that we have previously called servitude.'[27] These kinds of ideas have turned the certainties of the world upside down. The wholeness and integrity of concepts and the empirical entities and relations that they purport to represent can no longer be relied upon. Put crudely, the rejection by women and homosexuals of the status assigned to them has led to a wholesale assault upon the biological imperatives of sexuality. This in its turn has led to the elaboration of a social history of sexuality that seeks to demonstrate that sexuality is a *social construction* without natural essence. Anti-essentialism therefore is the *raison d'être* of this history. Its purpose is to establish the historical character of phenomena and relations that may have formerly been attributed to changeless nature, or may even have been simply described or alluded to, but remained unexamined.

As a consequence of this strange, multifarious and gradual genesis the history of sexuality is often thought of as emerging from the lacunae created by other historical interests. It is thought to flourish 'in the hazy region where demography, family and women's history, psychohistory, and the history of childhood overlap', where there is 'disagreement about the sources, methodologies, and even the questions to be asked'.[28] Alternatively, it may be presented as a terrain of scholarship, certain in its methods, and clear in its objectives:

> Sex has no history. It is a natural fact, grounded in the functioning of the body, and as such, it lies outside history and culture. Sexuality, by contrast, does not properly refer to some aspect or attribute of bodies. Unlike sex, sexuality is a cultural production: it represents the *appropriation* of the human body and of its physiological capacities by an ideological discourse. Sexuality is not a somatic fact; it is a cultural effect. Sexuality, then, does have a history.[29]

Neither perspective is adequate. The history of sexuality has not been fashioned out of the detritus left by older, grander disciplines. Nor has it grown out of a study of its own 'constitutive discourse' in the fields of nineteenth-century medicine, punishment, morality, law; it does not spring ready-made from modern critical theory via Jacques Lacan (1901–81), Jacques Derrida, Jean-François Lyotard and Michel Foucault. Rather it emerges from the intersection of philosophical, psychoanalytical, sociological, anthropological and demographic practice. The history of sexuality, *as a discrete concern*, is born out of this great ocean of human sciences from the history of *mentalities* and from the maturation of social history. It has been made *possible* by a process of systematic sophistication, throughout the century, of ideas concerning the relationship between mind and society. Its *necessity* has been proclaimed, in the academy and in political life, by its first victims: women and 'sexual deviants'.

Theoretical Strife

Like other fields of historical concern it is not without its theoretical strife and methodological confusion. Many theorists believe postmodernism and deconstruction to be vital. They believe that opposition to biologism and essentialism cannot be deployed without mounting a frontal challenge to the metaphysics and structuralism of more traditional epistemologies. And it is evident that many different sorts of analysis, abstraction and reasoning are enlisted, and muddled up, by the partisans of different writers and activists in the field. Issuing from philosophy, aesthetics and literary criticism, and having considerable refinement and subtlety, deconstruction is at times pressed into service to give a theoretical gloss to political pluralism and to positive initiatives by the state in North America, Britain and Western Europe.[30]

The privileges often awarded to philosophical reflection over and above other forms of exploration has produced other kinds of criticism. In her essay 'Envy: Or With Your Brains and My Looks' Rosi Braidotti grumbled:

> Well may the high priests of postmodernism preach the deconstruction and fragmentation of the subject, the flux of all identities based on phallocentric premises; well may they keep reading into feminism the image of crisis of their own acquired perceptions of human consciousness. The truth is: one cannot deconstruct a subjectivity one has never been fully granted; one cannot diffuse a sexuality which has historically been defined as dark and mysterious.[31]

Braidotti's argument is that the feminists need a political practice to act on 'in the *here* and *now* of our common world'.[32] In her call for theory rooted in experience Braidotti is doing little more than echo Luce Irigaray in her book, *This Sex Which is Not One*:

> A long history has put all women in the same sexual, social, and cultural condition. Whatever inequalities may exist among women, they all undergo, even without clearly realising it, the same oppression, the same exploitation of their body, the same denial of their desire.

Consequently, 'The first issue facing liberation movements is that of making each woman "conscious" of the fact that what she has felt in her personal experience is a condition shared by all women, thus *allowing that experience to be politicised*.'[33]

The caution being sounded here concerns a reluctance on the part of the oppressed to engage in the *deconstruction of their own identities*:

identities that have been painfully built up within the interstices of
sexuality. They are identities that may have proved useful in the battle
to cohere solidarity and defiance in the face of repression. Lesbian
theorists, for example, may be 'less willing to question or to part with
the idea of a "lesbian essence" and an identity politics based on this shared
essence'.[34] However, despite this sort of reticence modern critical
theory – deconstruction and postmodernism – enjoys widespread
currency in the discussion of sexuality. Notions of indeterminancy and
differance have conferred authority upon conceptions of sexuality which
are more or less political. To all intents and purposes, throughout a vast
tranche of the contemporary literature, *sexuality is the offspring* of its own
'constitutive discourse'; *it is a social construction*.

The significance of this is that just as the resistance to the phallocentric
certainties of sexuality are understood to have necessitated the articulation of deconstruction, so this process of deconstruction is credited with
having called into existence the history of sexuality. Whatever one thinks
about this, you cannot escape the conclusion that it is a process that has
produced an awful lot of history. In fact, it has been estimated that there
are more people professionally engaged in historical work today than
during the entire period between the death of Herodotus about 425BC
and 1960.[35] In the field of sexuality all this energy has pushed to the
fore the kind of historical outlook that attempts to eschew traditional
narratives. As F.R. Ankersmit explains:

> The choice no longer falls on the trunk or on the branches, but on
> the leaves of the tree. Within the postmodernist view of history, the
> goal is no longer integration, synthesis, and totality, but it is those
> historical scraps which are the centre of attention.[36]

Ankersmit continues:

> What remains now for Western historiography is to gather the leaves
> that have been blown away and to study them independently of their
> origins. This means that our historical consciousness has, so to speak,
> been turned inside out. When we collect the leaves of the past in the
> same way as Le Roy Ladurie or Ginzburg, what is important is no
> longer the place they had on the tree, but the pattern we can form
> from them *now*, the way in which this pattern can be adapted to other
> forms of civilisation existing now.[37]

What is being questioned here is the possibility of constructing an
historical narrative with the capacity to explain any development that
might be regarded as objective. Objectivity has been abandoned in

deference to the observation that any (more or less) traditional epistemology employed will determine the shape and the character of the relationships being studied. In its place the operation to 'represent the unrepresentable' has ensued. The sensibilities of modern artists; of modern painters, writers and philosophers are employed to posit the idea that the historical imagination is similarly constituted.[38]

As a consequence of this sort of outlook much of the theory of the history of sexuality has become shrouded in what Lyotard might call 'clouds of unrepresentable experience'. Extremely valuable interrogations of all manner of documents, artefacts, relationships and memories have been produced. More is known about attitudes to sex and about how modern sexuality came into existence than ever before. Detailed work of considerable variety, scope and sophistication is underway. However, the sort of outlook advocated by Ankersmit has resulted in a volitional conception of the plurality of experience. Guided by our direct experience, and a measured assessment of our emotions, it is argued that we can understand the fragments, but that we cannot attempt a wider perspective.

This distrust of the historical narrative and of grander visions of the past has not been the only innovation. The privileges accorded experience and emotion have legitimated the elaboration of specific racial and gendered epistemologies. The possibility of the 'grand narrative' is denied (and certainly abandoned) in favour of the particular 'perspective' – experienced – and thereby inhabited by the particular observer. As Alison Jagger, an advocate of a distinctive feminist epistemology, explains: 'Western epistemology has tended to view emotion with suspicion and even hostility. This derogatory Western attitude towards emotion, like earlier Western contempt for sensory observation, fails to recognise that emotion, like sensory perception, is necessary to human survival.'[39]

Her argument is that oppressed people 'have a kind of epistemological privilege' that enables them, via the expression of 'outlaw emotions', to understand better how to go about getting the kind of society in which all could thrive. According to this outlook women are thought to have a special kind of emotional acumen that enables them to understand the mechanisms of domination, and helps them envisage a freer way to live.[40] This, not surprisingly, has led to considerable distress among male academics. The distress is most sharply expressed by male theorists who attempt to inhabit this feminist epistemology. As Stephen Heath modestly put it at a conference of the Modern Language Association:

All I can say here and now in the MLA, in this context, is that we should probably start by trying to grasp *who we are as men,* asking that from feminism rather than wondering what 'they' want from an assumed male us. We need to drop the academic masks, to pose at every moment the sexual determinations of the discourse we develop as we teach and write, to stop knowing as we do, as we want, as we impose – and could 'men in feminism' today be anything but another strategy of that, of our imposition?[41]

Heath is not talking here about fixed identities. It has nothing to do with the division between biological men and women, 'but rather with categories that cannot be predetermined, are never fixed, and are constantly being rearticulated under different representational conditions'.[42]

Now, contrary to ruminations of this kind, the problems of difference, division and identity being alluded to do indeed have quite a lot to do with biology. Even those engaged in the project of challenging biological determinations often remain entranced by the body and its organic concerns. As Jean Baudrillard has despairingly noted:

> ... in the feminist movement it is quite astonishing how the refusal of this [anatomical] destiny – phallic by definition, and confirmed by anatomy – still leads to a fundamental anatomical and biological alternative ... It always concerns the body, if not the anatomical body, then at least the organic and erogenous body, – the functional body for which, even in this fragmented or metaphorical form, pleasure would be its destination, and desire its natural manifestation. This means one of two things: either the body in all this is only a metaphor (but then what is the sexual revolution and our whole culture of the body talking about?), or else we have permanently entered, with the discourse of the body and of woman, into anatomical destiny, into anatomy as destiny.[43]

 In our culture *biological* men and women are, with few exceptions, regarded as *social* men and women. For us not even the *berdache* operates.[44] The words 'men' and 'women' describe categories that (in our empirical knowledge of the everyday world) *are* predetermined, fixed and rarely disturbed, let alone 'rearticulated'. The same is true of our experience of sexuality and of its practical corollary, the sex-life *possessed* by the individual. Sexuality is experienced as a pretty much fixed, natural, expression of our biology. This is as much the case for 'deviants' who are, more or less, given over to pursuing *unofficial* desires as it is for those whose *unofficial* desires are mediated or eclipsed by *official* ones. This is also recognised in feminist descriptions of the diffuse erogeneity possessed by women: 'Fondling the breasts, touching the vulva, spreading the lips, stroking the posterior wall of the vagina, brushing against the mouth of the uterus, and so on. To evoke only a few of the most specifically female pleasures.'[45]

Desire, sexuality and biology appear to be inextricably linked. Not simply because we exist 'as', 'with' and 'in' our bodies, but because our sexual feelings (our sexual potential) continue to be represented and understood as expressions of our biological constitution. Yet somehow the idea that sexuality is an 'ideological imposition upon the body' – that is, a social construction – has taken firm root in the academy and among the political opponents of phallocentric sexuality. The dissonance between the theory of sexuality – the history of sexuality – and its lived practice continues unabated. It is a conflict between history and theory on the one hand, and life on the other. It has become more profound as sexuality has come to be understood as a product of history; an artefact; a social construction. The disharmony has not resulted from a recent or momentous clash, but is one that has been deepening and spreading with the application of modern critical theory – deconstruction and postmodernism – to representations of sexuality and gender.

Strangely, this dissonance is not manifested as a row between theorists who have their heads in the clouds of unrepresentable experience, and practical commonsensical activists. There is a striking degree of unity between the academy and those engaged in the lives of radical and alternative women's groups, lesbian centres and gay scenes. There are tensions which may concern the social gulf between these circles and the academy. There may also be disagreement (as mentioned above) occasioned by the practical desire of oppressed people to hang on to 'essentialist' identities in the face of detailed academic criticism. However, despite the ups and downs and difficulties experienced by these different milieux, there is broad agreement with the productions of modern critical theory on the history of sexuality.

The explanation for this common ground between the academy, feminists, activists, and a wider public of malcontents is the antithesis canvassed between biology and society.[46] The specific victims of phallocentric sexuality know the bitter consequences of an outlook rooted in nature. Biology apparently decrees a particular set of relations between women, children and men. It decrees, like the law, that lesbians and gays should be hunted down like criminals, along with the other 'monsters' and 'misfits' produced by the biological imperatives of sexuality. Consequently, the challenge mounted by philosophers, anthropologists and historians to the fixed determinations of biology (and the established systems of representation) have been received like manna from heaven by those 'driven to rebellion' against the status assigned to them by sexuality.

However, the outstanding problem remains: the impasse between biology and society. The social determination, even the *social construction* of sexuality, still stands balefully opposed to the 'appetites' and 'drives' of our *essential* organic constitution. This impasse has been repeatedly encountered throughout the century. In order to trace the configurations of this repetition this book has been written in the form of a critical review. It outlines and criticises the most influential work on sexuality, from Freud at the beginning of the century, to the productions of modern critical theory at its close. This approach has made possible the combination of an introduction to the history of sexuality with a critical commentary; a commentary that challenges both the essentialism of biology and the pluralism of social construction.

2   Between Mind and Body

Sigmund Freud and Creative Tension

Sigmund Freud embraced the impasse between biology and society in an entirely novel manner. He didn't attempt to deny it, nor to overcome it. He worked with it, manipulated it, investigated it, and maintained it. He attributed the difficult and indecipherable aspects of mental life to the existence of an unknown, unexplored and indefinite region between the surface of the mind and the body. This region he termed the unconscious. Its ethereal character, billowing diffusely from past and present, necessitated the strict separation by Freud of mind, body and society. As he attempted to describe their definite constitutive relations he was compelled to abstract mental life from social circumstance and organic disposition. It was upon this abstraction that he constructed his interpretation of dreams and his psychoanalytic theory. At all times the impasse between biology and society was maintained, not as a barrier, but as a creative tension that resulted in the elaboration of new kinds of knowledge concerning the evolution of the adult within the constitution of the person.

Consequently, Freud's work is marked by a strange ambivalent quality: rigorous science gives way to vague intuition; reactionary ideas are employed to reach revolutionary conclusions, prejudices are deployed to reveal startling innovations. He moves sentence by sentence through a paragraph, turning over ideas, accepting some and rejecting others. He then takes the entire consideration, not just the conclusions, through to the next paragraph.[1] This literary device is his method of considering and evaluating ideas. It is an elusive strategy which permits patriarchal certainties, commensurate with the outlook of Moses, to coexist with indeterminations of a literary and poetic kind. It is a distinctive literary style. It precludes the possibility of putting ticks and crosses against this hypothesis, or that *unhesitating assertion*. Every statement made is modified, qualified and undermined by subsequent statements. For example:

> From what I have seen of intuition, it seems to be the product of a kind of intellectual impartiality. Unfortunately, however, people are

are seldom impartial where ultimate things, the great problems of science and life, are concerned. Each of us is governed in such cases by deep-rooted internal prejudices, into whose hands our speculation unwittingly plays. Since we have such good grounds for being distrustful, our attitude towards the results of our own deliberations cannot well be other than one of cool benevolence. I hasten to add, however, that self-criticism such as this is far from binding one to any special tolerance towards dissentient opinions. It is perfectly legitimate to reject remorselessly theories which are contradicted by the very first steps in the analysis of observed facts, while yet being aware at the same time that the validity of one's own theory is only a provisional one.[2]

Freud's ruminations cannot be illuminated by strict definitions or justified by their conclusions. Always, the entire procedure – the method, the approach, the outlook – has to be considered.

In the light of all this it is interesting to note that Freud's work has been exposed principally to three sorts of criticism. The first centres upon the way that his social background and personal prejudices disfigured the structure and findings of his research. The second disputes the claims of psychoanalysis to scientific interest. The third is more serious, concerning Freud's views on biology and the destiny of women. If successful (and taken together), attacks upon this range of problems would erase the product of his thought. However, on closer inspection, Freud is substantial, not at all enigmatic, and less dogmatic than many of his opponents have suggested.

Freud was born into a family of itinerant traders at Freiburg in the Hapsburg province of Moravia in 1856.[3] His family was Jewish and he grew up at a time of change and dramatic upheaval. When he was three years old all legal restrictions imposed upon Jews in Austria were abolished; a year later his family moved to Vienna, the German-speaking capital of the empire. By the time he was 12 Jews had been granted equal political rights. This emancipation was both a product and a cause of the decay of Jewish handicrafts and petty trading in the small towns and villages of Moravia, Galicia, Poland and Russia. Jews in these areas had for centuries been confined within ghettos or compelled to live as itinerant pedlars. Their outlook was dominated by religious orthodoxy and the hidebound rules and etiquette of closed communities.[4] It was rapidly dissolved by mass migration from remote rural areas to bustling progressive cities. Between 1840 and 1880 the Jews of Europe became an urban people.[5] The religious and parochial heirarchy of Jewish life was broken. For the first time, Jews were granted access to the institutions and professions of European legal, scientific and artistic life. The result was nothing less than a Jewish renaissance; an outburst of brilliant scientific and artistic activity. Freud's education and outlook was a product of the intellectual upheavals wrought by these transformations.[6]

Attempts to understand Freud as a product of a kind of 'Victorian' stability dominated by overstuffed furniture and bearded patriarchs are doomed to failure. It is true that Freud's career was composed of an extraordinarily steady climb from the vulnerable petit bourgeois to the upper ranks of a well-to-do profession.[7] He was certainly no firebrand. In fact the imperial army assessed him as an 'honest, firm and cheerful' officer; a man who enjoyed the confidence of the soldiers and civilians alike.[8] However, we have no reason to suppose that this made him conventional or narrow in his clinical or scientific concerns. As a matter of course, Freud 'was a child of his own times'.[9] But 'his own times' were characterised by incessant technical innovation, and vibrant scientific, artistic and political change. Throughout the most active period of Freud's life German science, in physics alone, witnessed the formulation of quantum theory (1900), the promulgation of the special theory of relativity (1905), the general theory of relativity (1916), and the uncertainty principle (1927).[10] At the age of 75 Freud enjoyed a pleasure trip in an aeroplane at Berlin, but from the moment of their invention he hated the radio, the telephone and even the typewriter. He liked motor cars, and detested his children's bicycles.[11] He thoroughly enjoyed the vacations he took without his wife, but he also hoped that most women would occupy themselves exclusively with the affections of a man: in youth as a daughter (or as an adored darling of the 'sweetheart' variety), and subsequently as a wife and mother.[12] Prejudices of this sort undoubtedly shaped the life of Sigmund's wife and daughters, but they were not the source of his psychoanalytic findings concerning mental life or the evolution of women.[13]

Freud's theoretical interest in sexuality grew directly out of his clinical practice. But nothing happened suddenly. There was no moment on the road to Damascus. He entered the university of Vienna as a medical student in 1873, but did not graduate until 1881. He had been doing research and publishing papers on physiology and neuropathology since 1876, however.[14] In the mid-1880s his professional interests gradually shifted from neurology to psychopathology. As he candidly explained: 'From the material point of view, brain anatomy was certainly no better than physiology, and, with an eye to pecuniary considerations, I began to study nervous diseases.'[15]

His marriage to Martha Bernays in 1886 and the birth of their first child, Mathilde, during the following year necessitated a steady and growing income. Preoccupied with earning money Freud set up private practice in nervous diseases, and continued his work on cerebral palsy in children at Vienna's Kassowitz Institute. As he prospered he began detailed work on aphasia and upon other groups of physical symptoms that seemed to be nervous in origin.[16] The result of this work was the publication in 1895 by Freud and Josef Breuer (1842–1925) of the celebrated *Studies on Hysteria*. In the case history on *Anna O* Josef Breuer reported how Anna's symptoms disappeared, one by one, after she had told Breuer in detail of the circumstances surrounding the particular symptom's first occurrence.[17] *Anna O* described this procedure as the 'talking cure'.[18] Both men, and their patients, had stumbled upon something that was very strange. Freud was disconcerted:

> I have not always been a psychotherapist. Like other neuropatholo-gists, I was trained to employ local diagnoses and electro-prognosis, and it still strikes me myself as strange that the case histories I write should read like short stories and, as one might say, they lack the serious stamp of science. I must console myself with the reflection that the nature of the subject is evidently responsible for this, rather than any preference of my own.[19]

Originally Freud had emulated Breuer in the use of hypnotic suggestion, but he was unhappy about the uncertain effects and inter-ferences that accompanied hypnosis. As an alternative he gradually developed the 'talking cure' into the technique of free association or *freier Einfall*. Freud came to assume that the content of free association (literally the ideas that spontaneously entered the patient's mind) would, however bizarre and apparently irrelevant, be related to the subject designated. However, he had to account for the fact that any rational connection between the patient's talk and the particular matter in hand often appeared to be absent. He had to account for connections that were unrecognisable. This he did by postulating the existence of *resistances* that obstructed the patients' access to their own unconscious. It became the task of analysis to assist the analysand to overcome such resistances.

It necessitated the elaboration by Freud and his colleagues of an entire symbolic universe where the raw material of free association, the patient's words, had to be reinterpreted by both the analyst and the analysand. The greatest single step forward in this process was made with the publication by Freud of the *Interpretation of Dreams* at the close of 1899. In it Freud established a distinction between the *manifest* content and the latent content of dreams. It was a distinction strictly analagous to the distinction between the conscious, and the unconscious, employed by analysts using free association. The manifest content (the dream-content) is what is available to consciousness, but it is the latent content (the dream-thought) that holds the meaning of the dream. As Freud explained: 'It is from these dream-thoughts and not from a dream's manifest content that we disentangle its meaning.'[20]

He conceived of the dream-content as a transcript of dream-thoughts into 'another mode of expression, whose characters and syntactic laws it is our business to discover by comparing the translation'.[21] Dream-thoughts were *displaced* and *condensed* into the material that eventually appears to the mind in the form of the manifest content. But:

> You must not suppose that we think nothing of this endless diversity in manifest dreams ... But for the moment ... we ask the dreamer, too, to free himself from the impression of the manifest dream, to divert his attention from the dream as a whole on to the separate portions of its content and to report to us in succession everything that occurs to him in relation to each of these portions – what associations present themselves to him if he focuses on each of them separately.[22]

Freud freely acknowledged the manner in which dreams are 'distorted and mutilated by memory', but he did not consider this to present any more of an obstacle than that presented by condensation and displacement.[23] However, Freud did not attempt to minimise the difficulties inherent in attempting to understand the means of representation in dreams.[24] He did not possess a pack of Tarot cards with its *minor* and *major arcana* to provide all the components necessary for an 'on-the-spot' revelation. The symbolic meaning of particular thoughts could not be read off from a tabulation. They could only be understood as part of the particular history of the particular patient. Freud took the view that only the most painstaking and careful analysis, lasting months, if not years, would produce reliable results.

The interpretation of dreams opened the way to the unconscious. It was an entry effected circuitously by deep analysis of the spontaneous product of the analysand's mind. Of course, interest in spontaneous or automatic thoughts was not new; not even in 1900.[25] What was novel, however, was Freud's systematic attempt to apply it to the analysis and alleviation of a large range of nervous disorders.[26] Freud was particularly aggrieved by attempts to show that his method of free association and analysis was unscientific. He was stung by Henry Havelock Ellis's (1859–1939) essay 'Psycho-Analysis in Relation to Sex'. In it, apart from likening Freud's method to that of the Swedenborgian mystic and poet, Dr J.J. Garth Wilkinson, Ellis claimed psychoanalysis for art. He said of Freud:

> His activities are, above all, plastic and creative, and we cannot understand him unless we regard him as, above all, an artist. He is indeed an artist who arose in science, and to a large extent remains within that sphere, with disconcerting results alike to himself and his followers when he, or they, attempt to treat his work as a body of objectively demonstrable scientific propositions.[27]

This confusion of Freud's method of free association and pyschoanalysis with art sprang from a misunderstanding of Freud's scientific background. Freud thought of himself as a positivist. He wanted nothing to do with the older German doctrine of *natur philosophie* nor with the 'germ plasm', 'genetic energy' and *vitalism* of his French contemporary, Henri Bergson (1859–1941).[28] However, it remained the case that speculation and intuition had an important and entirely honourable part to play in Freud's science.[29] Positivist, or not, he came from the tradition of Eduard von Hartmann who explained his method thus:

> I hold all speculation to be be baseless, which contradicts the clear results of empirical investigation, and conversely hold all conceptions and interpretations of empirical facts to be erroneous, which contradict the strict results of a purely logical speculation.[30]

Throughout the nineteenth century German science progressed triumphantly through this subjection of science to the products of philosophical speculation, and the exposure of the resulting hypotheses to rigorous empirical investigation. Its metaphysics threw up vast speculative structures; fantastic creations that were demolished, modified or rebuilt on the basis of empirical findings. But always this creative tension was maintained between the metaphysics and the physics; between the ideal and the real; between singular reality and Johann Friedrich Herbart's 'multiplicity of the "reals"'.[31] It would be foolish to conceive of German physics, chemistry, physiology or neurology developing *in spite* of this idealism. On the contrary, the maintenance of the dialectic between the reality of thought, and thoughts on the materiality of the world, permitted gigantic strides in science.

Freud's work was an integral part of this tradition. Building on the physiological work of the positivists Ernst Wilhelm Brucke (1819–92), Maynert (1833–92) and Siegmund Exner (1846–1926), he was able to commence the development of his elaborate and *mythological* metapsychology.[32] Freud was able to draw upon their speculations concerning the structure of the mind and its relations with the brain in order to develop psychoanalytic theory and push its clinical practice forward. As Henri Ellenberger explains in his excellent discussion of Freud's antecedents:

> Freud was the author of a powerful synthesis in which it is an almost impossible task to discern what came from outside and what was his personal contribution. In fact, many of Freud's theories were known before him or belonged to contemporary trends. Freud drew from his masters, his colleagues, his friends, his associates, his patients and his disciples.[33]

For the 20 years before his development of psychoanalysis Freud was engaged in microscopic anatomy and in clinical and theoretical neurology. He brought this experience to bear in his development of psychoanalytic theory. However, the demands of his clinical practice in nervous disorders moved him decisively beyond the limitations of empirical knowledge of both thought and what he regarded as its material *parallel* or *substratum*, the brain. In order to conceive of movements in the mind he was compelled to postulate an entire energetic economy; a mental economy composed of quantities and exchanges of energy that are channelled, dammed up, converted, deflected and, finally, discharged. Laplanche and Pontalis regard this idea of psychical processes as 'economic' as the 'most hypothetical' concept of Freud's metapsychology. In view of the fact that they also describe his metapsychology as 'an ensemble of conceptual models which are more or less far-removed from empirical reality' it can be seen that we are being edged decisively towards the mythological.[34]

It will be readily understood from all this that any exclusive focus on the scientific status or claims of psychoanalysis would preclude the possibility of understanding Freud's outlook. Whether it is scientific or not is no longer of the slightest importance. It was important for Freud because he had to dispose of charges of quackery and mysticism. But it is of no importance to us. Neither does it matter whether Freud ever actually cured anybody or not. No doubt this was of great interest to his patients, and perhaps continues to concern modern analysts and their analysands. For our present purposes, however, the effectiveness or otherwise of free association is irrelevant. Above all, we are interested in the ensemble of mental concepts employed by Freud. What matters is the way that his metapsychology sought to explain the importance of sexuality, and the mysteries of mental life in the evolution of the person. Rather than dwelling upon the efficacy or validity of Freud's outlook and practice we need to know better the kinds of questions and answers his approach canvassed within the history of sexuality.

Instinct, Drive and Envy

This way of looking at Freud brings us to the most confusing concept deployed by psychoanalysis: *instinct*. The belief that physical attraction and erotic practice have an instinctual basis is perhaps the most common way of understanding sexuality. It is when we reach the question of instinct that it appears that classical psychoanalysis intersects, for the first time, with a more ordinary – less abstract – approach. We are soon disappointed, however. In Freud's work instincts are not to be confused with the predisposition of bees to build hives or of birds to build nests. In psychoanalytic theory instincts are psychical movements; psychical movements that lie 'on the frontier' *between* the mental and the physical. They are not physical. Nor are they mental. They merely represent a stimulation originating in physical life to the life of the mind. More precisely, instincts are psychical movements that represent a continuously flowing source of stimulation from within the body.[35]

An instinct must be understood as a charge of energy from a source in the body; the aim of which is to eliminate the tension expressed by the stimulation. It is easy to see from this that the concept of instinct lies at the centre of Freud's conception of an energetic economy of the mind, and of relations between the mind and the body. It is as if Freud had taken on board Franz Anton Mesmer's (1734–1815) 'animal magic', or more directly, the conception of psychic energy pioneered by Gustav Fechner (1801–87). It seems that Freud's view of the mind as the centre of an energetic economy is derived from *natur philosophie*. Or at least from subsequent theories of nervous energy and mental energy; theories that emphasised parallels between physical energy and an imagined physical aspect of mental processes.[36] It is in this manner that the instincts discussed by Freud must be understood to represent the body to the mind.

Instincts have a source (within the body), and an aim (in the elimination of tension at the source), but their object (the manner in which the instinct seeks satisfaction), is undetermined. In the sexual instinct this mode of satisfaction is, to begin with, polymorphous: it aims at the elimination of tension but without attachment to a specific object. The instinct does not register normal desires or perverse desires; it does not register particular genders or particular sorts of practices as its object. Consequently, the sexual instinct may be conceived as representing stimulation within a range of erotogenic zones. But, essentially, it is a 'homeless' instinct; an instinct without a definite object or destination.[37] Freud dealt with this difficulty by postulating the existence of the *libido*. The libido is the energy that 'finances' the transformations that enable the instinct to realise its aim in an attachment to a specific object.[38] In Latin *libido* means desire; in Freudian parlance libido means the dynamic manifestation of the sexual instinct in the mental history of the individual.

Matters become further complicated, however, with Freud's introduction of the hypothesis of phylogenetic inheritance. Not satisfied with the idea that a disposition towards particular sorts of psychical response arise within the history (or the lifetime) of an individual, Freud admits the possibility that dispositions (or modes of reaction) might, together with traces of ancestral experience, be inherited.[39] Clearly, Freud preferred the idea of ontogenetic explanations that set every disposition, instinct and memory within the lifetime of the individual.[40] However, he attributes common mental phenomena, for which he can find no explanation in the history of the subject, to phylogenetic inheritance. For example, Freud learned of many accounts of people observing parental intercourse during childhood. He was also told of seductions in childhood by fathers and uncles, and of boys being threatened with castration. He was disposed to believe all of this in some cases, but not in all of them. He did not believe that such fantasies could be true in every, or even in most of the cases reported to him. So he felt obliged to attribute them to his phylogenetic hypothesis: 'These scenes of observing parental intercourse, of being seduced in childhood, and of being threatened with castration are unquestionably an inherited endowment, a phylogenetic heritage, but they may just as easily be acquired by personal experience.'[41]

These are the *primal* fantasies and their universality is always attributed in psychoanalytic theory to the 'fact that they constitute a phylogenetically transmitted inheritance'.[42] They are found in every subject and inform human sexuality: 'Sexuality cannot therefore be explained solely in terms of the endogenous maturation of the instinct – it has to be seen as being constituted at the core of intersubjective structures which predate its emergence in the individual.'[43]

What this means is that according to classical psychoanalytic theory sexuality is composed of a portion of inherited and a portion of acquired instincts and memories. However, no portion may be said to be ready-made. Sexuality is not solely a product of biological evolution or of the historical experience of the individual. It is the dynamic product of both phylogenetic and ontogenetic factors. In infancy it is diverse, covering all those excitations that seek pleasure (in the release of tension) which are not already explained by eating, breathing and excreting. As Freud emphasises:

> Impressive analogies from biology have prepared us to find that the individual's mental development repeats the course of human development in an abbreviated form; and the conclusions which psycho-analytic research into the child's mind has reached concerning the high value set on the genitals in infancy will not therefore strike us as improbable.[44]

These intimations of infantile sexuality were originally derived from detailed studies of hysteria and neurosis. As Freud explained:

> A formula begins to take shape which lays down that the sexuality of neurotics has remained in, or been brought back to, an infantile state. Thus our interest turns to the sexual life of children, and we will now proceed to trace the play of influences which govern the evolution of infantile sexuality till its outcome in perversion, neurosis or normal sexual life.[45]

It was observed that the 'mental life of all neurotics (without exception) shows inverted impulses', and the 'fixation of their libido upon persons of their own sex'.[46] However, for the first time, the conditional character of normality was noted. Although the neurotic were invariably perverse, the perverse were not necessarily neurotic.[47] By 'perverse' Freud meant lengthy foreplay and the use of the mouth and the anus as 'genitals' in sodomy, fellatio and cunnilingus. In his discussion of 'anatomical extensions' he made clear that he was depicting purely social definitions of perversion. He emphasised this with his view that normal behaviour also required explanation. In 1915 in the course of a consideration of homosexuality he wrote:

> Thus from the point of view of psycho-analysis the exclusive sexual interest felt by men for women is also a problem that needs elucidating and is not a self-evident fact based upon an attraction that is ultimately of a chemical nature. A person's final sexual attitude is not decided

until after puberty and is the result of a number of factors, not all of which are yet known; some are of a constitutional nature but others are accidental.[48]

Furthermore, the discovery of the constitutional root of the sexual instinct (derived phylogenetically and ontogenetically) within infantile sexuality revealed the germ of perversion within the sexual history of every person. In every childhood the sexual instinct is unregistered. It is always a polymorphous instinct. Thus experience of the sexual instinct as an instinct without a specific object or mode of satisfaction is universal. For Freud, it became clear that a disposition to perversion was, to some extent or another, innate in everyone. It was noted that normal sex-life was achieved only after a lengthy process of psychical and physical maturation within society.[49]

As a consequence of work on the aetiology of neuroses and infantile sexuality, psychoanalysis discovered that 'the libidinal relations to the parents' were 'the centre and the acme of the development of childish sexuality'.[50] Clinical observations and the need for theoretical coherence indicated the fundamental part played by sexual rivalry between the child and the parent of the same sex. This very early innovation in psycho-analytic theory gave rise to the *oedipus complex*. This complex manifests itself as 'a desire for the death of the rival – the parent of the same sex – and a sexual desire for the parent of the opposite sex'.[51] It is said to exist in all societies and is only overcome by the emergence of a particular object choice. The oedipal arises from the preoedipal during which the attachment of infants of either sex is for their mother. However, this preoedipal mother-attachment always gives way to the oedipal phase which lasts until the child is five or six. The oedipal effect then goes into abeyance during the years of sexual latency, only to return in a modified form at puberty; finally dissolving into identification with the parents via object choice and the development of sublimations.

The oedipal complex is experienced by children of both sexes.[52] However, this apparent similarity must not be allowed to obscure an important difference between the way boys and girls encounter the same developmental phase. For the boy the shift from the preoedipal to the oedipal does not entail a shift away from mother. On the contrary, his preoedipal attachment to his mother simply gets very much stronger and assumes an erotic aspect. It is on the basis of this, and upon his appre-hension of the relations between his mother and father, that there arises a murderous hostility towards his father. His father becomes his rival in his desire for his mother.

For the girl, however, matters are more complicated. Not only does she have to dispense with her preoedipal attachment to her mother, she has also to change her attitude to her own body. She has to replace her clitoris in favour of the vagina. She has to move from the 'male' relationship to her clitoris to a 'female' relationship to her vagina. As Helene Deutsch explained in 1925:

> The man attains his final stage of development when he discovers the vagina in the world outside himself and possesses himself of it sadistically. In this his guide is his own genital organ, with which he is already familiar and which impels him to the act of possession.

In complete contrast: 'The woman has to discover this new sexual organ *in her own person*, a discovery which she makes through being masochistically subjected by the penis, the latter thus becoming the guide to this fresh source of pleasure.'[53]

This idea is based upon the observation made by Freud that little girls are dismayed by the inferiority of their clitoris:

> They notice the penis of a brother or playmate, strikingly visible and of large proportions, at once recognize it as the superior counterpart of their own small and inconspicuous organ, and from that time forward fall a victim to envy for the penis.'[54]

In contrast, boys experience no such difficulties. The boy retains his mother as object and retains his orientation towards his genitals.[55] The oedipus complex reveals not only the task faced by little girls in the drastic shift away from preoedipal to oedipal – from mother towards father – but also the shift away from their clitoris (as penis) towards a recognition of their female status in the vagina. The girl has to give up her desire for a penis because it 'is incompatible with actual possibilities'. As Juliet Mitchell explains: 'The only legitimate form (or the only form legitimated by culture) is that the idea (the representation of the wish) is displaced and replaced by the wish for a baby which is entirely compatible with reality.'[56]

It is in observations of this sort that Freud's theory, and its labyrinth of hypotheses, encounter their most serious objections. Freud believed that women have little sense of justice because envy is predominant in their mental life; their smaller capacity for sublimating their instincts resulting in weaker social interests.[57] Taken together with his belief in the 'natural sexual passivity of women', these ideas place him squarely in the camp of biological determinism.[58] However, the minute this conclusion is reached we come across the contrary: 'But we must beware in this of underestimating the influence of social customs, which similarly force women into passive situations. All this is still far from being cleared up.'[59]

He makes the point that psychoanalysis 'knows nothing' about how the differentiation between the sexes came about:

> In conformity with its peculiar nature, psycho-analysis does not try to describe what a woman is – that would be a task it could scarcely perform – but sets about enquiring how she comes into being, how a woman develops out of a child with a bisexual disposition.[60]

What kind of response is possible to all of this from those opposed to the conception of natural roots for the social subordination of women? It goes without saying that psychoanalysis is not 'an equal opportunity theory'.[61] But is it also a theory that must depict the subordination of women as an expression of biological inferiority? This is a question to which there seems to be no satisfactory answer. It is possible to accept Freud's observations of penis envy as a social phenomenon; as a deep psychical presentation of the social domination of women by men. It is possible to accept classical psychoanalysis without regarding the inferiority betrayed by penis envy as inevitable. According to Simone de Beauvoir (1908–86),

> the childish desire for the penis is important in the life of the adult woman only if she feels her femininity as mutilation; and then it is a symbol of all the privileges of manhood that she wishes to appropriate the male organ.[62]

So, even

> the psychoanalytic portrait of the female as a failed male has been accepted as the deepest analysis available of the effects of patriarchy (or the nuclear family as the carrier of patriarchy) on men's attitudes toward women and women's attitudes toward themselves.[63]

According to Elizabeth Young-Brueuhl this kind of approach has become more influential. For many it is an interpretation that appears a little too sanguine. In 1937 and again in 1938 Freud made clear his belief that the 'repudiation of femininity can be nothing else than a biological fact, a part of the great riddle of sex.'[64]

Although in 1913 he had made explicit his belief that psychoanalysis 'can lay claim to no special psychical characterisation' of differences between the sexes he was not deterred from espousing biological determinism. He designated masculine and feminine as active and passive *qualities*. However, he was careful to specify that they were qualities determined by their aims not by the instincts themselves.[65] This was a shrewd explanation because it accommodated activity on the part of women taken in order to achieve the aim of passivity. But it does not modify the theory of instincts. According to this the sexual aims are the same for both male and female: the elimination of tension at sites of erotogenic excitation. It must therefore be the different character of the somatic sites in men and women that contributes decisively towards the different manner in which the instinct seeks satisfaction. In Freud's system activity and passivity are derived from the different physical forms of men and women, that is, from their biology. But again Freud is well aware of the nagging difficulties: 'In truth, it is hardly possible to give a description which has general validity. We find the most different reactions in different individuals, and in the same individual the contrary attitudes exist side by side.'[66]

There are other difficulties with Freud's work that will be touched upon in later chapters. However, for the moment, the difficulty in hand is the most surprising one: it concerns his unquestioning acceptance of sexuality as the problem it appeared to be. Why did Freud assume that the revelations concerning sexual evolution within mental life were true? Why did he accept their presentation in the form of hysterical symptoms, and their role in the aetiology of neuroses? Why did he regard the constitutive role of sexuality in the psyche as authentic? This question is not raised in order to repeat the oft-made charges of 'pan-sexualism' and 'sexualism'.[67] It is raised in order to focus attention on the fact that Freud, like the sexual pathologists, assumed that sexuality and maturation towards normality or perversity was an important scientific matter.[68]

Freud assumed that sexuality, normal and perverse, was a matter for medicine and for science. The value of this approach may seem self-evident, but few people (if any) would have thought like this before the last third of the nineteenth century.[69] For all Freud's concern with the evolution of the person – his concern with the history of the individual subject – he paid scant attention to the historical location of his work. *Totem and Taboo, The Future of an Illusion, Civilisation and its Discontents* and *Moses and Monotheism* discuss society in relation to the evolution of the individual, but do not seek to identify the historical character of the interest deployed by psychoanalysis in sexuality.[70] For Freud sexuality is a constitutional impulse, a somatic excitation, whose evolution and mode of satisfaction lie at the heart of the psychogenesis of mankind, and through the employment of libidinal forces, structure the mental life of the individual. He does not ask the question: why is sex so important? He assumes an ahistorical role for sexuality in the prehistory of the adult and in that of the infant. Freud does not challenge (or even question) the reason for his relentless construction of hypotheses that concern the manifestations of sexuality in mental life. Evidently this is a modern question that has to be both posed (and answered) by the unfolding history of sexuality.

However, despite the problems bequeathed to us by Freud it is remarkable that he was able to maintain the tension between biological determinism and the psychogenesis of the individual (and of the species) within society. It is true that he believed that 'for the psychical field, the biological field' played the 'part of the underlying bedrock'.[71] But his practice of constantly repudiating his own assertions, or at least reducing them to the status of hypotheses (or even speculations), enabled him to develop the most systematic, and the most creative, investigation into the part played by sexuality in the formation of character-disposition-personality.

It is in the self-conscious manner with which Freud insisted upon the maintenance of the opposition between biology and society that we can see his brilliance. It enabled him to present the life of the mind and the life of the body, normality and perversion, maturity and immaturity, masculinity and femininity, as evidence of constitutional ambivalence. He presented oppositions of this sort as both permanent and necessary. But there was a price to pay: the systematic abstraction of mental life from social life, and the abstraction of social life from biological circumstance. This procedure was essential for Freud's establishment of an economy of dynamic transactions in tensions, and the means of their relaxation.

Dealing in tensions was Freud's stock in trade; shrewdly he demanded their displacement, sublimation or discharge by their oppositions. This economy of oppositions had to be maintained in order to prevent a final settlement. Evidently Freud believed that every concept must honour the debt that it owes to its opposing idea. Grasping this refusal of conclusion, or more fashionably, *the rejection of closure*, is the key to understanding Freud's work. It was, no doubt, a procedure indicated by the problems of clinical and theoretical analysis, but its principal effect has been to enhance rather than dispel the mystery surrounding sexuality and the life of the mind. It is a mystery in which the fictitious and metaphorical aspects of Freud's system have all but eroded the claims of psychoanalysis to scientific interest.[72] Consequently, it is as literature, not as science, that Freud's work survives. It is because of their insistence on the ambivalence and ambiguities of sexuality (their rejection of conclusion and closure) that these writings continue to arouse great public interest. This is, therefore, an appropriate juncture to turn our attention towards those who seek to dispel the mystery of sex with a more 'parsimonious vision of the universe'.[73] Our interest must turn from the overdeterminations of classical psychoanalysis to those who wish to trade in the closures and conclusions of natural science.

3 The Nature of the Body

The Deployment of Biology

Because our sexual feelings appear to arise from within our bodies they are thought of as constitutional. They are inseparable from us, and who we imagine ourselves to be. Consequently the built-in ambivalence noted by Freud between normality and perversion, maturity and immaturity, masculinity and femininity, is disturbing. The conception that perverse desires are, at some stage or another, within the experience of everyone may be fascinating, but it is not reassuring. We are unsettled by such revelations. Instead of home truths and certainty we are offered metaphor, mythology and mystery. In our journey through infancy, childhood and adolescence, we are guided by mortal fears, obscene desires, and murderous passions. Instead of the ideals of innocence, and the diversions of romance, psychoanalysis depicts a negotiation between pleasure and unpleasure, between egotism and guilt, between envy and fear; the misfortunes of Oedipus are visited upon us all.[1] Our development, instead of being regarded as the sum of our physical growth and conscious experience, is said to be the product of our tragic and unconscious nature.

Throughout the twentieth century *biological determinism* has been employed to despatch this nightmare. The constitutional character of sexual desire is admitted readily. But the emphasis is shifted from our psyche to our physique. The strength of biological determinism lies in the idea that the source of sexual desire is both beyond reason and yet remains available for rational investigation. The biological determinist is able to defend the subrational aspect of sexual desire and to sponsor, simultaneously, the rational evaluation of the phenomenon. The fact that sexual feeling is elaborately contrived and utterly spontaneous, highly controlled and wildly uncontrollable, is known by everyone, but understood by very few. Consequently, the view that sexual desire is simply one of the modes of existence of biochemistry is very helpful. It permits the view that sexual desire is an entirely natural and unstoppable force requiring powerful social institutions and inducements to direct its energy towards constructive and socially acceptable purposes.

Biological determinism directs our attention towards natural processes that must be worked *with* and not against; it encourages society to cut *with the grain of nature* rather than against it.

In this way biologistic accounts are able to admit readily the plasticity of erotic expression – the cultural and social components of sexual behaviour – while presupposing that sexuality is simply a function of our organic constitution. Biological determinism is able to conceive of social arrangements and cultural conventions as inevitable corollaries of natural impulses. Indeed, because human life is inconceivable without set institutions and practices governing sexual behaviour, these conventions might almost be considered to be 'natural' themselves. It is along the route of such reasoning that we arrive at the idea that courtship, marriage and infidelity are 'natural'. Determinists do not argue that such human contrivances are immutable, but they do believe that they must be commensurate with the template of the human organism provided by biology.

Thus, armed with the warrant of nature and the authority of science, biological determinism is able to develop an explanation of sexual impulses in keeping with the ambivalence of our experience. It has the appearance of being true. Sexuality does indeed appear to arise within the body and to require strong ethical practices, and tensile social arrangements to absorb the shock of its energy, and to keep it under control. By 1850 this view was being widely canvassed: 'Sexual love may become a powerful engine for good, but only on the condition of placing it under rigorous and permanent discipline.'[2]

This approach permits biological determinism to dispense with psychic hobgoblins and mental uncertainties. It can accomplish all with the idea that it is the job of science to figure, and society to transfigure, what is given to us by nature. However, what might now appear to be 'common sense' rests upon profound changes in scientific outlook. During the opening years of the nineteenth century the earlier teleological concerns of scientists and philosophers began to abate. A much more powerful impulse to determine proximate causes began to erode and weaken traditional interest concerning ultimate determinations and the absolute ground of knowledge. This trend was known as *positivism*. It boldly contrasted the 'relativism' of most nineteenth-century philosophy and science with what it clearly regarded as outmoded concerns for first and final causes.[3] It dispensed with the need for a miracle-working God. God was allowed, but only if he agreed to stick to the fixed laws of nature. John Stuart Mill (1806–73) explained it well:

Positive Philosophy maintains, that within the existing order of the universe, or rather the part of it known to us, the direct determining cause of every phenomenon is not supernatural but natural. It is compatible with this to believe, that the universe was created, and even that it is continuously governed, by an Intelligence, provided we admit that the intelligent Governor adheres to fixed laws, which are only modified or counteracted by other laws or the same dispensation, and are never either capriciously or providentially departed from.[4]

Under the influence of this 'deist' confinement of God crude forms of materialism began to flourish. They began to rival spiritual and ideal explanations of human behaviour. The origins of moral disposition, of psychological temperament and of sexual conduct were increasingly sought in the physical aspect of the human condition, and in the energy and discharge inherent in the way that the motion of matter was conceived. Consequently, what has been called the 'positive spirit' reduced quality to quantity.[5] All realms of existence were reduced to measurable, weighable quantities. Society, man and nature could all be investigated by the new science using conceptual tools – ways of thinking and modes of analysis – developed in physics. In the 1830s the principal exponent of these ideas, Auguste Comte, wrote of biology that:

The study has assumed a scientific character only since the recent period when vital phenomena began to be regarded as subject to general laws, of which they exhibit only simple modifications. This revolution is now irreversible, however incomplete and however imperfect have been the attempts to establish the positive character of our knowledge of the most complex and individual of physiological phenomena, especially that of the nerves and brain. Yet, unquestionable as is the basis of the science, its culture is at present too like that to which men have been always accustomed, pursued independently of mathematical and inorganic philosophy, which are the only solid foundations of the positivity of vital sciences.[6]

Comte understood the world as an unfolding of potentiality, from matter at one end, to life and spirituality at the other.[7] He hoped science would reveal the essence of human life by the elaboration of a more and more complex aggregate knowledge of life's physical components and causes. The accumulation of such knowledge, he believed, would enable 'social physics' to indicate the determinations of moral conduct, and the necessity of particular social institutions.

This new science [of social physics] is rooted in biology, as every science is in the one that precedes it; and it will render the body of doctrine complete and indivisible, enabling the human mind to proceed on positive principles in all directions whatever, to which its activity may be incited. Imperfect as the preceding sciences are, they have enough of the positive character to render this last transformation possible; and when it is effected, the way will be open for their future advancement, through an organisation of scientific labour as must put an end to the intellectual anarchy of our present condition.[8]

This scientism facilitated unparalleled scientific advance while at all times leaving room for the social prejudices that reside in naturalistic and biologistic accounts of human conduct. In Germany positivism was laced with a heady mixture of idealism; in England with a phlegmatic and unperturbable empiricism. Whatever its local form, or its specific political register, the manifold incarnations of positivism came to dominate scientific thought by the end of the nineteenth century. The barriers to cultural or social change were invariably attributed to the human condition, the nature of man, the consequences of evolution. Yet, for the first time, all this could be grasped and understood by the steady, painstaking evaluations of science. The unfitness of the working class for political power, and the inferiority of 'savage' peoples could be tested, measured, demonstrated within the frame of a profoundly adaptable and flexible outlook.

Positivism could demonstrate that the position of women in Europe during the 1850s, and of the form of family preferred by the mid-century middle classes, were in perfect harmony with the immutable physical laws of nature:

Her mission is so uniform in its nature, and so clearly defined, that there seems hardly room for much uncertainty as to her proper social position. It is a striking instance of the rule that applies universally to all human effort – namely, that the order of things instituted by man ought to be simply a consolidation and improvement of the natural order.[9]

Consequently: 'In all kinds of force, whether physical, intellectual, or practical, it is certain that man surpasses woman, in accordance with the general laws prevailing throughout the animal kingdom.'[10]

In this way the 'precision of science' and the strict evaluation of quantity granted passage to successive waves of impressionism and prejudice. For example, it permitted Charles Darwin (1809–82) to derive the intellectual inferiority of women from Francis Galton's (1822–1911) 'law of the deviation from averages'.[11] These averages could then be applied to the small brains of women. But Darwin was cautious: 'His brain is absolutely larger, but whether or not proportionately to his larger body, has not, I believe, been fully ascertained.'[12]

His caution concerning the different cranial capacity of males and females ebbed away when he considered the social achievements of women:

> The chief distinction in the intellectual powers of the two sexes is shewn by man's attaining to a higher eminence, in whatever he takes up, than can woman – whether requiring deep thought, reason, or imagination, or merely the use of the senses and hands.[13]

It is not sufficient to see these ideas as merely 'a product of their times'. Not only were they not shared by everyone, but they were the subject of the most sustained and reasoned attack by figures as eminent and diverse as the English liberal, John Stuart Mill, and the German socialist, August Bebel (1840–1913).[14] However, even the rejection of the social prejudices of Comte, Darwin or Galton, did not damage positivism or weaken its sanction of biological determinism. This was because of the immense authority conferred upon it by the apparently limitless capacity of science to dissect, analyse and explain natural phenomena. As Isaiah Berlin explained, Comte's philosophy indicated 'one complete and all-embracing pyramid of scientific knowledge; one method; one truth; one scale of rational, "scientific" values'. It satisfied a 'naive craving for unity and symmetry.'[15]

The resulting scientism reduced the impact of much social criticism. While it was perfectly possible to enumerate the social obstacles that prevented women from rivalling the achievements of men, it was not possible to discount entirely the importance of physical difference. You could, like Bebel, seek explanations in unfair social arrangements, but you could not disprove biological determinations.[16]

By 1875 the tendency towards technical progress, social upheaval, and the perpetual transformation of all the possibilities of thought and life, had become permanent. A much more diverse and subtle culture started to come into existence. The perpetual revolution of technique in science, art, industry and commerce that we associate with modernity owes its origin to this period. Ideals of peace, progress and prosperity had to coexist with wars of conquest, poverty and the business cycle. Similarly, there was no iron correspondence between materialism and the scientific method, or between spiritualism and the advocacy of a priori knowledge of things mysterious.[17] Apprehension and irrationality about natural and social phenomena existed cheek-by-jowl with the most ruthless confidence in humanity's capacity to conquer all that lay before it.

These contradictions were accommodated and explained by biology and the new social sciences, and were underpinned by evolutionary theory. For Darwin and George John Romanes (1848–94) our kinship with apes and with pre-historic man was disturbingly indicated by the bearing and behaviour of the 'savages' that they had encountered.[18] It was argued that the social and mental life of human beings evolved, by natural selection, in much the same way as the morphology and instincts of animals. And because 'natural selection' worked 'solely by and for the good of each being' it was assumed that 'all corporeal and mental endowments' would 'tend to progress towards perfection'.[19] In this way, a picture of society and of the individual emerges in which the evolution of mind and body, disposition and morphology, is determined biologically, by the tendency of those best adapted to flourish, and the tendency of those less well endowed to fail. Simple or imperfectly adapted cultures would succumb to the more sophisticated and complex, as assuredly as inferior individuals would succumb to their superiors.[20]

At this juncture it is important not to attribute the political dimension of these ideas to Charles Darwin or to the impact of the ideology of 'Social Darwinism'. Florid attacks on Darwin's ideas for their racism merely serve to obscure their deep roots in the science of the nineteenth century.[21] Recognition and discussion of the struggle for survival of both man and beast, against each other and against the elements, informed all social thinking. This was so much the case that *struggle* itself assumed an elemental status. It was conceived as the manner in which 'God keeps all well balanced'.[22] It was reflected in the prevailing ideas of charge and discharge in the perpetual motion of matter. Individual men and women, their morphology and their mental capacity, their moral sense and their cultural level, their institutions and their societies, were all a product of the great struggle in which humbler and less complex forms give rise, perpetually, to more complicated objects and interactions.

Thus, from the war of nature, from famine and death, the most exalted object which we are capable of conceiving, namely, the production of the higher animals, directly follows. There is grandeur in this view of life, with its several powers, having been originally breathed into a few forms or into one; and that, whilst this planet has gone cycling on according to the fixed law of gravity, from so simple a beginning endless forms most beautiful and most wonderful have been, and are being, evolved.[23]

Because this outlook dominated most social and scientific thinking, memory, imagination, consciousness itself, was regarded as a product of biological evolution. In 1888 Romanes explained this idea in the grand manner:

For he [mankind] has begun to perceive a strong probability, if not an actual certainty, that his own living nature is identical in kind with the nature of all other life, and that even the most amazing side of this his own nature – nay, the most amazing of all things within the reach of his knowledge – the human mind itself, is but the topmost inflorescence of one mighty growth, whose roots and stem and many branches are sunk in the abyss of planetary time.[24]

Mental life is an analogue of physical life. And it has, like the body of animals, evolved over millennia from lower, less complex forms, to higher, more complex forms. All human consciousness came to be understood as the specific and direct products of movements within the brain. More than this, thought itself became a physical process:

There is no certainty that the distinctions are real unless they correspond to the physiological facts that create or are synchronous with psychic manifestations. Every mental fact has some physical expression. The test, therefore, of the reality of a psychic distinction is its correspondence to a physical difference, and this test should be applied in defining terms.[25]

Here, the cerebral cortex is not simply a necessary condition of thought; it is the material dimension of mental activity. The mind is conceived as having a thought-by-thought correspondence with physical movements within the tissue of the brain. Every thought is registered physically rather like the creases in a folded map. It may be unfolded and the creases 'forgotten' (or smoothed out); and they may be 'remembered', quickly, when we fold the map neatly away along the lines of its original creases. Similarly, it follows: 'that the tendency of ideas to *recur* in the same order as that in which they have previously *occurred*, is merely a psychological expression of the physiological fact that lines of discharge become more and more permeable by use.'[26]

Despite the preponderance, around 1900, of ideas of this sort, they continued to arouse considerable hostility. The view of man, and all organic life, as an ensemble of material properties arranged according to the mechanical laws of the physical universe was widely held to be absurd. The strict application of Newtonian mechanics to human life had always been offensive to Christian theology. By 1800 Kantian philosophy had arisen to do battle with the dismal conviction that man was merely the sum of his mechanical and physical sensations.[27] Whether or not life was understood as *deus ex machina* there was something more to it, and to mankind, than a mechanical orchestration of physical properties. Physical reductionism could not accommodate the freedom conferred upon humanity by God. Nor could it explain moral sense or the appreciation of the sublime. Paradoxically, it was progress in scientific knowledge that strengthened these idealist objections. 'Like Kant in his later years, most biologists realised that organisms are different from inanimate matter and that the difference had to be explained not by postulating some vital force but by modifying rather drastically the mechanistic theory.'[28]

Physicalism was regarded as unsuited to the task of understanding the dynamic complexity and variety of living things. Consequently real barriers to understanding human nature continued to be recognised. However, it was felt we could continue to address our 'animal natures' by analogy with the 'animal kingdom'. Although the source of our higher intellectual and moral functions would, no doubt, continue to prove elusive, it was noted that many 'emotions which we ourselves experience, are likewise recognisable in less perfect, or sometimes more perfect, expression in higher animals'. Especially those emotions 'which are associated with sex and reproduction' like 'love of mates, love of offspring, lust, jealousy, family affection' and 'social sympathies'.[29] It was the capacity of this approach to explain so much that seems vital, passionate, instinctive and irrational, that accounted for the continued progress of biologistic accounts of human behaviour.

Appetite, Function and State

Instead of concern for man's special status within the Creation the focus of biologistic attention shifted toward human kinship with the beasts.[30] But deterministic trends continued to conceive human biology as an irreducible base upon which a social and cultural superstructure is erected. If anything, this sort of determinism enjoyed more support during the twentieth century than either 'wilful' idealism or the 'life force' of vitalism.[31] Bronislaw Malinowski (1884–1942), a major exponent of this more popular trend, went into great detail concerning our mortal coil:

By human nature, therefore, we mean the biological determinism which imposes on every civilisation and on all individuals in it the carrying out of such bodily functions as breathing, sleep, rest, nutrition, excretion, and reproduction. We can define the concept of basic needs as the environmental and biological conditions which must be fulfilled for the survival of the individual and the group.[32]

Malinowski, an anthropologist, went so far as to tabulate a series of sequences that move from the biological 'Impulse' through the culturally mediated 'Act' to the experience of 'Satisfaction'.[33] Colon pressure leads to defecation which leads to abdominal relaxation. Similarly sex appetite leads to conjugation which leads to detumescence.[34] He does the same for hunger, thirst, fatigue, restlessness, somnolence, bladder pressure, fright and pain. He noted that these sequences incorporated in all impulses are 'permanent' vital sequences incorporated in all cultures.[35] In doing so he conceded that the 'additional complexity' assumed 'a less self-evident value and utility'.[36] But he insisted that 'human nature imposes on all forms of behaviour, however complex and highly organised, a certain determinism.'[37] His idea was that a universal set of basic needs calls forth a corresponding cultural response. 'Function', says Malinowski, 'in this simplest and most basic aspect of human behaviour, can be defined as the satisfaction of an organic impulse by the appropriate act.'[38]

Malinowski's approach is compelling, but it does have a serious flaw. In conflating 'impulses' and 'reflexes', and the 'individual' with the 'group', Malinowski's biological determinism permits false assumptions about sexual intercourse and reproduction. Whereas every individual must eat, rest, sleep, defecate, breathe and so on, sexual intercourse is not a condition of survival for any particular man or woman; conjugation is not necessary for the survival of the organism. Of course, some men must fertilise some women. That is necessary for the survival of the species. But sexual intercourse is not vital for the survival or physical well-being of the organism. Irrespective of any ideas we may have concerning our psychological or emotional equilibrium our sexual 'appetite' is not comparable to our appetite for oxygen, water, food, or our need to urinate or defecate.

Despite this problem, the approach canvassed by Malinowski had, and continues to have, broad appeal. Somewhere, underneath all that civilisation, lies the 'natural', 'gritty', 'primitive' human being. Strip away our culture and self-importance and an irreducible organism is revealed: the body that is the fundamental particle of human society. The body, as a product of nature, is conceived as the bearer of organic needs and impulses that are given specific texture and disposition by culture.[39] It is thought that sexual impulses come naturally from this body, and are shaped normally (or perverted) by the social experience of the person that culture fashions from (and within) this body. This sort of biological determinism has sustained the popular prejudice that we are *two-fold* creatures. Like the centaur we are apparently both man and beast: a rational front-end joined to a bestial rear.

This tendency to see human nature as the product of the conflict between our animal side and our self-conscious, reasoning side, closely resembles Christian concepts of the conflict between body and soul. Or, according to taste, the struggle between the vigorous natural man, and the weak hot-house product of civilised moralities. This battle is between the flesh and the passions on the one hand, and morality, restraint and reason on the other. It is an eternal struggle with no decisive outcome. It is a perpetual conflict between the profane and the divine; between the irrational and the rational. Even Freud sought the constitution of our psychology in a highly strung constitutive tension between innate drives on the one hand, and civilisation on the other. At their most sophisticated such dualities envisage humanity as an authentic synthesis of the struggle between our deep primitive self, and our brilliant and imaginative social life. More crudely, we are conceived as having one foot in the beast's den, and the other firmly planted in the world of our own making.

This tension between the profane and the divine, between body and soul, beast and man, biological base and cultural superstructure, was sustained by the rudimentary character of our understanding of living things. Mechanistic, vitalist and idealist conceptions of life perpetually vied with each other in opposition, in unhappy combinations and in unstable syntheses. Since the middle of the twentieth century, however, developments in the biological sciences have greatly strengthened reductionist and physicalist sorts of biological determinism. Of course, this ultra-rationalism has many opponents, and we should always bear in mind Mary Midgley's warning that: 'One cannot cast out myth by rationalism, because pure rationalism is itself a myth. In any case, myth and science have always been intimately associated.'

Consequently, 'The rational intelligence must therefore fight on two fronts and against two kinds of superstition – superstition as conventionally known and that other form of superstition, reductionism.'[40]

Midgley is responding to a startling paradox. Modern biology has furnished us with undreamed-of complexity and indetermination, and yet has produced, simultaneously, entirely new variants of physicalism and biological determinism. This modern reductionism has been ushered into existence by better science. Paradoxically, it is the decisive defeat of the mechanistic ideas of the seventeenth century, and the eclipse of their nineteenth-century incarnations, that has given biological determinism a new lease on life. The substantiation of the old positivist themes, the quantification of behaviour, and the chemicalisation of physiology, needed the development of:

> powerful new machines and techniques for the determination of the structure of the giant molecules, for observing the microscopic internal structure of the cells, and, above all, for studying the dynamic interplay of individual molecules within the cell. By the 1950s it had begun to be possible to describe and account for, in the mechanistic sense, the behaviour of individual body organs – muscles, liver, kidneys, etc, – in terms of the properties and interchange of individual molecules: the mechanist's dream.[41]

This sour response doesn't really do justice to the process. Greater knowledge has led to an astonishingly sophisticated account of the mechanisms of life. A sure-footed understanding of biological systems and processes has resulted in a clearer conception of the relationship between living things and the laws of physics and chemistry. Life has no special substance, it is not an object or a force.[42] The *process* of living can be defined, but *life* cannot. Life is a process that operates within the laws of physics and chemistry – it violates none of them – but it cannot be explained by them.

> The explanatory equipment of the physical sciences is insufficient to explain complex living systems and, in particular, the interplay between historically acquired information and the responses of these genetic programs to the physical world. The phenomena of life have a much broader scope than the relatively simple phenomena dealt with by physics and chemistry. This is why it is as impossible to include biology in physics as it is to include physics in geometry.[43]

The confidence expressed in this observation stems from the new biology that arose in the middle of the twentieth century. Between 1935 and 1955 the electron microscope was invented, and the concept of analysing systems from the point of view of information exchanges and programmes was developed.[44] As a consequence of theoretical and technical innovations of this order, striking empirical discoveries were made. The function of deoxyribonucleic acid (DNA) was conceived and its structure described. The study of genetics was reestablished on an entirely new basis. Biochemistry gave rise to molecular biology. Scientists began to deal 'with the biology of molecules, their modifications, interactions, and even their evolutionary history'.[45]

At this point it is important to grasp what sort of processes molecular biology deals with. It must be appreciated that,

> the word 'gene' does not refer to a substance in the same way as does the word 'water'; rather it refers to a concept as does the word 'molecule', or 'atom', or 'electron'. Although hereditary material consists of nucleic acid, a substance, the unit hereditary determinants are identified only on the basis of their biological activity. Consequently, these units can be defined only in an operational way; our concept of them is only a logical inference from a vast array of observations.[46]

It is not possible to give an account here of molecular biology, endocrinology or neuroendocrinology.[47] But it is important to bear in mind the character of the processes at work. They involve chemical releases that initiate other releases, and so on. Complex sequences of singular events lead on to complex arrays of sequences. Thus, for example, one hormone binds to one receptor and leads to the activation of ten transducer proteins. One transducer protein activates ten enzyme molecules. Each active enzyme produces, in turn, ten molecules of second messenger. So the binding of each hormone molecule induces the production of 1000 molecules of second messenger.[48] This catalysing system has the advantage of considerable flexibility within the confines of a relatively simple series of communications.[49] It employs a hierarchy of messengers in order to allow 'the various individual cells, which have to respond to hormones in a widely different manner, to utilise identical signalling systems to elicit the appropriate response'.[50]

Hormones, like genes and chromosomes, are concepts, events and substances that play a vital part in the catalytic series that bring about morphological change in embryo and at puberty. Hormones also prepare the body for coital sexual activity. However, there appears to be no evidence that hormonal catalysts determine or direct conduct – except in the sense that they bring about physiological changes that facilitate certain activities. For example, androgens in men appear to be necessary *but not sufficient* for usual libido. There is no evidence, concerning men or women, that particular hormonal states will dictate or determine a particular type, or level, of sexual interest and activity.[51] Work on spotted hyenas, captive wolves, Japanese quail and many other creatures abounds in the literature, but in human beings the relationship between hormones and behaviour continues to prove problematic.[52]

It is noticeable that when molecular scientists and biochemists discuss hormones and human sexual *behaviour* they stray off into citing psychiatrists and psychologists. They move away from biological science. This shift is prompted by the entirely different problems and kinds of knowledge required. Findings concerning cell signalling and complex series of catalysing and synthesising events do not equip one to pronounce upon the behaviour of whole organisms. By definition, the behaviour of a whole organism has an extracellular dimension. It also lies beyond the systemic functions of particular processes and organs. In approaching the problem of human behaviour from a biochemical point of departure we are moving from the arrangement of the living process within the organism, to the living interaction of the organism with a myriad of plants and other animals. Biochemically induced events (for example, puberty) do indeed have social ramifications. Similarly, socially induced events (such as stress) have biochemical implications.[53] However, just because two entirely different processes, the social and the biochemical, react to each other does not at all mean that such processes can be conflated without damage to our understanding of both processes.

Unfortunately, conflation of this sort occurs quite frequently. Different kinds of knowledge are employed to draw analogies between different sorts of events, leading to illegitimate analogies between different sorts of processes. For example, C.R. Badcock thinks that:

> From the all-important point of view of evolution, the T4 bacteriophage and a human being are functionally identical: both are protein-packaged, organismic encapsulations of the vital element in evolution: genetic information. The fact that human beings are such complex encapsulating organisms and T4 bacteriophage such a simple one is neither here nor there as far as evolution is concerned.[54]

Well, one can see what he means, but it leads him on to soppy conclusions. He ends up arguing that essentially selfish genes cooperate in order to best secure their future, and that this effect can be seen in economic life when essentially selfish individuals and classes find it to their mutual advantage to cooperate with each other![55] Leaving biochemically inspired political economy to one side, it is important to remember that genes cannot be 'selfish', 'cooperate' or behave as if they know anything.

Genes and DNA ... are precise names given by scientists to specific little bits of complex goo. And little bits of goo, however complex, cannot design or engineer anything. Of course it is quite true that this particular consignment of goo is by ordinary standards very special and important – but only because it is liable to turn into organisms, and organisms are, by ordinary standards, important; indeed they are the condition of anything's being important.[56]

The truth of this is widely acknowledged despite the currency of sociobiology and reductionist accounts of human behaviour and consciousness. Consequently, the view that the modern biological determinist generally seeks to reduce our idea of the human person to the sum of the movements within the organism is outmoded. This is not the register in which they write or speak. Despite the extremes of sociobiology and the assumptions of model builders in artificial intelligence, most modern biology does not sanction the cruder sorts of physicalism.[57] Biology, anthropology, ethology, reflex psychology and behaviourism have been synthesised into an account that tends towards a description of the human person as an ensemble of interactive appetites, functions and states.[58] 'A person is not an originating agent: he is a locus, a point at which many genetic and environmental conditions come together in a joint effect.'[59]

The assumption here is that human beings arise out of the interaction between their genetic make-up and their (social) environment. Interactionism of one sort or another is the modern position. This approach now extends from the field of artificial intelligence to that of endocrinology. Appetite, function and state are component expressions of corresponding physical processes. They are processes that interact with the environment (of physical circumstance and social relationships) to constitute the person. The result is a person that may be analysed as an objective entity composed of appetites, functions and states. In the field of sexuality it might be appropriate to think of *desire*, *reproduction* and *arousal* as corresponding to the ensemble: appetite, function and state.

Because sexual feelings and desires are experienced as sub-rational, they must have a source which lies beyond reason. However, there must also be an explanation that can account for the social and cultural dimensions of sexuality. Simple mechanistic reductions of sexuality to our 'animal spirit' or even directly to the operation of hormones do not entirely satisfy. Modern experience has called forth a much more sophisticated account. It is one that brings biology and society together in a naturalistic explanation that has the appearance of doing justice to the complexity of the phenomena. The old antagonistic dualisms of body and soul, man and beast, biology and society have been brought up to date. This has been done by the interactive account. By employing the latest discoveries, modern biological determinists can declare, *ultimately*, that the source of sexuality is biochemical. In the 'last analysis' sexuality can be said to be a physical effect of our biology. The determinists can continue to discover the secret of sexuality within the nature of our bodies. The appetites and drives of our organic constitution – the impulses of our sexual essence – have been concocted into a much more elaborate theoretical account. It is one that willingly concedes that society modifies physical circumstance, but unerringly awards the honours to biology.

So the impasse between biology and society remains. Biological determinists have renovated and deepened their arguments, but they have not swept all before them. Consequently, we must turn our attention to the tradition that always canvassed a more positive role for society (and for social transformation) in the realm of sexual expression.

4   Society and Self-realisation

Virtue through Health and Hygiene

The idea that good conditions will produce good people and conversely
that bad conditions will produce rotten ones continues to have broad
appeal. It also forms the basis of what is most distinctive in the radical
account of sexuality. From the middle of the nineteenth century
Marxists, anarchists, socialists and liberals subscribed to the idea that virtue
would be made real through social improvement. In relation to sexuality
this meant that the emancipation of women and the abolition of
exploitation would liberate the most intimate aspects of human life from
the disfiguring effects of domination, violence and repression. In 1884,
while envisaging the future, Frederick Engels asked:

> But what will there be new? That will be answered when a new
> generation has grown up: a generation of men who never in their lives
> have known what it is to buy a woman's surrender with money or
> any other social instrument of power; a generation of women who
> have never known what it is to give themselves to a man from any
> other considerations than real love, or to refuse to give themselves
> to their lover from fear of the economic consequences. When these
> people are in the world, they will care precious little what anybody
> today thinks they ought to do; they will make their own practice and
> their corresponding public opinion about the practice of each
> individual – and that will be the end of it.[1]

In this passage Engels is expressing a point of view, and an aspiration,
that was typical of a broad spectrum of radical opinion. It was thought
that bad social conditions both harboured (and gave rise to) sexual
perversion and sexual problems of all kinds. It was a belief that strengthened interest in economic and social determinations without ever
unseating biological ones. It permitted consideration of sexuality to focus
upon the ways in which society modified physical circumstance without
ever challenging the conception that in the 'last instance' sexuality was
a physical effect of our biology. In this respect socialist thought, and left-
wing opinion generally, was closer to mainstream liberal and conser-

vative views than either left or right has ever cared to admit. They shared many prejudices and many objectives, but above all, they shared a similar enthusiasm for science and for evolutionary theory. As Anton Pannekoek (1873–1960) explained in 1912:

> The scientific importance of Marxism as well as of Darwinism consists in their following out the theory of evolution, the one upon the domain of the organic world, of things animate; the other, upon the domain of society. This theory of evolution, however, was in no way new, it had its advocates before Darwin and Marx; the philosopher, Hegel, made it even as the central point of his philosophy.[2]

A more or less positivist enthusiasm for science, for evolutionary theory, and for a conception of materialism that traced all psychological and social phenomena back to physiology, and to physical causes, became the hallmark of socialistic movements and currents of opinion.[3] This meant that the most extreme forms of social criticism that arose in Europe and North America were, in all essentials, informed by a similar kind of outlook as that expressed by mainstream liberals and conservatives. In the field of sexuality it meant endorsing hatred of perversions and sexual irregularity; it meant supporting campaigns for improved breeding and the proliferation of better physical types. Across a broad range of issues the common theoretical approach of the left – positivist science and an evolutionary view of man and society – was buttressed by support for the crude prejudices of the day.

Numbered among these was an endorsement for the popular hatred of the 'unnatural vice' that was thought of as the deepest and strangest taint of Greek civilisation.[4] In a letter to Karl Marx (1818–83) in June 1869 Engels described the beginnings of the struggle for homosexual rights as: 'War on the cunts, peace to the arse-holes.' The salacious vulgarity of this letter is also accompanied by expression of the sinister desire 'to wheedle out ... the particulars of pederasts in high and top places'.[5] This epistle was, of course, not meant for publication. However, Engels did venture into print in a diatribe worthy of St Paul:

> The [Greek] men, who would have been ashamed to show any love for their wives, amused themselves by all sorts of love affairs with *hetaerae*; but the degradation of the women avenged itself on the men and degraded them also, till they fell into the abominable practice of pederasty and degraded alike their gods and themselves with the myth of Ganymede.[6]

Ganymede, it will be remembered, was a Trojan lad who was so beautiful that Zeus abducted him to Olympus so that he could be the cupbearer of the gods. Evidently, the founders of scientific socialism found this sensuous mythology very distressing. August Bebel, the leader of the German Social Democratic Party, was of a similar opinion:

> Another evil, which is being developed more and more by the present state of things must be cursorily alluded to. Too much sexual indulgence is even more injurious than too little ... The number of old and young *roués* is immense, and all surfeited, palled by superfluity, feel the need of keener irritants. Some resort to the unnatural practices of Greek times, others seek stimulation in the abuse of children ... Thus we see that vice, depravity, error, and crime of all kinds, are bred by our social conditions.[7]

In the translation of Bebel's views made by the American socialist Daniel De Leon (1852–1914) lesbians are included in the account of shocking depravity:

> The number of young and old *roués* is enormous, and they require special irritants, excess having deadened and surfeited them. Many, accordingly, lapse into the unnatural practices of Greek days. The crime against nature is to-day much more general than most of us dream of: upon that subject the secret archives of many a Police Bureau could publish frightful information. But not men only, among women also have the unnatural practices of old Greece come up again with force. Lesbian love, or Sapphism, is said to be quite general among married women in Paris; according to Taxal, it is enormously in practice among the prominent ladies of that city. In Berlin, one-fourth of the prostitutes are said to practice 'tribady', but also in the circles of our leading dames there are not wanting disciples of Sappho. Still another unnatural gratification of the sexual instinct manifests itself in the violation of children, a practice that has increased greatly during the last thirty years.[8]

Here, in the great socialist classics concerning the family and the emancipation of women, homosexuality is associated, simultaneously, with the upper class and with the *lumpenproletariat*, with decadence and self-indulgence, and with child abuse.[9] Paradoxically, opinions of this sort were often held by people who opposed criminal sanctions and endorsed campaigns that aimed at the decriminalisation of homosexuality. Ferdinand Lassalle (1825–64), the founder of the *Allgemeiner Deutscher Arbeiterverein* (Universal German Working Men's Association), is known to have had extremely liberal attitudes and certainly did not support the state repression of homosexuality.[10] In the 1890s the great socialist theoreticians Karl Kautsky (1854–1938) and Eduard Bernstein (1850–1932) publicly associated themselves with calls for the repeal of the statute in Germany that prohibited consenting sexual relations between adult males. These calls were not calls for acceptance of homosexuality, but they were informed by the opinion that the repression of homosexuality by the criminal law was both unfeeling and ineffective. August Bebel made similar calls in the Reichstag.[11]

However, it was the sentiments of Marx and Engels that prevailed – particularly when the rich and powerful were involved. In 1902 Alfred Krupp, scion of the great armaments family, died in mysterious circumstances. A week before his death he had been expelled from the isle of Capri for sexual misconduct. The socialist newspaper, *Vorwarts*, made the most of the scandal. It intoned:

> The case must now be discussed in public with due regard to seriousness ... because it offers a picture of capitalist culture in the most garish colors ... The horrible picture of capitalist influence is not especially toned down by our discovery that this is a man of perverse orientation. The pity due the victim of a fateful error of nature must be denied when millions have been placed at the service of that sickness's gratification.[12]

In 1906 the socialist weekly *Die Zukunft* took matters further by denouncing aristocrats and associates of the Kaiser for jeopardising national security by their 'secret immorality and unnatural vices'.[13] However, some socialists still spoke up against repression, and even called for full acceptance. A year earlier, the socialist deputy, Adolf Thiele, had argued in defence of homosexuality in the Reichstag saying that, 'I wouldn't even admit that this is something sick; it's simply a deviation from the usual pattern nature produces.'[14] In response, the socialist deputy, Von Vollmar, rushed to isolate Thiele:

> ... my colleague Thiele, as every other colleague who speaks on this matter, is taking a purely personal stand on the issue, and the Social Democracy has as little to do with this issue as any other party. (Quite right! on the Left. Hear! hear! on the Right.)[15]

It seems that Von Vollmar was speaking for the vast majority of the left. The early homosexual rights campaigners got some support, but not much. Broadly speaking the left stood with the right on the matter of homosexuality. There was some disagreement on the efficacy of repressive laws, but, by and large, an abomination was as much an abomination for a socialist leader as it was for a Catholic or a conservative politician. As James Steakley notes:

> With the sole exception of August Bebel, the left Social Democrats maintained silence on the issue of homosexuality. Reichstag opposition to penal reform was led by the Center Party, and only a few members of any party other than the Social Democracy voted in its favour.[16]

The reason for this dismal record lay in the acceptance by radicals and socialists of mainstream conceptions of biology, nature, morality and social danger. Whatever socialists might argue concerning wages or social insurance, when it came to sexuality they identified the same problems and were motivated by the same fears and nightmares as many of their political opponents. Because of this, the desire to support the decriminalisation of homosexuality and other liberalisations was always eclipsed by fear of the grim consequences of sexual licence and perversion. For most radicals progress in matters sexual meant the end of the moral and physical enervation produced by capitalism. As Emma Goldman (1869–1940), the anarchist and feminist agitator, explained: 'Girls, mere children, work in crowded, overheated rooms ten to twelve hours daily at a machine, which tends to keep them in a constant over-excited sex state.'[17]

Emma Goldman is echoing the warning sounded much earlier by August Bebel. Bebel had observed that among upper-class women sexual feeling was raised 'to the highest pitch of excitement' because, in an idle atmosphere heavy with exquisite perfumes, they overdosed on music, poetry, and on every other 'so-called artistic enjoyment'. Whereas:

> In the case of the poor, various kinds of fatiguing but mostly sedentary employments occasion a determination of blood to the pelvic organs, while sexual impulses are stimulated by the pressure of constant sitting. One of the most injurious and most widely spread of these employments is working at the sewing machine. Its effect on the nervous and sexual system are at the same time so exciting and wearing that a working day of ten or twelve hours is sufficient to ruin the best constitutions in a few years. Undue sexual irritation is also caused by long hours of work in a high temperature, for instance, in factories for refining sugar, for bleaching and calico printing; by nightwork in overcrowded, gas-lighted rooms in which both sexes often work together.[18]

Because of fears of this sort radicals fought for a world where the young would grow straight and strong; they fought for more *natural* conditions so that perversion would wither and die. Under socialism, perversion (if, indeed, it ever got started) would be treated and most probably cured.[19] The libertarian Paul Lafargue (1842–1911) expressed the hope, common on the left, that with the abolition of private property, 'Motherhood and love will permit woman to regain the higher position which she occupied in primitive societies, the memory of which has been preserved by the legends and myths of the ancient religions.'[20] By the end of the nineteenth century socialists believed that sexual ignorance and repression would, if unchecked, lead to insanity, suicide and the distortion of nature. They believed that sexual incontinence threatened all with impotency, sterility, spinal complaints, idiocy, imbecility and numerous other derangements. Mostly they believed that: 'A healthy manner of life, healthy employments and a healthy education in the broadest sense of the word, combined with the natural gratification of natural and healthy instincts must be brought within the reach of all.'[21]

The association of sexuality with social danger had not always taken this form among radicals. Earlier in the nineteenth century a greater emphasis was placed upon the positive harm done to young people by inadequate sexual congress. In the 1820s Richard Carlile (1790–1843), the London radical, asserted that 'want of sexual commerce' was often a cause of illness and even death among young women. Of both sexes he said: 'They, therefore, who abstain from sexual intercourse, are generally useless for the purposes of civil life. They seldom possess either the common cheerfulness or the gaiety of well-supported animal life.'[22] However, in the course of his instructions on how to prevent 'the semen of the male' from remaining 'in the genital vessels of the female', Carlile made clear that:

> We desire to bring about a cessation from all these bad and disease-producing practices by the recommendation of natural and healthy commerce between the sexes. We recommend chaste and proper commerce in preference to all the artificial and unnatural means that are extensively in use, to subdue, for the moment, the passions of love.[23]

This kind of apology for the advocacy of sexual pleasure and of contraception arose in response to earlier dissent and agitation in England. In 1793 the publication of the *Enquiry Concerning Political Justice* by William Godwin (1756–1836) provoked considerable discussion. Godwin's book, employing a novel form of utilitarian-anarchist criticism, attacked the government, marriage and many other institutions cherished

by the English gentry. On their behalf Thomas Robert Malthus
(1766–1834) replied. In defence of the rich against the complaints of
the poor, he insisted that 'population is necessarily limited by the
means of subsistence', and that population 'invariably increases where
the means of subsistence increases, unless prevented by some very
powerful and obvious checks'. Those checks were 'all resolvable into
moral restraint, vice and misery'.[24] The consequences for the labourer
were clear to Malthus:

> This duty is intelligible to the humblest capacity. It is merely, that he
> is not to bring beings into the world, for whom he cannot find the
> means of support. When once this subject is cleared from the obscurity
> thrown over it by parochial laws and private benevolence, every man
> must feel the strongest conviction of such an obligation. If he cannot
> support his children, they must starve; and if he marry in the face of
> a fair probability that he shall not be able to support his children, he
> is guilty of all the evils, which he thus brings upon himself, his wife
> and his offspring.[25]

Malthus also made it plain 'that the rich do not in reality possess the
power of finding employment and maintenance for the poor'. Consequently, he explained, it was 'in the nature of things' that the poor did
not 'possess the *right* to demand' their maintenance from the rich.
Godwin's response was that mankind was the master of his own fate and
that within very wide limits indeed there are no evils 'that man is not
competent to cure'.[26] However, at the time, Godwin's optimism was
not shared by all. In 1822 the prominent radical, Francis Place
(1771–1854), altered the terms of the debate with his *Illustrations and Proofs
of the Principle of Population*. In it he rejects the brutal fatalism of Malthus
and the buoyant optimism of Godwin. Instead he argued that:

> If, above all, it were once clearly understood, that it was not disrep-
> utable for married persons to avail themselves of such precautionary
> means as would, without being injurious to health, or destructive of
> female delicacy, prevent conception, a sufficient check might at
> once be given to the increase of population beyond the means of sub-
> sistence; vice and misery, to a prodigious extent, might be removed
> from society, and the object of Mr Malthus, Mr Godwin, and of every
> philanthropic person, be promoted, by the increase of comfort, of
> intelligence, and of moral conduct, in the mass of the population.[27]

He followed this up with the publication and distribution of two
leaflets, known in the literature as the 'Diabolical Hand Bills'. These

leaflets were widely circulated in London and in the industrial districts of the north of England. They were also reprinted by several radical newspapers.[28] Their appearance was followed up by the London publication of Richard Carlile's *Every Woman's Book* (1826). This was soon followed by Robert Dale Owen's (1801–77) publication in New York of his *Moral Physiology*. In 1831 the most popular of these early instruction books, the *Fruits of Philosophy*, was published by Charles Knowlton in New York. All of these publications provided women with explicit instructions on how to prevent conception with the use of a vaginal sponge and a piece of ribbon. They all discuss the use of sheaths and the practice of withdrawal. And, they all regard the vaginal sponge as the most aesthetically pleasing and reliable method of contraception.[29] Most importantly, they all promoted sexual pleasure and contraception as a principal means of fighting vice and protecting health. Robert Dale Owen was very firm in his rejection of prurient or improper interest in his work:

> Libertines and debauchee! this book is not for you. You have nothing to do with the subject of which it treats. Bringing to its discussion, as you do, a distrust or contempt of the human race – accustomed as you are to confound liberty with licence, and pleasure with debauchery, it is not for your palled feelings and brutalized senses to distinguish moral truth in its purity and simplicity. I never discuss this subject with such as you.[30]

Sexual pleasure, in its own right, and for its own sake was promoted as a positively good thing.[31] But the freer and more frequent sexual intercourse facilitated by contraception was justified principally for the protection that it was thought to afford from the peevishness of the celibate, and from prostitution, disease, perversion, and from the masturbation that prevailed 'to a lamentable extent, both in' the United States of America and in England.[32] In fact: 'A temperate gratification promotes the secretions, and the appetite for food; calms the restless passions; induces pleasant sleep, awakens social feeling, and adds a zest to life which makes one conscious that life is worth preserving.'[33]

Good Breeding and Birth Control

No doubt the prominence of this concern to promote virtue and the welfare of society was intended to calm the outraged feelings of the censorious. However, it also seems likely that it represented the heartfelt sympathies and prejudices of English republicans and American radicals.

Most social critics were appalled by the ignorance and squalor of great masses of the poor.[34] They regarded self-restraint, self-consciousness and temperance as necessary for the survival of the labourer and his family. Such virtues were vital if the poor man or woman was to have any hope of combating the misery of their conditions. Consequently, socialists, anarchists and liberals supported the promotion of good manners and good breeding. It is interesting to note how early all of these features are present. For example, Charles Knowlton introduced the desire to promote healthy *conception* into his advocacy of contraception in 1831.[35] He was appalled by how careworn and weighed down with toil many women were, and he was disturbed by the incidence of hereditary diseases and social inadequacy:

> Others there are, who ought never to become parents; because, if they do, it is only to transmit to their offspring grievous hereditary diseases, which render such offspring mere subjects of misery throughout their existence. Yet such women will not lead a live [sic] of celibacy. They marry. They become parents, and the sum of human misery is increased by their doing so.[36]

As the century progressed such concerns overlapped with those of people promoting social purity, and a more or less rigorous Christian moral discipline. This confirmed the absence of a distinctively socialist or left-wing outlook, but it ensured (in the face of prosecutions, fines and imprisonment) the advance of contraception, and a better understanding of sexual matters. However, it was utilitarian and positivist ideals that came to define the objectives of social improvement rather than the specifically Christian outlook of social purity.[37] Morality mattered but in a context where it was seen by more and more people to derive its authority from positive social facts rather than the verities of the Pentateuch or the Decalogue. As the influential anthropologist, Edward Westermarck (1862–1939), put it:

> Could it be brought home to people that there is no absolute standard in morality, they would perhaps be somewhat more tolerant in their judgements, and more apt to listen to the voice of reason. If the right has an objective existence, the moral consciousness has certainly been playing at blind man's buff ever since it was born, and will continue to do so until the extinction of the human race.[38]

It was this kind of outlook, in the mainstream of intellectual life in Europe and the United States of America, that permitted the emergence of social hygiene and eugenics as the organising ideas around which the drive to raise the spiritual and physical level of the population was concentrated. As Havelock Ellis explained in 1911:

> It is undoubtedly true that the growth of eugenical ideals has not been, for the most part, due to religious feeling. It has been chiefly the outcome of a very gradual, but very comprehensive, movement towards social amelioration, which has been going on for more than a century, and which has involved a progressive effort towards the betterment of all the conditions of life.[39]

In the course of this development the collision between social conditions in big modern cities, and primordial biological processes, began to be regarded with dismay. Ancient moral codes appeared to be losing their efficacy and relevance. Deliberate, scientific management was now required. In 1885 Jane Clapperton put it succinctly:

> In the savage epoch of our history, the force of natural selection produced survival of the fittest. From that epoch we have long since passed into a humanitarian semi-civilized epoch, in which sympathetic selection produces a miserable state of indiscriminate survival; and now we want the solution of the above problem, to pass onwards to a rational, wholly civilized epoch, when intelligent selection will systematically secure the birth of the morally, intellectually, and physically fit.[40]

In his *The Tasks of Social Hygiene* (1912) Havelock Ellis, in broad sympathy with Clapperton's views, explained:

> Eugenics constitutes the link between the Social Reform of the past, painfully struggling to improve the conditions of life, and the Social Hygiene of the future, which is authorized to deal adequately with the conditions of life because it has its hands on the sources of life.[41]

Ellis, a liberal advocate of social hygiene and eugenics, regarded tramps, prostitutes, paupers, criminals and inebriates as members of a degenerate class who all tended to be born a little defective.[42] He wanted to rid society of them, not simply by improving social conditions, but by encouraging responsible parenthood, contraception and the voluntary sterilisation of the hopeless and the inadequate.[43] Of the feeble-minded he said:

> Feeble-mindedness is an absolute dead-weight on the race. It is an evil that is unmitigated. The heavy and complicated social burdens and injuries it inflicts on the present generation are without com-

pensation ... The task of Social Hygiene which lies before us cannot be attempted by this feeble folk. Not only can they not share in it, but they impede it; their clumsy hands are forever becoming entangled in the delicate mechanism of our modern civilization.[44]

This was the socialist perspective. Or, at least, a very influential strand of socialist opinion. Ellis believed that there could be 'no socialism without individualism' and no 'individualism without socialism'. It was an aspiration that could only be achieved by 'enlisting finely selected persons' in the context of a 'highly organised social structure'. All this was necessary in order to escape from unimproved humanity:

> But these human things, made to be gods, have spawned like frogs all over the earth. Everywhere they have beslimed its purity and befouled its beauty, darkening the very sunshine. Heaped upon one another in evil masses, preying upon one another as no other creature has ever preyed upon its kind, they have become a festering heap which all the oceans in vain lave with their antiseptic waters and all the winds of heaven cannot purify.[45]

Of course, not all socialists shared this neo-Malthusian horror of the 'great unwashed'. August Bebel was untroubled by the population question, and even regarded abstinence from reproductive sexual intercourse, and the use of 'repellant preventive measures' as injurious.[46] However, this was not a view shared by many socialist or radical women. On the whole, socialist opinion couched its social desires in a combination of demands for the material improvement of social conditions, and neo-Malthusian rhetoric expressing concern for the physical and moral quality of the existing stock of human beings. If they did not endorse the outlook of the English campaigner Marie Stopes (1880–1958), they were often prepared to acquiesce to it. This meant putting up with imperious calls for the 'low grade' to have fewer children:

> Apart from the needs of individual patients, a word should be said of the national, indeed the racial position. For want of contraceptive measures the low-grade stocks are breeding in an ever-increasing ratio in comparison to the high-grade stocks, to the continuous detriment of the race. Hence the medical practitioner who has a practice among the poor and ignorant, and particularly among the low-grade elements, has a double duty to inculcate contraceptive knowledge, a duty to his individual patients and a duty to the State.[47]

The American campaigner, Margaret Sanger (1883–1966), liberally mixed her pity for the pathetic 'chronic masturbator' with the usual desire to sterilise the insane and the diseased. She wanted something done about the feeble-minded, and people of the lower grade:

> The statistics indicate at any rate a surprisingly low rate of intelligence among the classes in which large families and uncontrolled procreation predominate. Those of the lowest grade in intelligence are born of unskilled labourers (with the highest birth-rate in the community); the next high among the skilled labourers, and so on to the families of professional people, among whom it is now admitted that the birthrate is voluntarily controlled.[48]

Neither these attitudes, nor her explicit hostility towards Marxism and the 'class war' did much damage to Sanger's radical credentials. Her audacious campaign for 'a saner and healthier attitude on the sex subject', and for thorough sex education for boys and girls assured her place in the pantheon of progress.[49] The commitment of the twentieth-century birth controllers to the emancipation of women, to sex education, and the positive endorsement of sexual pleasure, guaranteed the support of anarchists, socialists and communists.[50] Ruth Hall summed up the contradiction nicely when she noted:

> The paradox was that the birth control movement, the greatest liberalising force of the twentieth century, and Marie Stopes, its archprophet, had each fed off a philosophical base that by the [nineteen] seventies was regarded as too 'illiberal' to be hinted at even by a right-wing Conservative.[51]

So, although the left was, in general, motivated by the impulse to liberate the body, the psychology and the emotional life from the stifling atmosphere of conventional morality it proved incapable of developing a philosophical, anthropological, sociological, biological or psychological outlook that it could call its own. In all essentials the Marxists, the anarchists and the social democrats relied upon the most utilitarian and rationalist ideas developed within the mainstream of European and American society. This lack of independence from the authorities was to prove disastrous. It meant that the left was compelled to attempt the emancipation of the individual by anchoring the socialist dreamboat on the rock of materialist psychology. A positivist commitment to the reality of proximate causes, and to the exclusive authority of material circumstance, inevitably gave priority to the eradication of social danger through social hygiene. Sexuality was to be emancipated from the conditions that stunted it, perverted it, made it disgusting and dirty.

The Revolutionaries and the Radicals

In the midst of the Russian Revolution the cornucopia and cherubim of ancient times were conjured up by the Bolshevik Alexandra Kollontai (1872–1952):

> Make way for healthy, blossoming children; make way for a vigorous youth that clings to life and its joys, which is free in its sentiments and in its affections. Such is the watchword of the communist society. In the name of equality, of liberty, and of love, we call upon the working women and the working men, peasant women and peasants, courageously and with faith to take up the work of the reconstruction of human society with the object of rendering it more perfect, more just, and more capable of assuring to the individual the happiness which he deserves. The red flag of the social revolution which will shelter, after Russia, other countries of the world also, already proclaims to us the approach of the heaven on earth to which humanity has been aspiring for centuries.[52]

There is no doubt that the grandeur of what was attempted by the Russian Revolution justified this hyperbole. No matter how wretched the poverty, or brutal the encirclement of the revolution became, Alexandra Kollontai's speech, 'Communism and the Family', was entirely in keeping with the times. It was delivered in Moscow in 1918 to more than a thousand women who had struggled through the chaos of the Civil War to get to the congress of working and peasant women. Simply their attendance at such a gathering signalled the potential of the revolution. Women were to be emancipated, of that there could be no doubt. As early as 18 December 1917, by a decree of the People's Commissars, the old ties of marriage were swept away. Henceforth divorce would be obtainable in a week or two:

> In place of the indissoluble marriage based on the servitude of woman, we shall see rise the free union, fortified by the Love and mutual respect of the two members of the workers' state, equal in their rights and their obligations.[53]

But, the injunction to the young and healthy was still to love each other, to be happy, and to 'give your country new workers, new citizen children'. Because the 'society of the workers is in need of new working forces', and 'it hails the arrival of every newborn child in the world.'[54] The main purpose of sexual reform was the harmony and well-being of society in the interests of the working class. Despite the 'chaos and contradictions of sexual relationships' sexuality was a discrete phenomena that must be given effective form by the elaboration of a new working-class morality.[55] As Lenin (1870–1924) put it in 1920:

> We do not believe in an eternal morality, and we expose the falseness of all the fables about morality. Morality serves the purpose of helping human society rise to a higher level and rid itself of the exploitation of labour.[56]

This outlook led Soviet jurists to emulate the *Code Napoléon* in decriminalising homosexuality.[57] The Bolshevik government swept away all statutes inspired by religion and archaic prejudice. Their outlook was akin to that of August Bebel and the best elements of the German Social Democracy.[58] As Gregorii Batkis, Director of the Moscow Institute of Social Hygiene, explained in 1923: '[Soviet legislation] *declares the absolute non-interference of the state and society into sexual matters, so long as nobody is injured, and no one's interests are encroached upon.*[59]

Batkis also made the point that the Soviet law regarded homosexual intercourse in the same light as 'the so-called' natural intercourse; all forms of sexual intercourse were regarded as private matters so long as force and duress of any sort was absent.[60] As late as 1930 the Great Soviet Encyclopedia, while it denounced Western governments for hypocritical laws aimed at suppressing homosexuality, could boast that 'Soviet law does not recognize "crime" against morality ...'[61] None of this survived the onset of the bureaucratic dictatorship led by Joseph Stalin (1879–1953). Alexandra Kollontai was out of favour as early as 1923, and by March 1934 the revolutionary new rights and laws had disappeared without trace.[62] They disappeared without trace (as campaigning issues) in the West too. And, it was not until the end of the 1960s that the socialist movement in Europe and the United States of America would actively fight for the liberation of women, or even dream of supporting demands for the emancipation of homosexuals.

This was not because of the defeat of the Bolshevik Revolution. It was because, in common with the rest of the socialist movement, the Soviet Power did not establish any new way of looking at the problem of sexuality. It decreed formal equality and it did all in its power to destroy the sway and mystery of the priests. But, like the radicals elsewhere, it relied on evolutionism, positivism and social hygiene:

The task of sexual pedagogy in the Soviet Union is to bring up healthy individuals, members of a future society in whom there is complete harmony between their natural drives and their great social tasks. To this end everything that is creative and constructive in the natural drives must be furthered, and everything that could become harmful to the development of the personality of the member of the collective should be eliminated.[63]

Lenin was in full agreement with this line.[64] And, in it there is nothing that the enthusiasts of eugenics and social hygiene in the West, Stalin in the East, nor Trotsky in exile, could disagree with. It was a blank cheque, to be drawn on the 'bank of nature and social danger', whenever its directors determined that society was threatened by malformation and perversion.[65] The socialist tradition could not overcome its anthropological commitment to the idea of a 'natural man'. It was a commitment to a struggle in which 'man' was to be emancipated *and* refashioned by a new society so that his essential nature might, for the first time in history, be truly made real. In the Soviet Union this outlook gave rise, during the 1920s, to a complex debate concerning the development of a strictly materialist or *objective* psychology that claimed insight of mental functioning through linguistic theories rooted in the division between mental and manual labour, and from speculations concerning the evolution of social life.[66] However, V.N. Volosinov spoke for many in the Soviet Union, and for millions throughout the international socialist movement when, in 1927, he wrote:

All periods of social decline and disintegration are characterised by *overestimation of the sexual* in life and in ideology, and what is more, of the sexual in an extreme unidimensional conception; its *asocial* aspect, taken in isolation, is advanced to the forefront. The sexual aims at becoming a surrogate from the social. All human beings are divided above all into males and females. All the remaining subdivisions are held to be inessential. Only those social relations that can be sexualised are meaningful and valuable. Everything else becomes null and void.[67]

In an analysis replete with the 'break-up of the Greek city states', Petronius' *Satyricon*, and the 'decline of the Roman Empire', Volosinov treads the well-beaten path to assert that 'Freudianism – the psychology of the déclassés – is becoming the acknowledged ideological persuasion of the widest strata of the European bourgeoisie.'[68] This view was not the product of Stalinism, Leninism or Bolshevism. It sprang from the evolutionism, the anthropology and the positivism of the nineteenth-century radical tradition. Attempts to derive all behaviour from an objective material 'substratum' provoked a profound distrust of both ancient mythologies and modern psychologies.[69] As Karl Kautsky made plain in the same year it was a view shared from the left to the right of the socialist movement:

> As Freud imagined them, primitive men are a bizarre hybridization of robust stallions snorting with rage and decadent weaklings from the literary circles and demimonde of Vienna. Primitive men, according to Freud's assumption, were sexually aroused to the utmost and lusted after women so strongly that they murdered their fathers in order to get them.[70]

Coarse attacks of this kind were not always the order of the day. Between 1928 and 1955 Wilhelm Reich (1897–1957), Erich Fromm (1900–80) and Herbert Marcuse, to name just three, were all engaged in attempting to determine a socialist course for psychology and sexology. Reich worked for many years on attempts to give material and practical expression to an 'oceanic' release of instinctual energy.[71] Fromm and Marcuse worked on developing conceptions of instinctual forces and social forces that could be brought together to form a new consciousness and a new reality consistent with man's biological, social and psychic needs. Marcuse wanted to create conditions in which the reactivation of polymorphous and narcissistic sexuality ceased to be a threat to culture. Free sexuality could 'itself lead to culture-building if the organism exists not as an instrument of alienated labor but as a subject of self-realization – in other words, if socially useful work is at the same time the transparent satisfaction of an individual need.'[72] A deal was to be struck between instincts and reason so that harmony could be established between 'instinctual freedom and order'. A new ethic was to be devised by the social transformation of the instincts and the psyche in a regression to the more harmonious instinctual infancy of man. Paradoxically, this would not involve a descent into barbarism because it would occur at the 'height of civilisation'.[73]

No matter how bizarre or avant-garde this sort of approach may seem, when compared with more prosaic agendas, it is informed by the same outlook as social hygiene. More cosmic in its rhetoric than calls for better contraception and better sex education, it is nothing more than a species of social hygiene. It shares the common assumption that sex is something wonderful (though potentially dangerous) that arises on the basis of a biological substratum. It understands that it is the job of society to ensure that the individual enjoys and make real this sexual potential in a manner consistent with the policy of the state and the needs of society.

Thus social hygiene, under the rubric of progress, self-expression and the full development of the individual, became the principal organising idea in the management of sexuality. Those who concentrated on the social dimension of sexuality became ensnared in the struggle for the realisation of human nature. While 'social hygienists' fought for the rational organisation and reorganisation of matters sexual, the materialist and positivist assumptions of the biological determinists lay more or less undisturbed. In pursuing this course the militants of social hygiene incurred the wrath of religious groups and sometimes of the state, but by the middle of the twentieth century they had succeeded in defining and policing sexuality.[74] In the century that followed Auguste Comte's death (in 1857) sexuality became a great natural force for good. It came to be understood that it could be sublimated, emancipated, even liberated, but also that it must always be kept under strict surveillance and firm social control. Consequently, while the radical tradition gave impulse, voice and expression to numerous changes to the way in which sexuality was understood and managed, it failed to overcome the impasse between biology and society. For that a move beyond the anthropological imagination was demanded.

5 Enemies of the Oedipal Triangle[1]

Escaping the Biological Impasse

The effort to understand sexuality has struggled beyond the anthropological; it has battled beyond biology, nature and the problems of social management. In the process it has become more truly wonderful and mysterious than it was before the adventure began. A form of analysis has arisen that refuses to be addressed, and refuses to give answers, in the old manner. It is an approach that announces its inability to answer (or even to recognise the question) at the very first meeting. It is of the opinion that 'everything that can be analysed is sexual', but that not everything that is 'sexual is accessible to analysis'.[2] It is in webs of such conundrums that the conventions of reason and intelligibility have become entangled. They have been snared and cocooned by those who wish to dispense altogether with the impasse between biology and society. Moving through the work of André Breton, Georges Bataille, Claude Lévi-Strauss, Roman Jakobson, Jacques Lacan, and the incomprehensible Jacques Derrida, we have arrived at a point where a wholesale assault upon progress, reality and humanity is being promoted by the diabolical Jean Baudrillard.[3]

This kind of approach has been spun from very fine scholarship, and deploys considerable literary subtlety. It rejects the didactic role of those who wish, in some way, to improve the public. It refuses even to make a pedagogic promise. It is not concerned with realising the potential of the existing social relations by conservation, reform or revolution. In this respect it appears peculiarly irresponsible. It is a kind of politics without the political. Many look to it for aesthetic rewards and amusement, while others sink helplessly into the multi-layered mesh of its tricks and allusions, infuriated by its determined indeterminations. The problems and subtleties of this postmodernism are indeed ethereal, tenuous and without substance. But for all that they refuse to melt away. In respect to sexuality they seep, then bubble, and finally, stream, from the work of Freud.

Freud's brilliance lay in his refusal to permit the opposition between biology and society to be resolved. It was kept open like a wound.

Neither was ever allowed stable or authentic priority. A series of gaps were posited and maintained. The gap between the mind and body, between the unconscious and the conscious, between perception and consciousness. Even perception was effaced as its traces passed into memory. As Jacques Lacan was to argue, Freud attempted to find desire, indestructible and timeless, in the unconscious, the gap which is neither being, nor non-being, but the unrealised. We meet the thought that thinks before it attains certainty, in a cause that cannot be rationalised. It is a quest that leads us into the shades. It leads us into a world that is opaque and inexplicable. It is a world where the thought is a thought – it is not a dialectical figure, it is not in a state of becoming – it is already a thought that lacks certainty. Such a thought is, according to Lacan, already an enterprise without the prospect of success.[4] Psychoanalysis is an encounter, an appointment to which we are always called with a real that eludes us:

> The real has to be sought beyond the dream – in what the dream has enveloped, hidden from us, behind the lack of representation of which there is only one representative. This is the real that governs our activities more than any other and it is psycho-analysis that designates it for us.[5]

According to this way of understanding the unconscious, and the general flow of Freud's thought, the mythological and the ambiguous always undermine the certainties of the biological 'substratum'. Whatever Freud hoped for and whatever he worked for, it is evident that his conceptions were distilled, along with other elements present in modern thought, into a spirit strong enough to destroy the stability of perception. Why this concoction was brewed first in France cannot be discussed here, but we must consider the process of its manufacture in some detail.

In 1925 André Breton launched the Surrealist movement with the publication in Paris of the First Surrealist Manifesto.[6] Surrealism set out to undermine the conventions of perception; to overturn the way experience was understood. It sought to challenge the conventions of language, representation and reality. Although its forerunner, the Dadaist movement, was rather more anti-real than Surrealism, André Breton's initiative was still considered pretty strong medicine.[7] The first manifesto did not question either the existence of madness or the designation of different sorts of mental states but it lashed out at 'the Tower Babel constituted by the various classifications of mental illness'. The Surrealists considered that many mental 'disturbances' had a positive value. Hysteria in particular appealed to them: 'For the Surrealists, hysteria was a language, a realm of expression, a work of poetry whose subversive form ought to be championed against art itself, against literature.'[8]

The Surrealists were clearly less concerned with Freud's views than with the revolt they seemed to symbolise; a fact which applies just as much to their concerns with Tarot cards, automatic writing and the paraphernalia of occultism. As Elizabeth Roudinesco explains: 'Fundamentally, Breton identified with the Freudian adventure in its most resolutely modern aspects, which is why his spiritism, and that of his friends, was more like a strident demonstration of iconoclasm than an appeal to the crystal ball.'[9]

The Surrealists were also resolutely opposed to the employment of psychoanalysis for strictly 'medical' purposes and proposed 'a radical break between psychoanalysis and the ideals of medicine'.[10] In fact, it was during the course of the dispute over what Freud termed 'the far from simple relations between psycho-analysis and medicine' that the decisive split among Freudians in France took place.[11] This occurred because what the Surrealists proposed ran directly counter to everything that the Société Psychoanalytique de Paris (SPP) had been trying to achieve. The SPP had been working hard against formidable obstacles to improve its standing by stressing the scientific and medical interest of psychoanalysis.[12] Consequently, the antics of Breton and the Surrealists were regarded with dismay by Princess Marie Bonaparte and the other leaders of the SPP. The rupture was so profound that no section of the organisation was prepared to grant the Surrealists any credence. It meant that the profound cultural impact of psychoanalysis in France took place without the participation of what might be termed the 'official' leadership:

> One consequence of such a split was to create an incommunicability between the psychoanalytic movement and the modernist vanguard. Although they were divided among themselves, none of the twelve founders of the SPP acknowledged the importance of the Surrealist movement in the infiltration of Freudian ideas in France. At the same time, they turned their backs on the entirety of a literary intelligentsia deemed to be dangerous.[13]

As a result, the development of Surrealism, and of the battles within Surrealism, assumed greater importance than the fate of the SPP. These battles reveal the nature of Breton's understanding of Freud, and the stark limitations of Breton's radicalism. In 1928 he participated in two open discussions concerning sexuality. On both occasions several poets gathered around a table and spoke, under the direction of Breton, of their sexual experiences and interests. The discussions ranged from masturbation, through prostitution, voyeurism, fellatio, to the desecration of the Host and the communion chalice with excrement. However, on both occasions Breton angrily drew the line at 'pederasty'; he was fulsome in his condemnation of homosexuality and in expressions of hatred for homosexuals.[14] This intrinsic conservatism was revealed further in the course of the rows between André Breton and the writer Georges Bataille. Their work expressed the sharp contrasts and the opposing tendencies of their respective *Surrealisms*.

In 1928 André Breton published *Nadja,* and Georges Bataille brought out the *Story of the Eye*.[15] The contrast between the two Surrealisms was pointedly made. Whilst Breton sets out to produce a new figure of beauty in the form of the female hysteric, Nadja, Bataille produced a book filled with desecrations, torments and monstrous pleasures which appear as sufferings. Breton ends with a call for a new beauty: 'Beauty will be *CONVULSIVE* or will not be at all.'[16] Bataille finishes his novel with a chapter relating the whole work to a gruesome family story of blindness, death and madness. Aesthetically the two works could not be further apart. For all its subversion of literary form Breton's work is mainstream. It is still concerned with beauty. Bataille on the other hand is unmistakably on the side of ugliness and presents sexuality as intimately bound up with darkness, death and murder.[17]

The antagonism between Breton and Bataille became more pronounced in 1929 when Bataille became involved in setting up a new journal, *Documents*, which rivalled more orthodox Surrealist productions. In the fourth issue he wrote an article called 'Eye' in which he stated: 'It seems impossible ... to judge the eye using any word other than *seductive*, since nothing is more attractive in the bodies of animals and men. But extreme seductiveness is probably on the boundaries of horror.'[18]

With the publication of this journal Bataille announced himself a Surrealist rebel. This was too much for Breton. In 1930 he published the *Second Surrealist Manifesto* which denounced Bataille in no uncertain terms:

M. Bataille's misfortune is to reason: admittedly he reasons like someone who 'has a fly on the end of his nose', which allies him more closely with the dead than with the living, but *he does reason*. He is trying, with the help of the tiny mechanism in him which is not completely out of order, to share his obsessions: this very fact proves that he cannot claim, no matter what he may say, to be opposed to any system, *like an unthinking brute*. What is paradoxical and embarrassing about M. Bataille is that his phobia about 'the idea', as soon as he attempts to communicate it, can only take an ideological turn.[19]

Breton gave full play to his hostility towards the dirt and degradation of Bataille's imagination, and he used the manifesto to announce the progressive and positive aspirations of Surrealism: 'Everything remains to be done, every means must be worth trying: in order to lay waste to the ideas of *family, country, religion.*'[20]

This commitment to revolt was tied to experimentation on a broad range of matters. Most important, however, was the question of language:

> The problem of social action, I would like to repeat and to stress this point, is only one of the forms of a more general problem which Surrealism sets out to deal with, and that is *the problem of human experience in all its forms.* Whoever speaks of experience speaks of language first and foremost. It should therefore come as no surprise to anyone to see Surrealism almost exclusively concerned with the question of language at first, after some foray into another area, as though for the pleasure of travelling in conquered territory.[21]

The concentration on language was only one side of Surrealist action. Language was connected intimately to experience but the greatest experiences were connected with woman:

> The problem of woman is the most wonderful and disturbing problem there is in the world. And this is so precisely to the extent that the faith a noncorrupted man must be able to place, not only in the Revolution, *but also in love*, brings us back to it.[22]

Breton has connected language, experience, woman, love and the revolution. This luscious confection was put forward as the desire of 'the noncorrupted man' who wishes to realise virtue. It is a view that Breton rightly conceived as directly opposed to the filthy M. Bataille. Firm in his opposition, Bataille continued to be preoccupied with the struggle to avoid 'any return to pretentious idealistic aberrations' implicit in Breton's programme.[23] He hoped that:

> By excavating the fetid ditch of bourgeois culture, perhaps we will see open up in the depths of the earth immense and even sinister caves where force and human liberty will establish themselves, sheltered from the call to order of a heaven that today demands the most imbecilic elevation of any man's spirit.[24]

It was in such terms that Bataille bitterly rejected the project of realising ideals by the elevation of men and women through the means made available by the reality (or even the surreality) of the existing conditions. Whereas Breton wanted to reinvigorate the Idea of revolt (realised in the uncorrupted man) Bataille wished to explore the baseness of human–nature combinations in order to defeat Capital through the extension not of the Idea but of the body. These differences were also expressed in the dispute between the two wings of Surrealism concerning the philosophy of Hegel and the possibility of employing dialectics to resolve the contradictions between dreams and material life.[25] As Elizabeth Roudinesco explains, Breton had an inspired approach to the arcane demands of Hegel's thought:

> Breton had 'intuited' Hegel in a philosophy class. He impregnated himself with the texts 'convulsively' in the manner of a hysteric: 'Any specialist', he declared in 1952, 'would be able to show me up so far as exegesis is concerned, on his subject, but it remains no less true that since I intuited him through the sarcasms heaped upon him in or around 1912 by my philosophy teacher, a positivist, André Cresson, I have impregnated myself with his views and for me his method reduces all other to indigence. Where the Hegelian dialectic does not function, there is for me no thought, no hope of truth'.[26]

Breton's approach to Hegelianism was thus expressed through an inspired logic. It was a peculiar hotchpotch that could not spread much outside the direct range of Breton's circle. Bataille published an article in 1932 that he had written with Raymond Queneau in which he dissociated himself entirely from such an overboard commitment to Hegel's work. They made the point that they were dissatisfied with the *Philosophy of Nature* and that this dissatisfaction had led them to oppose, entirely, the orthodox understanding of Marxism: 'To link facts as different as the transformation of electricity into heat (or any other change in nature) and class struggle in fact makes no sense – and in fact no practical sense.'[27]

While Breton's approach permitted idiosyncratic twists it could not move beyond the orthodox account of Hegel. Bataille, however, followed the movement of Hegel's thought much more closely in order to develop constructions of his own. This enterprise was greatly strengthened by the teaching of Alexandre Kojeve, which not only brought a much more coherent conception of Hegel to French intellectual life, but also served as a meeting point for figures like Bataille, Lacan and Lévi-Strauss.[28] The conception of Hegel fashioned by Kojeve was rooted in the *Phenomenology of Mind*.[29] Everything else was read through the rubric of the *Phenomenology* which was itself read and re-read continuously in the seminars. The reading that resulted was one that was pursued in an anthropological and humanist fashion:

> Man is self-consciousness. He is conscious of himself, conscious of his human reality and dignity; and it is in this that he is essentially different from animals, which do not go beyond the level of simple sentiment of self. Man becomes conscious of himself at the moment when – for the 'first' time – he says 'I'. To understand man by understanding his 'origin' is, therefore to understand the origin of the I revealed by speech.
>
> Now the analysis of 'thought', 'reason', 'understanding' and so on – in general, of the cognitive, contemplative, passive behaviour of a being of a 'knowing subject' – never reveals the why or the how of the birth of the word 'I', and consequently of self-consciousness, that is, of the human reality ...[30]

Kojeve's account takes the generalised view of self-consciousness's self-alienation (which divides from itself to produce a self which wishes recognition from itself for itself by itself) as a statement about human reality. Humans are thereby classified as self-conscious and contrasted with animals on the grounds that the latter have no language and thus no notion of an 'I'. He thus uses Hegel's analysis of self-consciousness to found a whole anthropology: 'the human reality can be formed and maintained only within a biological reality, an animal life. But, if animal Desire is the necessary condition of Self-Consciousness, it is not the sufficient condition.'[31]

Animality is the first necessary stage for man's self-consciousness but to realise this self-consciousness he has to engage in productive destruction: 'the I of Desire is an emptiness that receives a real positive content only by negating action that satisfies Desire in destroying, transforming, and "assimilating" the desired non-I.'[32]

The I produced by this action on a thing will still only be an animal I, a 'thingish' I. It is only when Desire turns on Desire (when conscious transformation turns to another conscious being) that the animal is transcended. The proposition is that Desire gives rise to an awareness of the presence of the absence of reality. This absence is itself a reality that is essentially different from the object desired. Consequently, Desire directed towards another Desire will create an I (a presence) quite different from the animal I. Consummation never takes place. A point

of final satiation is never reached. This I reproduces Desire in its satisfaction of its Desire. It is a process in time in which Desire perpetually
gives rise to Desire.[33] Thus man is understood as being primarily a
creature of action who realises himself in history. The stress on action
(which produces conceptions) is more akin to Fichte than Hegel.[34] It
is a view that leads Kojeve to understand the Desire of Desire for
Desire to be the human condition. An ingeniously unsensual conception
of love is the result:

> ...in the relationship between man and woman ... Desire is human
> only if the one desires, not the body, but the Desire of the other; if
> he wants 'to possess' or 'to assimilate' the Desire taken as Desire – that
> is to say, if he wants to be 'desired' or 'loved', or rather, 'recognised'
> in his human value, in his reality as a human individual.[35]

It was along such a route that the idealism of Breton, and his anthropological assumptions about an 'uncorrupted man' was overcome.
Through the work of Kojeve on Hegel's *Phenomenology*, Bataille, Lacan
and Lévi-Strauss came into possession of a much more sophisticated way
of understanding the distinctively human. This outlook, although it lay
resolutely within the camp of philosophical anthropology, opened up
a trajectory of development that permitted a more imaginative and fruitful
line of enquiry than that available to those gathered around the
Surrealism of the *Second Manifesto*. However, it would be wrong to
imagine that these intellectual machinations went on without considerable intercourse between the different and opposing schools of
thought. For example, Jacques Lacan, who became a pivotal figure in
making war on naturalistic and biologistic accounts of Freud, was
active across a broad spectrum of interests. His enthusiasms extended
from Dadaism to monarchism. In his youth he even flirted with fascism.
Roudinesco reports the paradoxical effects: 'Without adhering to any
principles of anti-Semitism, he occasionally participated in meetings of
the Action Française and found in monarchism the wherewithal to
abandon his belief in God.'[36]

His medical training provided him with an entirely organic explanation
for mental illness. However, in 1931, while working on his thesis on
paranoia Lacan met the Surrealists of the André Breton camp, including
Salvador Dalí, whose ideas on the capacity of paranoia to deliver a final
blow to the world of reality made a lasting impression on him.
Henceforth he understood paranoia not as a product of organic processes
but rather as entwined with the range of meanings available for a
subject to understand and interiorise his experience. Lacan dubbed

this new configuration 'concrete psychology'. In 1934, two years after the publication of his thesis, he joined the SPP. It was an important moment for psychoanalysis in France, for although it remained marginal to French medicine, and hostile to the French literati, in Lacan it acquired a new line of communication. He attended Kojeve's seminars on Hegel, published articles on style and paranoia, and did prescient work on paranoid criminals. In 1938 he also won official recognition when he was invited to write an article on family complexes for the *Encyclopie Française*.

Lacan weathered the storm of the Second World War by concentrating on learning Chinese. After the Occupation he came more under the influence of Lévi-Strauss, commencing a serious study of linguistics through the work of Ferdinand de Saussure (1857–1913) and that of Roman Jakobson.[37] He was also inspired by Martin Heidegger's (1889–1976) idea of 'idle talk' – the talk which constantly avoids all important questions – to instigate a revolutionary shortening of therapeutic sessions.[38] He proposed a new swift form of analysis in which the talk would pursue the important questions throughout by directing free association towards certain key themes. Simultaneously, a split was developing in the SPP over a number of other questions concerning therapeutic practice. Lacan's new methods were attacked by most factions. However, he subsequently joined the group that broke away from the SPP and became the Société Française de Psychoanalyse (SFP). As a result of these intellectual and organisational upheavals the 1950s proved a fertile decade for Lacan. His earlier anthropological perspective was radicalised through his contact with linguistics. And, this radicalisation led him to reassess and reinterpret what Freud could have meant by the unconscious.

The importance of Lacan's work lies in the challenge that it threw down to accepted notions of self. Through a critical assessment of language he was able to both derive and explain the self and the unconscious in a new way. He drew out that when we enter the symbolic dimension of language we become subject to its laws – the laws of signs and symbols inherent in language – and, simultaneously, we become a home for these signs and symbols – we are inhabited by them. This is what Lacan means when he says 'the unconscious is structured like a language.'[39] It is what he means when he says that man is 'decentred'. For Lacan, just as much as for Lévi-Strauss, man is the object of a law which transcends him. He is the creature of signs and symbols, and it is only through their exchange and transaction that his self is constituted, his being known, and his unconscious deduced:

Before any experience, before any individual deduction, even before those collective experiences that may be related only to social needs are inscribed in it, something organises this field, inscribes its initial lines of force. This is the function that Claude Lévi-Strauss shows us to be the truth of the totemic function, and which reduces its appearance – the primary classificatory function.[40]

So, before strictly human and social relations are established: 'Nature provides – I must use the word – signifiers, and these signifiers organise human relations in a creative way, providing them with structures and shaping them.'[41]

It was this approach that ensured that Lacan's *elucidation* of Freud produced such radical results. It was rather more ambitious than an 'elucidation'. Lacan was irritated by the staid character of psychoanalytic theory and was of the opinion that theoretical innovation was not only necessary, but inevitable: 'Was Freud really the first, and did he really remain the only theoretician of this supposed science to have introduced fundamental concepts? Were this so, it would be very unusual in the history of the sciences.'[42]

He rejected Freud's idea of a *dynamic* unconscious as wholly inadequate. As far as he was concerned, to say that the unconscious was 'dynamic' was merely 'to substitute the most common kind of mystery for a particular mystery'.[43] In explanation of this mysterious 'dynamic' Lacan introduced the notion of 'a gap': 'Well! It is at this point that I am trying to make you see by approximation that the Freudian unconscious is situated at that point, where, between cause and that which it affects, there is always something wrong.'[44]

This point, or gap, is 'the navel of dreams' that had been tied up. It was forgotten because of the activities of those busying themselves by psychologising analytic theory. By the deployment of the schemas and apparent certainties of the metapsychology all ambiguity was removed and the gap healed over.[45] However, this changed nothing because the 'gap of the unconscious may be said to be *pre-ontological*'. Its existence is pre-existence and 'what truly belongs to the order of the unconscious, is that of neither being, nor non-being, but the unrealised.' So the gap is also lack: 'The unconscious is constituted by the effects of speech on the subject, it is the dimension in which the subject is determined in the development of the effects of speech, consequently the unconscious is structured like a language.'[46]

And the nodal point by which the pulsation of the unconscious is linked to sexual reality is *desire*.[47]

Throughout this entire argument one is constantly assailed by what appears to be the intrinsically incomprehensible nature of drive/desire/instinct and its/their causation. Lacan's ruminations on Freud do not reveal the structure of the drive nor render it any more understandable. Like the Freudian 'dynamic unconscious', the Lacanian unconscious constituted by signs and signifiers is equally opaque and unknowable. It is a mysterious presence/absence that arises at the juncture of the unconscious and the preconscious. It is, simultaneously, expressive of human status because it constitutes an I (Self) that Desires the Desire of Desire. Lacan's structuring of the unconscious, like a language, does not make Freud's metapsychology any more tangible (and nor is it meant to). Always, as we approach the unconscious it closes up, vanishes, melts silently away before our ears can detect its vibration, before our minds can compose an adequate metaphor, or a distinct thought. This, as a matter of course, puts the constitution of desire, sexuality, and the erotic, beyond understanding.

The End of Humanism?

There is another way of looking at all this. Ever since writing 'The Use Value of D.A.F. De Sade' at the end of the 1920s Georges Bataille had proposed the reversal of the philosophical process (which can only express idealism) towards the elaboration of a science of the obscene.[48] Scatology – excreting, rather than appropriation – expressed the demand and the needs of the moment. He continued to be haunted by the possibilities of this anti-philosophy. In 1943 he published a book called *Inner Experience* in which the notion of non-knowledge is experimented with. In this way he attempted to continue the earlier project of a science of the obscene.[49] To enable this to continue he established the journal *Critique* in 1946. He also undertook to write a great number of articles, the majority of which have not been translated. However, his main work *L'Erotisme* was published in 1957 and it was first translated in 1962.[50] The work is organised in terms of Hegelian notions which it sets out to disrupt by presenting them continuously with the vantage point of non-knowledge which they cannot comprehend. He thus understands the activity of knowledge to be coterminous with the world of work (following Kojeve's presentation) and presents this dialectic with the non-knowledge it cannot comprehend: violence. Violence is all that disrupts work, all that diverts energy into areas not recuperable. Eroticism is such a force of violence: 'Only negative experience is worthy of our attention, to my thinking, but this experience is rich enough.'[51]

Eroticism is understood by Bataille as being something more than biological sexual activity. It is the pursuit of self-loss, it is a special manifestation of 'inner experience':

> Man achieves his inner experience at the instant when bursting out of the chrysalis he feels that he is tearing himself, not tearing something outside that resists him. He goes beyond the objective awareness bounded by the walls of the chrysalis and this process, too, is linked with the turning topsy-turvy of his original mode of being.[52]

In this way Bataille sought to develop a theory of excess that is constitutionally rebellious against work and reason. By opting for non-reason, non-knowledge, Bataille sought a transcendence that could never be incorporated by the inherent idealisms of philosophical systems. The focus of these sort of concerns is the untrustworthy nature of manifest appearances, coupled with the recognition that this problem of appearances could not be overcome by suppositions concerning their depth. Surfaces without depth; a present without a past; moments of appearance and disappearance, these perceptions form the ambience of the 'deconstruction' and the postmodernism that the work of Freud, Bataille, Lévi-Strauss and Lacan did so much to bring into our presence.[53]

All stable (or categorical) perceptions of the unconscious, of language, of self, and of desire have been utterly disrupted. As a result, perceptions of force and power have been radically altered. The idea that some kind of sexual kernel exists within every man and woman has been rendered absurd. It has been rendered absurd by the growing awareness of the indeterminations that exist between mind and body, between the conscious and the unconscious, between language, knowledge and meaning, between the past and the present. Consequently the idea that the social climate and the quality of the social soil will determine whether sexuality will grow strong and straight or perverse and twisted has also been pitched back into the 'fetid ditch'. This is because such ideas presuppose a special and privileged knowledge of being human. They reek of an ideal conception of men and women that make us (our consciousness, our bodies, our sexuality), *essentially this or that*. It is upon such philosophical foundations that all liberations, transformations, repressions and *managements* of sexuality are founded. Because of this insight many of those imbued with hostility towards stable orders of perception seek the disappearance of man and mankind. Michel Foucault explains:

> Strangely enough, man – the study of whom is supposed by the naive to be the oldest investigation since Socrates – is probably no more

than a kind of rift in the order of things, or in any case, a configuration whose outlines are determined by the new position he has so recently taken up in the field of knowledge. Whence all the chimeras of the new humanisms, all the facile solutions of an 'anthropology' understood as a universal reflection on man, half-empirical, half-philosophical. It is comforting, however, and a source of profound relief to think that man is only a recent invention, a figure not yet two centuries old, a new wrinkle in our knowledge, and that he will disappear again as soon as that knowledge has discovered a new form.[54]

Foucault thought this notion of man might be nearing its end. He thought it possible 'that man would be erased, like a face drawn in sand at the edge of the sea'.[55] More than this he argued that the end of the anthropological is necessary in order for us to be able to think.[56] For Foucault such a move beyond man opens up the possibility of knowledge. But knowledge is a new kind of movement in which no knowledge can be separated from the various experiences and perceptions that produce it. Gilles Deleuze explains the consequences of such an outlook: 'There are only practices, or positivities, which are constitutive of knowledge: the discursive practices of statements, or the non-discursive practices of visibilities.'[57]

So, knowledge of nature, of our bodies, of social life, ceases to be something that is *produced* by investigation and activity working upon the objects of interest. Knowledge also *produces* its own objects of interest. Knowledge in the course of its movement and articulation constitutes its own field and the kind of events and things that occur within it. This perception led Foucault to investigate how, in modern Western societies, an *experience* came to be constituted that caused individuals to recognise themselves as subjects of sexuality. How was it, Foucault set out to ask, that 'sexuality' (a term that did not appear until the beginning of the nineteenth century) was incorporated into 'changes in the way individuals were led to assign meaning and value to their conduct, their duties, their pleasures, their feelings and sensations, their dreams'.[58] Such questions led Foucault into a study of the slow formation of an interpretation of the self.[59] It also led him towards a particular conception of history:

> My field is the history of thought. Man is a thinking being. The way he thinks is related to society, politics, economics, and history and is also related to very general and universal categories and formal structures. But thought is something other than social relations. The

way people really think is not adequately analyzed by the universal categories of logic. Between social history and formal analysis of thought there is a path, a lane – maybe very narrow – which is the path of the historian of thought.[60]

This conception of history, along with knowledge that constitutes its object in the course of a social discourse, have given great credence to the idea that sexuality is socially constructed. The idea has certainly taken root among the splendid indeterminations and unrepresentable representations of postmodernist thought. Of course, this is only natural. It has been obvious for some time that the mysteries of the dark unconscious would provide an exceedingly fertile environment for the myriad spores produced by speculations on sexuality. And so it has proved to be. However, Michel Foucault's ideas concerning power, knowledge and history did not 'create' the idea of the social construction of sexuality. But they have lent it a certain style, and an impetus, that it has not earned and does not deserve. In fact social construction has rather less Gallic origins, to which we must now turn.

6 The Perspective of History

The Construction of Many Sexualities

Clearly, writing on sexuality employs a vast array of different theoretical approaches. More often than not, it does not carry any great or strong theoretical commitment. Yet the configuration of the writers' work is determined by the preferred angle of attack: literary, antiquinarian, historical, sociological, psychological, physiological. However, the legions of authors are much too precise in the focus of their preoccupations to evince much concern about theoretical consistency. They beg, conflate, borrow, overlap, and steal. They employ whatever revelation, observation or insight they think might prove useful in the struggle to make their most discrete point. Different schools of thought melt into one another, and words that used to mean several definite things quickly acquire several new and indefinite meanings. As Jacques Derrida said of 'deconstruction':

> For me, it was a word in a chain with many other words – such as trace or difference – as well as with a whole elaboration which is not limited only to a lexicon, if you will. It so happens – and this is worth analyzing – that this word which I had written only once or twice (I don't even remember where exactly) all of a sudden jumped out of the text and was seized by others who have since determined its fate in the manner you well know ... But for me 'deconstruction' was not at all the first or the last word, and certainly not a password or slogan for everything that was to follow.[1]

The theoretical outlook of most writers in the field is much too formless to be either denounced or embraced as eclectic. If one's particular concern is the sworn virgins of the Balkans, masochism in the novels of Leopold von Sacher Masoch, or the development of the homosexual bar as an institution, then a great many different bits, belonging to different sorts of theories, will be selected from the continuous background noise generated by the grand (and the not so grand) theories.[2] It matters not whether this is a 'legitimate' or an 'illegitimate' procedure; it is the procedure that determines the particular configuration. Most books on sexuality, and on the history of sexuality, are fashioned by this procedure and come to us along this route.

This is how we should understand the effects of Michel Foucault, the growth of the history of sexuality, and of the ideas that have led many people to suppose that sexuality is a social construction, or even an 'invention'. Foucault's proposition that sexuality had a discrete history was perhaps the most startling: 'The history of sexuality – that is, the history of what functioned in the nineteenth century as a specific field of truth – must first be written from the viewpoint of a history of discourses.'[3]

In line with his conception of the constitutive role of knowledge Foucault noted the importance of tracing the emergence of particular ways of knowing and talking about sex and the effects of these in the determination of the matrix of power relations that cover the entire surface of society. This, paradoxically, created a view of 'the discourse of sex' that was not actually about sex, or about the essence or nature of sex or sexuality. It was an investigation concerned with the part played by the discourse of sex in the production of truth about the self:

> Causality in the subject, the unconscious of the subject, the truth of the subject in the other who knows, the knowledge he holds unbeknown to him, all this found an opportunity to deploy itself in the discourse of sex. Not, however, by reason of some natural property inherent in sex itself, but by virtue of the tactics of power immanent in this discourse.[4]

This view resulted in the history of sexuality being regarded as a series of studies, within a concrete and historical framework, designed for the construction of an analytics of power. It was a view of sex that saw sexuality as an effect of power. Not of the power of law, sovereignty, and the theoreticians of right, but of a diffuse kind of power, a power that manifests itself (and, indeed, grows out of) all the relations that exist in society.[5] The diffusion of this power, and its constitutive role in the elaboration of discourses and knowledge – its role in the production of truth – was understood by Foucault to be the most decisive matter in determining the deployment of sexuality and in the production of its particular historical configuration. Despite the specificity of this kind of approach it appears to produce many points of contact with other accounts. It rejects the idea that sexuality is produced by some kind of rebellious biological energy. It also rejects the idea that sexuality is organised by repression. More importantly, it appears to view sexuality as an effect of power organised through social definition and social regulation.[6] It is at this point that Foucault's hypotheses appear to meet (if not quite gel with) the interests of a more staid kind of sociology: 'The need is to grasp the ways in which specifiable, historically produced meanings shape – and often damage – human experiences.'[7]

It is this sort of concern, and this view of Foucault, that has led the historian Jeffrey Weeks towards the suggestion that because sexual definitions are sites of contradiction and contestation that are historically formed they can be *re*formed by different types of intervention. It has led him to conclude that they can be changed; not just changed in the manner in which they are deployed, but changed fundamentally, both in the way in which they are constituted, and in the resulting practices, and sexual behaviour they describe and give rise to.[8] As Weeks would have it:

> Social processes construct subjectivities not just as 'categories' but at the level of individual desires. This perception, rather than the search for epistemological purity, should be the starting point for future social and historical studies of 'homosexuality' and indeed of 'sexuality' in general.[9]

By this kind of refraction through Foucault's work, as much as from any conscious rejection of purity, the outlook of social construction has arisen to a position of dominant influence. Sometimes its influence is expressed merely as a 'background noise'. Sometimes its influence is direct, conscious, even programmatic. Its success is so widespread that we must consider its direct origins in some detail. It comes from the confluence of sociological concerns stemming from criminology, from the study of deviancy, the development of labelling theory and from ethnomethodology.[10] Put more crudely, the idea that sexuality is a social construction comes from the interactionist wing of sociology.[11] In 1966 Peter Berger and Thomas Luckman argued that 'reality is socially constructed'. They went on to insist that it was the task of the sociology of knowledge to analyse the process in which this construction of reality occurs. Their point was a simple one:

> Sociological interest in questions of 'reality' and 'knowledge' is thus initially justified by the fact of their social relativity. What is 'real' to a Tibetan monk may not be 'real' to an American businessman. The 'knowledge' of the criminal differs from the 'knowledge' of the criminologist.[12]

Similarly, the observation that deviant behaviour is the subject of an active and contextual process of labelling was noted. As Kai Erikson explained: 'Deviance is not a property *inherent* in certain forms of behaviour; it is a property *conferred upon* these forms by the audiences which directly or indirectly witness them.'[13] It was noted that people attach the label 'deviant' to others and in the process *make* them deviant. However, it was also realised that because deviance arises in the course of interaction with others changes in interaction could produce significant changes in behaviour.[14] It is from such modest managerial beginnings that interactionism arose. In the course of time it has developed a surer focus on matters sexual. As John Gagnon and William Simon explained in 1973:

> Our concern here is to understand sexual activities of all kinds (however defined, good or evil, deviant or conforming, normal or pathological, criminal or noncriminal) as the outcome of a complex psychosocial process of development, and it is only because they are embedded in social scripts that the physical acts themselves become possible.[15]

They went on to argue that although the experience of sexual excitement appears to originate from secret sources within the body it is in fact a learned social process that the myth of naturalness conceals from us. In this way the kind of sociology that was interested in the flexible character of human experience and the plasticity of human responses began to build an interactionist account of the social construction of sexuality.

This interactionism is, above all else, a sociology that privileges the experience of the individual (often known as the actor) in the process of constructing the reality in which s/he lives, and which, in its turn, constitutes who s/he is. Consequently, the interactionist is preoccupied with the process by which meaning is created out of a world bereft of inherent meanings. Meaning has to be imposed upon the void. And standards have to be constructed which permit human beings to make judgements between better and worse. Ken Plummer explains:

> For the interactionist, these standards may be *internal* to this theory or *external* to it. Internal standards are derived from the social worlds that he is studying (that is, the rules the actor uses to construct his own reality, or the rules abroad in the objective reality in which he is enmeshed). External standards are derived from outside of the worlds being studied – in particular from the philosophy of science (which

entails a commitment to 'science'), or from various political and moral stances.[16]

Plummer's concern is with the way in which social reality is constantly constructed by people in everyday life. Behaviour is not understood as the product of pre-existing personalities, emotions, attitudes or drives. Nor is it thought of as the product of cultures, structures, organisations or roles. As Plummer explains the interactionist focuses upon emergence and negotiation. The interactionist is interested in:

... the processes by which social action (in groups, organisations or societies) is constantly being constructed, modified, selected, checked, suspended, terminated and recommenced in everyday life. Such processes occur both in episodic encounters and in longer-lasting socialization processes over the life history.[17]

However, it is important not to be too hard and fast about the precise configuration of interactionism. It is not the most theoretical kind of theory. It is generally much more interested in the findings of fieldwork and research than in theoretical refinement. Consequently, little energy is devoted to defining or defending an orthodoxy, and there is not a single 'official' form of interactionism. However, what interactionists do have in common is a belief in the idea of reflexivity: 'the folding back of consciousness on itself'.[18] What this means is that the observer is:

No longer simply a spectator of external events or an omniscient reasoner, he or she will be an integral aspect of those events, evolving as they evolve. The very being who views the world and gives it order will itself be seen and ordered.[19]

Everything that goes to make who one is and what one may do is the product of this process. It is the process that does nothing less than produce the self: 'The self is a symbolic representation, created when consciousness bends back on itself and becomes its own object. It is the result of reflexivity. Turned on itself, mind becomes both subject and object, "I" and "me", observer and observed.'[20]

This production of self does not render itself transparent and trouble-free. On the contrary, one's behaviour can often be surprising and unexpected to oneself. Selves are problematic and can often be quite unintelligible needing repeated attention to fathom them out. However, it is this social production of self – its construction in the course of the subjects' interaction with their surroundings – that is the defining feature of interactionism. This focus upon the self is not the product of any formal sort of individualism. It is rooted in the recognition that in the course of social life 'the discoverer is also discovered'.[21] Selves issue out of this dynamic interaction with society. They are dependent upon the recognition of others and upon their environment, and they do in their turn also contribute to the creation of that same environment – the environment that does so much to constitute them. 'They are emergent products, continually unfolding in ways that cannot be easily predicted. They are contingent, changing from situation to situation.'[22]

This outlook gives definition to the conception of the social construction of sexuality. It is also an outlook that gives expression to the ambiguity of the relations between self and society, and between what is personal and what is political. According to an interactionist the relationship between society and the individual, and between the personal and the political, are perpetually opaque and unstable. They are emergent and shifting oppositions that, if they make sense at all, could only be observed as momentary and contingent social facts; they would be facts that would lose their firm definitions very rapidly in the course of the movement of the self and the social.

This conception of the social is one in which the self (the individual) is always potentially both the subject and the object. The hare and the hound. The hammer and the anvil. The shaper and the shaped. It is the sort of outlook which has very definite sorts of political consequences. Not in terms of political affiliation, but in terms of political response to movement and change in society. It is an outlook that privileges every individual with some active, and potentially self-conscious role, in the constitution both of themselves and the others who surround them. In the field of personal relations it is seen as informing a humanistic sexual politics and practice 'which can free us not only from others' but also from 'ourselves'.[23]

This sort of outlook has given rise to a vast range of responses but at its most radical the stability of the self, the group or class is brought into question. The stability of particular institutions, and even the stability of the social, is undermined as all become embroiled, perpetually, in a constitutive flux that renders all fixed categories elusive. As Ernesto Laclau and Chantal Mouffe have expressed it:

> The limit of the social must be given within the social itself as something subverting it, destroying its ambition to constitute a full presence. Society never manages fully to be society, because everything in it is penetrated by its limits, which prevent it from constituting itself

as an objective reality. We must now consider the way in which this subversion is discursively constructed.[24]

As this argument proceeds it is evident that a plurality of influences and experiences must be presupposed. They will not be an orchestration of distinct elements that seek definition or precise articulation with each other. It is more likely that they will be precarious spaces and identities that cannot be understood or represented as a stable or reliable system of differences.[25] The implications of this pluralism between shifting, indeterminate, self-constituting selves is the dissolution of categories that have essence and definite form:

> But this would seem to imply that, insofar as this precariousness tends to make unstable the internal frontiers of the social, the category of formation itself is threatened. And this is exactly what occurs: if every frontier disappears, this does not simply mean that the formation is more difficult to *recognise*. As the totality is not a datum but a construction, when there is a breaking of its constitutive chains of equivalence, the totality does something more than conceal itself: *it dissolves.*[26]

Sociology, Struggle and Social History

Many proposals concerning the constitution of the self and the social construction of sexuality are derived from rather less novel forms of theorising than those spun by Laclau and Mouffe. The most popular stem from traditional forms of social history refracted through the sociology of interactionism and the conventional apparatus of social struggle. As Jeffrey Weeks has rather testily noted concerning his own practice in the late 1970s: 'The proposal that identities were historically shaped rather than products of nature was hardly radical for a historian familiar with contemporary debates.'[27]

This is certainly true. A form of social construction could quite easily have arisen without the mediating influence of Foucault, interactionism, or Laclau and Mouffe. Marxist historians of many different stripes could certainly have provided a huge array of socially constructed determinations dense enough to have dished anyone fool enough to give voice to the fatalism of biology or the essentialism of the repressive hypothesis.[28] However, this is not what happened. Modern social construction theory did grow through the refraction of Foucault's writings by the existing sociological procedures of interactionist practitioners, and by the concern of radical social historians to emphasise the capacity of the common man and woman to play a leading role in the determination of their own fate. The social construction of sexuality is now an important facet of this mythology. It is a mythology essential to those who desire self-determination.

In this respect the influence of the Marxist historian, E.P. Thompson, has proved decisive. His brilliant book, *The Making of the English Working Class*, published in 1963, threw down a massive empirical challenge to those who would argue that men and women are merely the creatures of circumstance, moulded, shaped, determined, by social forces beyond their control. In the course of more than 900 pages he chronicled the development of the beliefs and struggles and self-determinations of the working class that emerged in England between the last two decades of the eighteenth century and the passage of the great Reform Act of 1832. Much more than a chronicle, Thompson's book evokes the texture of that life and reveals that the tensions between the decaying and emergent social forces produced anxieties of such force and complexity that the designation 'politics' does not really do them justice. He sought to destroy the idea that there is some simple, unproblematic, ideological process which automatically issues from new social relationships to produce new ways of seeing the world. Thompson's purpose in writing the book was to challenge the idea that the working class was simply determined by the process of steam power and the growth of the factory system: 'I was polemicizing against this notion in order to show the existing plebian consciousness refracted by new experiences in social being, which experiences were handled in cultural ways by the people, thus giving rise to a transformed consciousness.'[29]

In adopting this strategy Thompson was opposing the more conservative academics who tended to view the development of the working class simply as a consequence of modernisation. More important than this (at the time), he was also seeking to undermine the 'Marxist' orthodoxy 'which supposed that the working class was the more-or-less spontaneous generation of new productive forces and relations'.[30] It was a dispute to which he gave full attention in 1978 in his famous essay, *The Poverty of Theory*.[31] His hostility towards certain 'Marxisms', which he dubbed 'theological' in character, earned him many friends across a wide political field. Even the right-wing philosopher, Roger Scruton, welcomed Thompson's broadsides against the economic determinist and reductionist enemy: 'Every reader of *The Poverty of Theory* must feel grateful for the existence of a left-wing thinker who is determined to retain both common sense and intellectual honesty.'[32]

However, Scruton also noted, rather obliquely, that it was a remarkable feature of the reading public in England always to be ready to regard an historian – however incapable he may be of theory – 'as a man of ideas'.[33] It is not known whether Sruton was being bitchy, but plainly he was drawing attention to a real tension between English Marxists and their (theoretically) well-endowed comrades in Western Europe. The result was a collision on the degree to which men and women could determine their own fate. It was a collision on the degree to which their own actions and practices are constitutive of the reality in which they have to live, that is, the reality in which they play a determining and active part in constructing. For the opposition, Louis Althusser made the point bluntly:

> That human, ie, social individuals are *active* in history – as *agents* of the different social practices of the historical process of production and reproduction – that is a fact. But, considered as *agents*, human individuals are not 'free' and 'constitutive' subjects in the philosophical sense of these terms. They work in and through the determinations of the *forms of historical existence* of the social relations of production and reproduction (labour process, division and organisation of labour, process of production and reproduction, class struggle, etc).[34]

Althusser went on to make the point that these *agents* could only be *agents* if they are subjects. However, their status as subjects does not make them in any sense the constitutive *subjects of history*. On the contrary, the 'subject-agents are only active *in* history through the determination of the relations of production and reproduction, and in their forms'.[35] The register and tone of this outlook, as much as its specific content, provoked much hostility among those who wanted to emphasise self-determination and self-definition. Consequently, the sort of Marxist social history pioneered by Thompson seemed to offer a safe haven. Thompson became a beacon for those appalled by the bleak litany of determinations issuing from Althusser and and his ilk. As Jeffrey Weeks remembered:

> E.P. Thompson, in *The Making of the English Working Class*, had powerfully demonstrated that class identities were as much products of self-activity as of the forces of nature beyond human control. The new social history, particularly in the work of the pioneering feminist historians of the 1970s, was beginning to demonstrate that other categories we assumed to be natural, such as 'childhood' and 'motherhood', had histories that could be traced.[36]

There is evidently a danger in this kind of outlook that the 'natural' and the 'social' will tend to be conflated. I would venture that there are not many people who would actually describe class identities as 'forces of nature', or as the products of the 'forces of nature'. However, some people would indeed insist that there are entirely *social forces*, which can and do produce relations and realities that lie beyond the capacity of individuals to be able to do very much about them. From this perspective it is perfectly possible to be subjected to the vicissitudes of social forces that are indeed beyond human control. It matters not whether such an outlook is denounced as depressing, dismal or even reactionary; it is clearly a perspective that can defend itself quite adequately against the continuous 'hip, hip, hurrah' of those who think they are (potentially) in complete (and constitutive) charge of their own destiny.

The point about all this is that one does not have to believe in essentialist or biological or economistic determinations in order to challenge the view that sexuality is a social construction amenable to conscious intervention and *re*construction. However, social construction theory issues from just such an insistence. It is characterised not so much by the conflation of nature and society, but rather more from the conflation of the 'self' and the 'social' in the manner of the interactionist account. Social constructionists tend to designate any manifestation of the social that violates the self-definitional as belonging to essentialist determinations: biology and economics (and class ideologies). Social constructionists list heavily towards the view that what is social *cannot* lie beyond the writ of the self or beyond the warrant of self-consciousness and self-activity. This is the case precisely because of the reflexivity of the self in the constitution of the social. Consequently, social forces never operate beyond the possibility of consciousness, or beyond the potential control/mediation of the individual; or beyond the potential control/mediation of social movements and interactionist social strategies and practices.

Social constructionists have erected a view of the world in which social realities are constructed and reconstructed by the self-aware self-activity of political and social movements, working more or less self-consciously to construct new communities, new forms of consciousness, and new practices. This process has been called 'collective self-activity' and:

> we must learn to see that sexuality is something which society produces in complex ways. It is a result of diverse social practices that give meaning to human activities, of social definitions and self-definitions, of struggles between those who have power to define and

regulate, and those who resist. Sexuality is not given, it is a product of negotiation, struggle and human agency.[37]

This version of self-determination and self-definition can prove very heartening. However, it does produce a number of difficulties, two of which spring readily to mind. First, we are confronted with the inscrutable 'I': 'Yet one aspect of the self, the *I* is relatively aloof and stable, scrutinizing situations and itself but defying direct scrutiny and control.'[38]

In other words, the I of the self remains opaque and almost always indistinct. This fact, in itself, presents something of an obstacle to self-definition and hence to self-determination. Secondly, because the self requires external as well as internal standards in order to be able to function, a philosophical, political, and/or moral 'stance' has to be *imported* by the self in order to save itself from triviality.[39] These two problems tend to lead social construction theorists headlong into a struggle to determine an appropriate ethical 'stance' that usually turns out to be some version of 'moral pluralism', or, more prosaically, 'freedom of choice'. Superficially, there is not much wrong with this ethical preoccupation, but it does harbour an *ideal* conception of man and woman. It is the bearer of an ideal view of men and women that sees humanity as being 'world open', that is, active and self-defining rather than instinctive and hidebound: 'Man occupies a peculiar position in the animal kingdom. Unlike the other higher mammals, he has no species-specific environment firmly structured by his own instinctual organisation.'[40]

This corresponds roughly to Arnold Gehlen's understanding of mankind as a 'world open' and undetermined 'acting being' who develops an attitude towards the world, and presents a problem to himself.[41] Gehlen's view was that because man is so frail he would be a wretched, indeed an impossible animal. Human beings have no claws, no fur, no hide, bad eyesight, poor hearing and a comparatively rudimentary sense of smell. Most animals are in some respect or another considerably better equipped. In the animal kingdom man is out-run, out-climbed, out-classed. Many animals are more agile and stronger than human beings; size for size most animals are quicker and more robust than man. Consequently, what is of paramount important about man is his active and world open intelligence:

Man's self-production is always, and of necessity, a social enterprise. Men *together* produce a human environment, with the totality of its socio-cultural and psychological formations. None of these formations may be understood as products of man's biological constitution, which, as indicated, provides only the outer limits for human productive activity.[42]

This is not quite the same as Immanuel Kant's vision of man as a reasoning, and therefore as a rational, animal, but it is not too distant from it:

> All we have left, then, for assigning man his class in the system of animate nature and so characterizing him is this: that he has a character which he himself creates, insofar as he is capable of perfecting himself according to the ends that he himself adopts.[43]

So the more one delves into the logic of social construction theory the more it is revealed as a particular sort of anthropological view. It is an outlook that sees human beings as socially constructed creatures; creatures that exhibit a degree of plasticity of disposition, behaviour and expression unique in the animal kingdom. Indeed, it is so flexible that the meanings and knowledges attached to the human body, and to the relations between it and the self, undergo a constant process of creation and re-creation. It is a relationship that is potentially in a state of flux within each individual. It is a network of social meanings that are perpetually being made, modified, and unmade, through a series of social and cultural processes.

The epistemological tension this produces is fairly evident. Social construction − or self-creation − implies the pre-existence of an essential natural self. Not quite the *tabula rasa,* but an entirely plastic 'world open' creature that is ready for anything. Most of all, social construction envisages a creature that is ready to make itself, interactively, in the course of constituting society and the relations that it will inhabit (and be 'inhabited' by). Many who share this aspiration are well aware that men and women have to make and remake themselves (and the world in which they live), in circumstances that are not entirely of their own making. Ideas of social construction are fashioned by people who have an acute understanding of the points of articulation between the determination of potential and its realisation. As the radical philosopher Kate Soper explains:

> The situations in which we act have not been deliberately brought about by any individual or group, and the consequences of our actions are often themselves unforeseen and unintended. Furthermore, political agents are not necessarily aware of all the factors which have

conditioned their feelings and actions, even though it is not ruled out in principle that they might come to a fuller understanding of these.[44]

It is by this sort of route, dare I say, by this sort of accommodation with 'reality', that social construction theorists arrive at the necessity of determining the desired type or range of types of their 'world open' men and women. They have to determine objectives, negotiate practices, decide for and against particular kinds of behaviour, and decide for and against particular forms of expression. The preference is usually for a plurality of sexualities, and a process of building respect for a huge array of different ways of doing sex, of being sexual, or even (if so desired) of diminishing the presence of the sexual. And whatever accommodations with oppressive relations, or with the commercialisation of sex, are canvassed, the main focus remains the development of a kind of politics that aims, not at the reconstruction of society, but at the reconstruction of sexuality. Or, to be more accurate, at a reconstruction of society through a reconstruction of personal relationships. As Frank Mort has put it:

> If a hundred and fifty years of sexual politics teaches us nothing else, it should be that a large part of winning the argument about groups' and individuals' need to change involves convincing them that their sexuality is capable of changing.[45]

The hope is for a world and a matrix of social relationships that lie in some way beyond the meretriciousness, restrictions and oppressions of the present.[46] It is a complicated tissue of aspirations that encompasses a broad swathe of opinion including feminists, socialists and liberals of many different political hues. However, the essential element in this outlook is a belief in self-determination, both as a practice that shaped the present in the past, and as a practice that will shape the future in the present. It is not a notion of self-determination that sees social construction as being an entirely volitional and subjective matter. On the contrary, the social construction theorists understand the historical construction of sexuality as a process of regulation, struggle, dissent and consensus. On the basis of this perpetually shifting ground a vision rooted in the conception of a life without alienation is conjured. It is the dream of a world in which 'true' selves and 'true' natures will be realised: 'We have the chance to regain control of our bodies, to recognise their potentialities to the full, to take ourselves beyond the boundaries of sexuality as we know it. All we need is the political commitment, imagination and vision. The future now, as ever, is in our hands.'[47]

Evidently, this is a bit of 'rhetorical' flourish, but it does express, authentically, and with clarity, the impulse behind the theory. It expresses a desire for the formation of ideal men and women who will be flexible, open, gentle, generous, democratic persons, whose greatest sexual pleasure is to share sexual pleasure with others. Such people may express these qualities through widely different tastes and sexualities; the plurality will be a plurality of different similarities. Not a lot wrong with that! However, it is inevitably a plurality of sexualities constructed out of the old singular sexuality. It is to be constructed by the *realisation of our contemporary sexual ideals*; the realisation of ideals that carry within them forms of knowledge and deployments of truth indistinguishable from those they seek to replace.

In the day-to-day struggle of *re*construction, within the bowels of 'actually existing capitalism', the social construction theorists have to contend with the paucity of the available imagination. They also have to contend with the problem of articulating the points of contact between the plurality of approved behaviours, and also the points of contact between those behaviours and the state. It is a process of perpetual negotiation and renegotiation that, in the fullness of time, produces political strategies and, it is hoped, positive public policies that will assist in the *re*construction of sexuality.

This brings us to the most important aspect of modern social construction theory. In the past, those who believed that an 'essential' free form of sexuality was disfigured and held down by repression advocated an implacable struggle against the authorities. They had a 'liberationist' model of change. Now, however, the more up-to-date 'aspirational essentialism' credits the state with the potential for a positive role in the construction and reconstruction of sexuality. Paradoxically this places the adherents of social construction theory firmly within the long tradition of sexual management – sexual formation and sexual reformation – that arose in the course of the nineteenth century. The notion that 'we have deconstructed the idea of sexuality' turns out to be, at best a hope, at worst an idle boast. Because it is now clear that the perspective of radical social history in the determination of sexuality has resulted in a continuation of that historical process of assembling and reassembling the forms of knowledge and truth produced by the sexual discourse.

I will return to this question in Chapter 8, but for the moment we must move on (undeterred) to a consideration of the vicissitudes of the relationship between sexuality and the state.

7   The Desire for Order

The Emergence of Consensus

Sexual conduct is often hemmed in, and desire reigned back, by economic considerations, by morality, by custom, and by law. Because of these factors it can appear that sexuality is pulled into directions and shapes that it would not otherwise assume. From this perspective sexuality is constrained, disastrously, by repression. Sexuality is conceived as Prometheus, chained to his rock, or as Gulliver in Lilliput, tied down by a myriad of petty and dishonourable restraints. It must be made free, liberated from the toils imposed upon it by capitalist development. Known in the modern literature as the 'repressive hypothesis' this idea credits the development of modern industrial societies with the inauguration of an age of increased sexual repression. It is a notion that is broadened out to include the belief that sexual repression is orchestrated by the state through family policy, moral panics and the management of deviancy, in order to encourage marriage and the perpetual formation and renovation of regular family life.[1] By these means, it is argued, the state employs the regulation (and the deformation) of sexuality as a means of imposing its authority.

To many who have found this outlook compelling, and entirely plausible, developments over the last decade, and particularly in the last five years, have proved perplexing.[2] These developments have in their way been as stunning as the fall of the Berlin Wall and the disintegration of the Soviet Union. Guided by the repressive hypothesis it was reasonable to assume that war, mass unemployment, chronic economic crisis, Reagan and Bush in America, Thatcher and Major in Britain, Christian Democracy in Germany, 'modernisation' in France, and the worldwide retreat and collapse of socialist political forces, would result in increased repression in the regulation of sexuality. It was axiomatic to those employing the repressive hypothesis that economic and political crisis would result in the militarisation of society. It was imagined that this process of militarisation would result in repressive social policies aimed at promoting and renovating regular family life while crushing and criminalising sexual deviancy. Always, reaction was conceived as a form of return to the past.[3] Nobody believed that history would repeat itself, but many did think that the 'content', if not the 'form', of the moral codes and sexual attitudes of the past would somehow be restored.

None of this has occurred. At least not in the manner envisaged by the adherents of the repressive hypothesis. The forward march of 'liberalisation' has been maintained. It has faltered here and there, on this or that issue, but there has been no general retreat. The trajectory of public opinion, social policy and legislation in modern industrialised societies continues to be towards the acceptance and accommodation of growing diversity in sexual tastes and in domestic arrangements. Consequently, we must look more closely at this process of 'liberalisation'.

As we have seen, the relationship between sexual pleasure, contraception and population management has been woven tightly together since the nineteenth century. The suppression of vice, and the prohibition of perversion, has never succeeded in effacing, or reversing, the development of a subtle and flexible conception of the relationship between sexual conduct, morality and the provenance of the law. At the same time as repression and censorship was widespread, books explaining the art of sexual pleasure were being widely distributed and widely read. As *Ideal Marriage* explained in 1926:

> The clitoris is an organ of voluptuous sensation exclusively. Accordingly it is provided with an abundant network of *nerves*, whose numerous fibres are chiefly clustered immediately beneath the surface of the *glans*, and are peculiarly apt to receive and transmit stimuli. The most sensitive portion is the junction of *glans* and *frenulum*. Even the lightest contact – and more especially a *light* and *gentle* contact – here arouses acute sensations of pleasure.[4]

This is followed up by an explanation, and even advocacy, of the 'genital kiss' that may be enjoyed by both partners.[5] The book is rounded off with a series of detailed colour-coded charts and diagrams of the genitals and the pace of sexual response. This book went through 42 impressions in Germany between 1926 and its suppression by the fascists in 1933. The English edition was published in 1928 by Heinemann and went through 43 printings, totalling 700,000 copies. And it is estimated that Random House sold around 500,000 copies in the USA between 1930 and 1945.[6] *Ideal Marriage* emphasises the importance of interaction between man and woman, the reciprocal joys of giving and receiving pleasure, and the necessity of learning how to do it.

Even the Roman Catholic Church, while explicitly opposing the achievement of equality by women, was prepared to endorse sexual pleasure, rather than procreation, as a legitimate motive for sexual intercourse.[7] As early as 1931 Pope Pius XI gave love, and the quieting of strong sexual desire, as sufficient reasons for having intercourse within the so-called 'safe' periods. It was buried in the less than explicit language of the encyclical, *Casti Connubbii*, but its meaning must have been plain to every confessor and parish priest in the world:

> Nor are those considered as acting against nature who in the married state use their right in the proper manner, although on account of natural reasons either of time or of certain defects, new life cannot be brought forth. For in matrimony as well as in the use of the matrimonial rights there are secondary ends, such as mutual aid, the cultivating of mutual love, and the quieting of concupiscence [strong sexual desire] which husband and wife are not forbidden to consider so long as they are subordinated to the primary end and so long as the intrinsic nature of the act is preserved.[8]

The Pope was engaged in an important rearguard action against the spread of contraception, and his cardinals obviously thought some form of accommodation was wiser than the outright condemnation of intercourse for pleasure. By the mid-1930s condom sales had reached 317 million per year in the United States of America alone. In 1936 Norman Himes described the situation as follows:

> The height of mechanized diffusion of contraceptives seems to have been reached in one respect in Germany and Holland, where for many years condoms have been sold by coin slot-machines! In the United States vending machines have been introduced; and more are sold in gasoline stations and tobacco shops than in drug stores. Thus enters a new problem of social control.[9]

Himes goes on to describe, in awe-struck vein, the introduction of modern mass production techniques for the manufacture and testing of condoms in huge plants and factories.[10] Evidently, from the Vatican to the filling station, the idea that sexual intercourse could be largely about pleasure, and only incidently about procreation, was well established before 1940. It became clearer that sexual intercourse within an ordinary family setting could be specifically aimed at pleasure, and not simply at the release of the husband's sexual tension, or the generation of babies. The idea of 'non-reproductive' sexual engagement was domesticated as it left the brothel and entered the home. As the years went by these developments were to have important implications for the understanding of masturbation, and of homosexual practices. Inevitably, there was an attenuation of the natural, purposeful, procreative, *defence* of regular sex. The charge against the perverse, that their sex was barren, unreproductive, and therefore unnatural, began to lose some of its force.

The sources and implications of developments of this sort have a depth and range that cannot be discussed here. However, it must be borne in mind that nothing in the twentieth century has been able to halt the perpetual transformation of all the technical and social circumstances of life. Not even the strategies of clerical and fascist movements. By and large, the military and industrial ambitions of European dictators resulted in such upheavals that, despite conservative ambitions and the killing of 'sexual deviants', the older forms of family life (and the sexual assumptions that went with them) were dislocated, or perished amid the destruction. It is also clear that the democratic state, and the religious authorities, have not felt able to respond to changes in sexual conduct simply by prohibition or repression. Research, discussion, and the development of a policy directed towards the management of change, seems always to have got the better of the bigots.

None of this should allow us to underestimate the degree of violence and the bitterness with which those opposed to sexual reform have attempted to delay, divert, and hold back change. Such people have tended to regard amendment of law, education, and medical practice as the source of changes in public attitudes and conduct. This has always been a mistake. Or, at best, an oversimplification. In most respects the authorities have *followed* rather than *led* reform. However, refusal to recognise the spontaneous element in the perpetual alteration of sexual life has always led reactionaries to charge legislators, campaigners, educators, and even researchers, with the erosion of respect for religion, tradition and morality. As the entomologist, Alfred Kinsey (1894–1956), discovered, even the *study* of sexual behaviour in the 1930s and 1940s provoked bitter hostility and harassment:

> There were attempts by the medical association in one city to bring suit on the ground that we were practising medicine without a licence, police interference in two or three cities, investigation by a sheriff in one rural area, and attempts to persuade the university's administration to stop the study, or to prevent publication of the results, or to dismiss the senior author from his university connection, or to establish a censorship over all publication emanating from the study.[11]

Clearly, those opposed to change did not want to know what was going on, and feared the consequences of such knowledge. As things turned out, their worst fears were realised. Among the 'worst' was the revelation that 37 per cent of white men in America had had sex with another man *after* adolescence. A quarter of the men in America had had more than incidental homosexual experience over a *three-year period* between the ages of 16 and 55.[12] It led to the conclusion that:

> Since only 50 per cent of the population is exclusively heterosexual throughout its adult life, and since only 4 per cent of the population is exclusively homosexual throughout its life, it appears that nearly half (46%) of the population engages in both heterosexual and homosexual activities.[13]

If these figures are startling today, their impact in 1948 was explosive. The public's fascination with Kinsey's findings could not be staunched. Interest spilled out well beyond the scientific and academic community:

> After commissioning a market analysis of the book's potential audience, the publishers ordered a first run of 5000 copies of *Sexual Behaviour in the Human Male*. But the huge demand for the 804-page tome brought the number of copies in print to 185,000 within two weeks of its official publication date of January 3, 1948. Both volumes spent several months high on the *New York Times* bestseller list, and each sold almost a quarter of a million copies ... The Indiana zoologist appeared on the cover of *Time,* newspapers made headlines out of critiques of his work, and a Hollywood producer tried to secure rights to the scientific treatise.[14]

It appeared that public findings and public discussion had caught up with the private practice of millions of Americans. Cold War hostilities led to witch-hunts of homosexuals and Kinsey's revelations did not do much to calm fears of the corrosive effects of perversion on the foundations of the republic. However, just as strongly, and in the long run much more effectively, Kinsey strengthened the hand of those engaged in the struggle to emancipate homosexuals from social and legal repression.[15]

In 1953 Kinsey's team followed up their earlier work with publication of *Sexual Behaviour in the Human Female* and announced that:

> homosexual responses had occurred in about half as many females as males, and contacts which had proceeded to orgasm had occurred in about a third as many females as males. Moreover, compared to the

males, there were only about half to a third as many of the females who were, in any age period, primarily or exclusively homosexual.[16]

As may be imagined, these sort of findings were not reassuring to conservative opinion. Even more alarming in the early 1950s were observations of this sort:

Of the thirty-three psychosexual stimuli which arouse the male erotically, only three – movies, reading romantic literature, and being bitten – aroused as many or more females than males. There is, of course, great individual variation, but there can be no doubt about the sex differences as a whole.

The Kinsey workers have reversed the traditional belief, now shown to be false, that women are creatures of sex while men are in control of sex. The opposite is true.[17]

It does not matter for our purposes whether ideas of this sort were well-founded or not because, whether true or false, they indicate the way such research and public discussion had the effect of turning the sexual world upside down. The effects were to have an enormous impact in Britain and throughout Western Europe. As early as 1952 the British writer, Gordon Westwood, was to make the point that:

It would not be surprising if a scientific investigation revealed that the incidence of homosexuality was even greater than Kinsey found in the United States. The unnatural restraint and prudishness of parts of our sex code might well be a source of a great deal of abnormality. Alex Waugh, Bruce Marshall and others have drawn attention to the dangers of frustrated sexual impulses in our all-male public schools. The intense cultivation of games in England has its echo in the Athenians' worship of the male human body.[18]

Westwood went on to calculate that: 'Even if we use the figures of 4 per cent which on the available evidence seems to be a very conservative estimate, this means that there are over 650,000 homosexuals in England and Wales alone.'[19]

The importance to the state of the scale and incidence of homosexual behaviour among men lay in the fact that it was illegal. Millions upon millions of men were violating, not only traditional moral laws, but the legal code as well. As the British Member of Parliament, Leo Abse, was to note, the chances of an illegal homosexual act leading to a conviction was about 30,000 to one. It is not clear how he calculated this, but his point was clear enough: blanket prohibitions of homosexual behaviour among men are unenforceable and consequently bring the law into disrepute.[20] It was thinking of this sort, well-larded with the desire not to punish people for behaviour and a sexual disposition that was not of their choosing, that led to substantial changes in the law, and gave impulse to the spread of increasingly liberal attitudes.

At any rate, there was to be no respite, either in the pace of change or in the degree of public discussion and detailed investigation to which sexuality was to be subjected. In Britain Parliament convened a committee, under the chairmanship of Sir John Wolfenden in 1954, to review the law on homosexual offences and on prostitution.[21] In the same year, William Masters and Virginia Johnson commenced their investigation in America into *Human Sexual Response*. The revelations concerning the widespread nature of homosexuality among men, and the lively and intense sexuality of women, continued to keep the sexual pot on the boil. As Masters and Johnson were to emphasise, women have very special characteristics when it comes to orgasm:

> The clitoris is a unique organ in the total of human anatomy. Its express purpose is to serve both as a receptor and transformer of sensual stimuli. Thus, the human female has an organ system which is totally limited in physiologic function to initiating or elevating levels of sexual tension. No such organ exists within the anatomic structure of the human male.[22]

As if this was not bad enough for the traditionalists, Masters and Johnson were to argue eventually that:

> The homosexual male always has certain advantages in being able to interact with a same-sex partner. There is a sense of identification and a level of subjective appreciation of fears of performance that perforce are lacking when a sexually dysfunctional man is interacting with an opposite sex partner.[23]

This led Thomas Szaz to turn more sour than usual: 'This is depressingly familiar. Masters and Johnson's research is merely a variation on the theme that the oppressed are morally superior.'[24]

In this response Szaz is expressing the kind of dismay that 30 years of relentless change and upheaval in sex knowledge, sex conduct and sexual manners have wrought. It seems that once out of the bottle the brazen *genie* of explicit discussion and public knowledge could not be put back. The old moral certitude, and former conceptions concerning the sexual behaviour of men and women were irreparably shattered between 1950 and 1980. Classicist Allen Bloom was working on a different timescale when he noted in 1987 that: 'The change in sexual relations, which now provide an unending challenge to human ingenuity, came over us in two successive waves in the last two decades. The first was the sexual revolution; the second, feminism.'[25]

It has been, according to Bloom, an unsatisfactory sort of experience, resulting in feelings of guilt, unease and confusion in young men and male university professors alike. The forward march of feminism has resulted in the onset of a sort of reign of terror.

> The new reign of virtue, accompanied by relentless propaganda on radio and television and in the press, has its own catechism, inducing an examination of the conscience and the inmost sentiments for traces of possessiveness, jealousy, protectiveness – all those things men used to feel for women. There are, of course, a multitude of properly indignant censors equipped with loudspeakers and inquisitional tribunals.[26]

Nostalgia of this sort – for the good old days when men were men, and women were silent, and everybody knew where they stood – is widespread. It has been issuing from every social pore in North America and Western Europe throughout the last 40 years. However, the state has had to respond to changes in sexual conduct and manners with less prejudice and rather more regard for the social order. It has had to do its best to absorb and regulate changes that it could not rationally deny, or efficiently suppress. Inevitably, this has involved jurists in a discussion of the provenance of moral laws and in the range and duties of the state in upholding them. As Kinsey noted in 1948:

> It is ordinarily said that criminal law is designed to protect property and to protect persons, and if society's only interest in controlling sex behaviour were to protect persons, then the criminal codes concerned with assault and battery should provide adequate protection. The fact that there is a body of sex laws which are apart from the laws protecting persons is evidence of their distinct function, namely that of protecting custom.[27]

In London in 1957 the *Wolfenden Report* on homosexuality and prostitution was published. It made a firm distinction between behaviour and the person, making the point that homosexuality is a state or condition, and as such cannot come within the scope of the criminal law.[28] The report noted that the law must apply to actions of particular sorts rather than to tastes or predispositions, and the law must be able to show that some particular damage to society flows from homosexuality. This the Wolfenden committee could not do:

> We have had no reasons shown to us which would lead us to believe that homosexual behaviour between males inflicts any greater damage on family life than adultery, fornication or lesbian behaviour. These practices are all reprehensible from the point of view of harm to the family, but it is difficult to see why on this ground male homosexual behaviour alone among them should be a criminal offence.[29]

The fate of Sodom and Gomorrah, the fall of Rome, feelings of revulsion and disgust – all these were discounted by Wolfenden when the committee made the point that:

> Unless a deliberate attempt is to be made by society, acting through the agency of the law, to equate the sphere of crime with that of sin, there must remain a realm of private morality and immorality which is, in brief and crude terms, not the law's business.[30]

It took a further ten years for these views to influence the framing of the law on homosexuality in England and Wales. However, a legal opinion rebutting Wolfenden came somewhat faster. In March 1959 Sir Patrick Devlin delivered the Maccabean Lecture in Jurisprudence which was published in the same year. He opened with the opinion that as a judge he did not feel that a complete separation of sin (that is, an infringement of morality) would be good for the moral law or the criminal code.[31] He argued that because all sexual immorality involves the exploitation of human weakness that there was virtually no field of morality which can be defined in such a way as to exclude the law. By reasoning of this sort he arrived at a parallel that must have delighted J. Edgar Hoover (1895–1972): 'The suppression of vice is as much the law's business as the suppression of subversive activities: it is no more possible to define a sphere of private morality than it is to define one of private subversive activity.'[32]

He defended this reaction by reference to what the man or woman 'in the street', or any 12 men and women selected for jury duty, might conclude was moral or immoral, because it is the power of common sense and not the power of reason that lies behind the judgements of society:

> No society can do without intolerance, indignation, and disgust; they are the forces behind the moral law, and indeed it can be argued that if they or something like them is not present the feelings of society

cannot be weighty enough to deprive the individual of freedom of choice.[33]

In response to all this the Oxford Professor of Jurisprudence, H.L.A. Hart, gave a series of lectures at Stanford University in which he argued that the morality of the enforcement of morals had also to be considered. Because of this, Hart insisted, morality enters into the discussion in two ways, and is rather more complicated than Devlin had suggested. Hart pointed out that in Boston in 1948 248 people had been arrested for adultery and he noted that:

In America a glance at the plural statutes of the various states of the Union reveals something quite astonishing to English eyes. For in addition to such offences as are punishable under English law, there seems to be no sexual practice, except 'normal' relations between husband and wife and solitary acts of masturbation, which is not forbidden by the law of some state.[34]

It is evident that Hart did not think that such statutes were necessary for the preservation of civilisation. He made the point that Devlin gave no evidence to support his contention that deviation from accepted sexual morality is a threat to the existence of society. Astutely, he noted that Devlin's argument was based on the assumption that all morality – sexual morality as well as rules that forbid killing, stealing and dishonesty – form a single seamless web, so that those who break one moral law are more likely to, or are even bound to, break all of them. This, Hart argued, was an entirely unproven and false assumption.[35] On his opponent's views Hart concluded:

[Devlin] appears to move from the acceptable proposition that *some* shared morality is essential to the existence of any society to the unacceptable proposition that a society is identical with its morality as that is at any given moment of its history, so that a change in its morality is tantamount to the destruction of a society.[36]

In making this point, Hart was recognising that the central function of law is the preservation of society and that this can no longer be regarded as synonymous with the preservation of some traditional or religious moral codes. Even when public attitudes may shift, for a time, in the direction of restoring more traditional attitudes, the state must take care. Thus, in Britain in the late 1980s, T.E. Utley urged caution upon the Thatcher administration:

So long as the state does not run counter to prevailing moral convictions (which, we are told, are becoming increasingly conservative) it can do something, if it wishes, to promote the cause of traditional morality; but it must not be strident and it must be circumspect.[37]

The Role of the State

The state, as the seat and defender of the law, exists to protect society. The state does not exist to guard some long-forgotten type of social set-up, or some kind of imaginary society of the future. It exists to preserve and protect society as it is presently constituted, and the process by which it is perpetually reconstituted. Consequently, the modern state is as fair and equal, and as unfair and unequal, as the market system will permit. Among other things, it must accommodate the right of individuals to own raw materials, machines and real estate, and it must preserve their right to hire labour in order to increase the combined value of this property.

However, just as important as protecting the ability of property owners to make profits from hired help, is the ability of the state to handle rapid development and change. This is because capitalist society is dominated by the perpetual displacement, replacement, renovation and renewal of all the technical and social circumstances of daily life. Today, the state must maintain order by regulating change. It must defend the dominant interests of the wealthy by being prepared to reform public policy incessantly, and to oversee the management of social and economic affairs in a flexible and prudent manner. If it does not do this the state will be overtaken by events, its laws will become archaic and outmoded, and it will no longer represent the needs of society.

It is true that the collection of disparate sorts of institutions that make up the state often seek to enhance their authority and legitimacy by reference to their great age, to old traditions, and antique ideas. However, integral to the claims of continuity, and the preservation of a highly 'cultured' patina of age, is a ruthless modernity; a modernity expressed in the ability of the state constantly to create and re-create itself, in much the same way that the society which it serves, more or less spontaneously, creates and re-creates itself. In capitalist society this is what *order* means: the ability to be able to manage change without serious disruption to the interests of the most influential and powerful sections of society. Order cannot, and does not, mean the defence of some kind of age-old tradition or the promotion of some kind of timeless morality. *Today, order is achieved only through change.* In relation to sexual conduct and sexual manners this has embroiled the state not simply in discussion of the niceties of jurisprudence, but in substantial social and legal reforms. These reforms have given expression to the trend towards the 'liberalisation' of public opinion; they are reforms that have been reflected in the increasingly tolerant attitudes of the public, and the authorities, towards new varieties of being sexual, and new kinds of domestic arrangement.

In Britain most of the major reforms were enacted during the terms of two Home Secretaries. The first, Rab Butler (Conservative Party), the second, Roy Jenkins (Labour Party). Sociologist Stuart Hall has provided us with the following handy summation:

> The first period – the 'Butler reforms' – included the limitation of the death penalty (the Homicide Act 1957), the Street Offences Act 1959 (dealing with prostitution), the Obscene Publications Act 1959, the Suicide Act 1961, and legislation affecting licensing, betting and gambling. Above all, it included the *Wolfenden Report* (1956–8), which enunciated the fundamental principles and doctrines that shaped legislation for the whole decade (HMSO, 1957). The second – largely coincident with the tenure of Roy Jenkins – included the Murder (Abolition) Act 1965, the second Obscene Publications Act in 1964, the Sexual Offences Act 1967 (dealing with homosexuality), the Family Planning Act 1967, the Abortion Act 1967, legislation on divorce (1969), theatre censorship (1968) and the law governing Sunday entertainments (1968).[38]

The purpose of all of these reforms was to bring the law into alignment with contemporary attitudes; their purpose was to ensure continued public respect for the capacity of the authorities to frame and enforce laws that could commonly be regarded as necessary and rational. This procedure was essential if the police, the probation service and the courts were to secure the degree of public consent necessary within a democratic state. This was their *purpose*. Their *effect,* by and large, was to enhance the rights of the individual citizen and to increase the range and quality of their freedom of expression and the kinds of choices available to them.

In the United States of America the battles have been more bitter, more hard fought, more violent, as befits a much more heterogeneous society. However, since the mid-1950s – when the American Law Institute published with its draft Model Penal Code a recommendation that all consensual relations between adults in private should be decriminalised – the trajectory of American public opinion, and of American public policy, has been towards enhancing the rights of the individual.[39] In relation to sexual conduct, and to abortion and contraception, the struggles waged in America have resulted in the wholesale transformation of the policy and the behaviour of the authorities in vast areas of the country.[40]

There has been a backlash and it has become a permanent responsive feature of all debates concerning sexual reform. From the days when a county sheriff attempted to put a stop to Alfred Kinsey's questions there have always been reactionary 'die-hards', opponents of change ready to fight against public discussion of sexual matters, and always prepared to offer resistance to reform. They range from popular religious figures and purity campaigners, to people well placed within the establishment: congressmen, parliamentarians, police chiefs and mayors. They represent those sections of society appalled by the changes in sexual manners occurring all around them. The British purity campaigner, Mary Whitehouse, spoke for millions when she pointed out:

> The natural repugnance which most people feel when homosexuality and lesbianism is mentioned can result in a harshness of attitude and thinking which is, at least, unhelpful and certainly as unchristian as the perverse practices which are condemned. But to go to the other extreme and elevate people suffering from such abnormalities into a norm for society not only threatens society but is dangerous to the individuals themselves, since it excludes them from the consideration of treatment.[41]

In this way, voice is given to those who are attempting to moderate, slow, or even stop, all development and change within the sexual life of society. For this reason, purity campaigners can never actually succeed. They cannot stop the process of perpetual change. However, they can, and do, slow down acceptance of change by the state, and often by the general public. They focus discussion around the threat posed by changes in sexual conduct to traditional forms of morality and to traditional social institutions. Like Lord Devlin, they equate sexual pluralism with immorality, general social disorder, and the imminent disintegration of society in a wave of vice and crime. They also object to the way in which liberalisation and sexual reform renders sayable what was formerly unsayable, and makes thinkable what used to be unthinkable:

> A cursory glance at the outcome of permissive legislation in the past 20 years leads one to the conclusion that it always leads to the opening of the floodgates and a whole range of new problems. In the

semantic revolution the unborn child becomes 'the contents of the womb' or 'a blob of jelly', abortion 'termination of pregnancy', paedophilia 'young love', the illegitimate child 'a love child' and the homosexual 'gay'. Thus the unthinkable becomes palatable; everything is relative and nothing normative.[42]

Neither these attitudes nor the legislative reversals suffered by women and homosexuals have bitten deeply into public consciousness; they have not restored the moral climate of former times. However, the fears of purity campaigners always act as a drag-break, slowing, but never actually stopping, reversing or diverting the process of reform in any fundamental sense. The other effect of their activity has been to prolong the currency of the repressive hypothesis. Reactionary state and local government officials, purity campaigners and right-wing journalists furnish those who favour the repressive hypothesis with ample evidence of the backlash against sexual reform being prepared by the moral rearmers, and their friends and allies in high places. More tangible are those campaigns aimed at amending or actually reversing reforms that are already in force, and have been so for some time.[43]

This, not unreasonably, causes supporters of the repressive hypothesis to fear a reimposition of old restrictions and a return of the old moral conditions. However, this is precisely what cannot happen, because the old conditions, and the old sort of social circumstances and sexual relationships, have vanished forever in the hubbub of economic, domestic and cultural change that characterises modern conditions. Both those trying to put the clock back, *and* those who fear that it will be put back, are labouring under the same misapprehension: they believe that sexual and social life are (or, at least can be) creations of the state and of public policy.

Both left and right tend towards a version of social construction theory, enabling both sides to fight passionately for their respective visions of the preferred (or most virtuous) modality for sexuality. The theorists of the left have a tendency to suggest that those on the right regard sexuality as an entirely natural phenomenon that must be kept in check by Mosaic laws. And fundamentalists, from Jewish, Christian and Muslim traditions, do believe in exactly that. But most of those who fight to defend traditional values do not regard the Koran, the Pentateuch or the New Testament as the last word on the matter, nor do they believe in appeals to the authority of nature.

The outlook of the right cannot be grasped at all unless this is properly understood. The mythological role of the concept 'natural' must be acknowledged. Those who say that something is 'natural' are, by and large, making a statement about how they feel about the thing (or the relationship) under consideration. They are saying that this or that is right and proper. By saying that something is 'natural' they are saying that it is fitting. They are not, as a rule, making the literal statement that the phenomenon described as 'natural' is *natural* in the sense that it is unmodified by humanity or by civilisation. It is important to bear this in mind because most modern purity campaigners regard sexuality as a social artefact. If they did not they would not fight so tenaciously to inculcate little boys and girls with the correct 'natural' impulses. It is evident that for them sexuality is a 'natural' potentiality or aspect of human feeling. As such, it must be fashioned by good discipline and by good example, and treasured by restraint. In this way, and by the internalisation of conventional conceptions of social responsibility, sexual manners and sexual conduct will ennoble the individual, adding to the stability of key social structures, and to the general welfare of society.

Thus the desire for order is expressed and met within the dominant – social construction/interactionist – sort of account. Except for the most narrowly biologistic, the most fundamentally biblical, and the most ruthlessly postmodern, most writers about sexuality fall within the parameters of the social constructionist account. It is an account that recognises the dynamic complexity of the relationship between the natural substratum and the social construction of sexuality and the person. It is an account that attributes a key role to the state, and to social engineering, in the realisation of comtemporary sexual ideals. The resulting outlook is one torn by dissent over what those contemporary ideals might be. But it achieves the status of a consensus in espousing the common belief that human free will, and self-determination, can be employed to construct, reconstruct and determine the configuration of sexual desire, and the kind (and range) of sexual practices to be preferred by society at large.

8 Beyond the Consensus

Conclusions for the Future

At the beginning of this book I focused the narrative of sexuality upon the impasse between biology and society. I did this because it appears to be within the parameters of this conflict that sexuality acquires its numerous meanings. I wanted to look at the problem in the way that it is most often understood. I wanted to see if the assumptions that many of us have about these different and opposing accounts of sexuality would withstand investigation. It turns out that they do not. The opposition between sexuality as a natural effect of our biology, and sexuality as a product of social construction, does not do justice to the complexity of the thinking at work. Quite apart from anything else, this bipolar argument conceals the extent to which opposing ideas are subsumed (or remain embedded) within each other. Specifically, it does not take account of the degree to which those who believe in 'natural' sex acknowledge the social constitution of human sexuality. Neither does it give notice of the extent to which social construction theorists have built upon a substratum of presuppositions derived from anthropology and the 'world open' nature of human beings.

As we have seen the history of the history of sexuality has its roots in the discourses of biology, anthropology, criminology, psychology, sociology, philosophy and social history. The process of their emergence (or development) as modern discourses (and academic disciplines) has formed the context in which the discourse of sexuality has acquired its particular social presence, its own politics, and its own social history. For this reason a history of the emergence of sexuality during the course of the last two centuries must be drawn from many different sources. Above all, it must dispense with the desire to take sides within the construction of the historical record. This is not a plea for 'objectivity', but it is a call for a disengagement with a particular sort of involvement. We must dispense with the idea that Margaret Sanger, Emma Goldman or Stella Browne were 'our' sisters, or that Walt Whitman, Havelock Ellis or Edward Carpenter were on 'our' team. They were not. They belong to the past, and the past does not ever prefigure the present in the manner beloved by radical social historians.

Thus, escape from entanglement in the historical constitution of sexuality will involve a refusal to be party to its different factions. Above all the history of sexuality must 'be realistic and do the impossible'. It must disengage from the discourse of sexuality. In other words, the history of sexuality must escape from the process that called it into existence. It must dispense with the impasse between biological determinations and social constructions. It must refuse participation in the constitution or reconstitution of sexuality (which, in any event, could only be a form of accommodation with the definition and redefinition of normality).

The difficulties are immense. The *raison d'être* of much of the history of sexuality has been to discover and express the manner in which the relations between oppressed and oppressor have constituted sexuality as a special field of power, knowledge and social regulation. The particular importance of this has been the felt necessity on the part of radical historians, sociologists and philosophers to participate with the activists of various social movements in the demolition of the idea of sexuality as a free-standing and monolithic structure. The idea of 'men', of 'women', of 'perversity', of 'normality' – the idea of working with the discrete and stable categories of the past – just had to go. They had to be demolished, or 'deconstructed', if the oppressed were to have any hope at all of reorganising public perceptions and social practice. This was evident because of the manner in which the discourse of sexuality had decreed particular sorts of sexual relations that, in turn, merged into particular sorts of sexual divisions. In other words, the history of sexuality had to reveal the *historical process* in which the personality, character and social status of everybody in the society came to be constituted by their gender and by the particular sorts of sexual behaviour they felt drawn towards.

This process of historicising what had formerly appeared to be natural is what constitutes the history of sexuality and it is what situates it within the twin traditions of radical social history and interactionist sociology. The struggle to understand the construction of reality as a social process merges within the history of sexuality into the idea of self-determination. It is an idea which appears to offer the oppressed the prospect of putting an end to their status as the creation of someone else's imagination. In the field of sexuality, self-determination of the oppressed opens up the prospect of self-definition for women, for lesbians, for homosexual men. This is an idea which empowers. Potentially, it emancipates the oppressed from the notions of themselves imagined by their oppressors. In this way the oppressed can establish positive images of themselves; they can turn the tables on the oppressor by establishing the historical character of the 'truth' and the 'knowledge' of sexuality deployed during the development and regulation of modern society.

This process intersects with many different kinds of struggle in society. However, the principal point of contact between the history of sexuality, and those other struggles, is a belief in the capacity of ordinary men and women to determine their own fate. What is shared is the belief that emancipation will be achieved within a process of self-determination initiated amongst the oppressed. This has led the history of sexuality, and its political constituency among the oppressed, inexorably towards the theory that sexuality is the product of social construction. And it is axiomatic that sexuality may be reconstructed in the course of social struggles and social trends that aim at the elaboration of new sexual practices and novel domestic arrangements. Along the way they have recruited all those people who are imaginatively committed to the extinction of the 'natural' conceptions of sexual practice that do survive.

Thus it emerges that social construction theory is an illusion. It is an illusion because it arises more out of the wish for it to be true than from any evidence that we may have. It is an illusion, not a necessary fiction. Some might think that in order to emphasise the capacity of human beings to determine their own fate they must emphasise the role of society over that of nature and biology. According to this approach, while the theory of social construction might not be entirely adequate, we need it in order to do battle with the idea that sexuality is an immutable unchanging sort of 'thing'. Presumably, some people do this because of the prejudice which holds that 'social' things and relations are, on the whole, more amenable to human intervention than those things given to us by 'nature'. This prejudice rests upon the false assumption that the condition *social* is synonymous with being open to endless deliberate variation and conscious change, while the condition *biological* is synonymous with an inflexible substratum upon which the social may be constructed.

This opposition is unhelpful because it avoids entirely the significance of the relations between the social and the natural in all modern societies. Social relations can and do move beyond human control, and natural relations do increasingly become social relations. Consequently, we are witnesses to the dissolution of the difference between nature and society. This process is inevitable. It is the result of the perception that every human intervention mediates and changes the meaning and status of the natural; and that the products of society frequently become elemental forces that rule over men and women as if they were ancient forces of nature. It is not therefore meaningful to argue that because sexuality is the product of human activity and movement in society, it may be reconstructed by a process of social action. If sexuality is, at any given moment, a product of human activity and movement in society, then it is most certainly a spontaneous, unintended and unplanned movement. The particular configurations of sexuality are not the product of design or public policy. Nor does the particular style, ideology or register of the discourse of sexuality, at any particular historical moment, bring about, determine, or even correspond to, the way in which people do sex, are sexual or live their sex-lives.

We can on occasions do a lot about nature and nothing much about society. At other times, we can do nothing about nature, but a lot about society. It is a not a distinction that tells us anything concerning the effectiveness of human agency or volition. The manner in which human psychologies, emotions and sexual dispositions are constituted within society is unknown. It is certainly an indeterminate process and provides a more fertile terrain for the sensibilities of artists than it does for those of social scientists and social historians. The threads that connect human sexuality, at any given historical moment, to society cannot be delineated. We cannot stand like telephone engineers disentangling one wire after another from a vast spaghetti of multicoloured connections. We cannot do this because the colours constantly change and the number, disposition and length of the connecting wires changes from moment to moment. Indeed, we can only posit a connection between social organisation and the constitution of sexuality because of the existence of this state of flux which we can demonstrate within the historical record. However, we will never be able to discern precisely what links exist between society and nature and the constitution of sexuality.

So the idea that sexuality is 'a social construction' that may be 'reconstructed' is an illusion. It is an illusion that has produced a great many positive developments within the discourse of sexuality. It has produced, like a conjurer, many sexualities where before there was only one. It has, like a free-marketeer, introduced choice where there was none before. It has, like a democrat, put everybody in charge of their own fate. It is an illusion that has empowered the individual, and has promised to move the boundaries of sexuality as far away as possible from those who were formerly marginal. It is an illusion that has done much. What it has not done, however, is break from the discourse of sexuality.

Radical sociologists and social historians are perennially engaged in determining what is, and what is not, appropriate in the field of sexuality, and within the range of many sexualities. The theorists of self-definition and self-determination are big players in the constitution and reconstitution of what sexuality means.

Thus they become involved in the struggle for the realisation of an ideal sexuality. The ineffable desire most of us have for love is represented as a desire for a movement beyond the alienation and reification of the present into a future where authentic feelings of community will open up the prospect of us being in touch with our feelings. The desire for all human relations to become transparent, to be, in other words, direct, face-to-face relationships of friendship and mutual respect, is at times too much to bear. It is not an exquisite pain, it is experienced as a dull ache, it is a sense of loss for which our ignorance of what we have lost does not compensate.

It is from such feelings that the mythology of having lost something that we must regain is born. In times past this was represented as a literal loss of grace or of liberty; in more subtle and sophisticated times this sense of loss, and the need to regain possession of ourselves, is an aspiration for what might be. It is by the endorsement of such a mythology that many of the productions of the history of sexuality confirm their position within the discourse of sexuality. The aspirations endorsed are very similar, if not actually the same, as those I can encounter at every moment of the day by turning on my radio, buying a magazine, walking into a record store, going to the movies or turning on the TV. The forms of appearance of sexuality have changed and are changing. Sexuality appears in more and more exotic guises, each one promising more than the last. But what is promised is, by and large, the same: self-possession through the abnegation of lover and beloved.

This perpetuation and intensification of the discourse of sexuality is often conflated with the continuing need to fight against oppression. It is thought that continued involvement in the discourse of sexuality is necessary if an opposition is to be mounted and sustained to the oppression of women, of lesbians, or of gay men. It is often thought that because the social status of the oppressed derives from their relative positions within the discourse of sexuality it is imperative to change its meaning. Hence the ensuing struggle to redefine normality, to refurnish the idea of family, to reorganise the meaning of 'woman'. However, the prospect of redefining reality offered to us by the theory of social construction turns out to be poison bait. The realisation of the ideal eludes us, but we continue to slide towards the creation of an ideal type of sexuality or range of types of sexuality. We are drawn towards considerations of relationship and kinds of relationships that entangle us in the web of the discourse of sexuality. The more we struggle the firmer we are held in place.

This entanglement rests on the misconception that because the oppressed (in the field of sexuality) are the victims of the discourse of sexuality their salvation lies within the 'deconstruction' of that discourse. Yet it is precisely that process of 'deconstruction' that keeps us ensnared within the discourse. It is the idea that changing what we mean sexually will emancipate us, make us normal, or offer us the prospect of self-possession, that is utterly false. It is false because such a process must involve the oppressed in making representations to the authorities. Such representations inevitably take the form of reassuring the public that we are not what people thought we were. That after all, we are just like them: clean, home-loving, family types, who believe in God, Democracy, Loyalty and Love. By convincing ourselves, and by convincing the public, that we can all live happily together within the discourse of sexuality, we condemn the struggle against oppression to the triviality of the process of normalisation and renormalisation. Advances are made, improvements won. Life is better with them than it would be without them, but the oppression of the oppressed remains intact. Oppression is not a stick to be whittled down. Nor is it a stone to be worn away. Sexuality is not deconstructed or reconstructed by this process of normalisation. Sexuality remains what it always was, an entirely responsive ideology produced by the desire to understand and regulate the lonesome and atomised individual spontaneously constituted by all the circumstances of life in modern cities.

Paradoxically, the extent to which women have improved their relative position in society, the extent to which lesbians and homosexual men are treated as citizens, possessing the same rights and duties as everyone else, has been the extent to which the aspirations of the oppressed have become incorporated in the devices, strategies and possibilities of 'actually existing capitalism'. The most successful strategies pursued by the oppressed have been precisely those that have acknowledged their place in the vibrant process of individuation and atomisation that has been gathering momentum throughout the century. I write that this is a paradox because most of the ideologues of the oppressed, and most of those engaged in fashioning the radical history of sexuality, have been opposed to the commercialisation and even the commodification of sex. However, we have all been compelled to observe that this is precisely what has carried the day.

The advances made by the victims of phallocentric sexuality have not been made through coming together, getting in touch with their feelings, or with the creation of anything that could be described as a 'community'. Such communities as there are, are the products of the ruthless exclusion of those who cannot, for one reason or another, be granted a seat at the banquet. And where deliberate exclusion does not operate, market forces do. Consequently, self-possession has not been on offer as anything other than a rather sad and wistful aspiration. This has been a genuinely normalising experience. The oppressed can feel just as sad and wistful as everyone else. They can long for love, for that sense of belonging, they can long, too, for family and for friends, just as much as the rest of the population. They can share in the mythology of loss and recovery along with everyone else.

This is the best that can be hoped for within the discourse of sexuality. The effect of the theory of social construction has been to endorse the idea that these gains are the work of radical action, that is, that they are the product of a long tradition of contestation and struggle in which radical strategies seeking self-determination and self-definition have brought about a restructuring of sexuality and a 'deconstruction' of the discourse of sexuality. This is not the case. It is the perpetual flux in all the technical and social circumstances of life, and the perpetual shifting of the locus of the social life of highly industrialised societies towards the individual, and towards the configuration of the consumption and life*style* of the individual, that have found their most startling expression within the reform of sexual manners. Of course, all sorts of struggles have influenced these developments determining, to some extent, their specific colouration and their particular register. But, self-determining, self-defining movements have not, on the whole, determined the direction, trajectory or tempo of these changes.

I am well aware that such assertions will cause anguish, and may even evince cries of pain from a veteran campaigner or two, but I think that the jury has returned, and the verdict is in. The changes that have occurred have not been the result of agitation or organisation. On the contrary, agitation and organisation on the sex question have been the product of these spontaneous changes in the manner in which sex-life is conferred, organised and regulated. The agenda, strategy and tactics of the campaigner have always been directed by the actual drift of events in society, rather than in any determination to remake society, or the terms on which it is constituted. Adaptation to the prevailing ideas and ideals, rather than resistance to them, has been the dominant theme. This may have been an expression of quite limited and specific goals. It may even have been the result of 'realism'. Whatever it was – programmatic modesty or practical politics – the aggregate effect has been that the changes taking place within the possibilities of sex-life have all been ones commensurate with the choices, freedom and atomisation of the individual. They all reflect this dominant line of development.

This is not a counsel of despair or a rejection of a history of sexuality committed to radical purposes. What I am suggesting is that we need to think more about the way in which all the circumstances of modern life, particularly the twin processes of incessant change and atomisation, constitute the individual and his/her sex-life. I think that this would require much deeper investigations into the specific effects of agitation and organisation. It also underlines the need for the development of a proper assessment and analysis of the contemporary role and meaning of sex-reformers in the past. A frank recognition that they were not our audacious predecessors is also essential if we are to move forward. Above all, developing an effective history of sexuality means abandoning the illusion of social construction theory. It means abandoning the illusion that this theory can dissolve 'natural' determinations by bringing the whole of sexuality into the realm of self-determination, and conscious social and political intervention.

Over the last 30 years the labour that has forged the synthesis between interactionist sociology and radical social history has been enormous, and its achievements have been considerable. Without doubt we have a richer understanding of the history of sexuality because of its development. However, it is time to go boldly beyond its confines.

Notes and References

Chapter 1

1. For association of sexuality with the legion-of-honour see 'From Roland Barthes by Roland Barthes', 1975, in R. Barthes, *Barthes: Selected Writings*, 1982, introduced and edited by Susan Sontag (Collins: Fontana, 1983), p.421.
2. S. Hite, *The Hite Report on Male Sexuality*, 1981 (Ballantine Books, 1982), p.450.
3. R. Scruton, *Sexual Desire* (Weidenfeld & Nicolson, 1986), p.254.
4. Ibid., p.348.
5. See E. Evans-Pritchard, *A History of Anthropological Thought*, edited by André Singer and introduced by Ernest Gellner (Faber and Faber, 1981); M. Fortes, *Kinship and the Social Order: the Legacy of Lewis Henry Morgan*, 1969 (Routledge & Kegan Paul, 1970); A. Kroeber, *The Nature of Culture* (University of Chicago Press, 1952). For a discussion of the idea of culture and changes during the nineteenth century of the structure of meaning and the structure of feeling see R. Williams, *Culture and Society 1780–1950*, 1958 (Penguin Books, 1961).
6. See Chinua Achebe's novel concerning the impact of colonisation on the Ibo, *Things Fall Apart*, 1958 (Heinemann Educational Books, 1988). It is important to bear in mind the role of missionary and colonial activity in the formation of anthropology and in its early empirical studies. Morgan, for example, took much of his material on the native people of Australia from the work of the Rev. Lorimer Fison (an English missionary), the Rev. W. Ridley, and T.E. Lance, published in the *Proceedings of the American Academy of Arts and Sciences for 1872*. See L.H. Morgan, *Ancient Society, or, Researches in the Lines of Human Progress from Savagery, through Barbarism to Civilisation* (Henry Holt & Co, 1877), p.52. E. Westermarck explicitly offered anthropology as an instrument of colonial rule: 'I am convinced that in our dealings with non-European races some sociological knowledge, well applied, would generally be a more satisfactory weapon than gunpowder. It would be more humane and cheaper too.' E. Westermarck, *Sociology as a University Study* (John Murray, 1908), p.31. W. Rivers also expressly advertised anthropology as an instrument of colonial policy. See W. Rivers 'The Government of Subject Peoples' in *Science and the Nation*, edited by A. Seward (Cambridge University Press, 1917), p.307.

7. E. Tylor, *Primitive Culture*, 1871. Published as *Origins of Culture* with an introduction by Paul Radin (Harper & Row, 1958), p.1. See also Fortes, *Kinship*: Tylor's book comes at the end of 'the phenomenal decade which started with Maine's *Ancient Law* (1861) and Bachofen's *Das Mutterrecht* (1861) and ended with Morgan's *Systems [of consanguinity and affinity of the human family]* (1870) ... Not only that, for Darwin's *Origin of Species* (1859) and *Descent of Man* (1871) appeared at the beginning and the end respectively of this intellectual explosion' (p.6).

8. R. Wheaton, 'Observations on the Development of Kinship History 1942–1985' in *Family History at the Crossroads*, edited by T. Hareven and A. Plakans (Princeton University Press, 1987), p.286.

9. Morgan's *Ancient Society* exerted considerable influence on Karl Marx and Friedrich Engels and provided much of the anthropological thinking for F. Engels, *The Origin of the Family, Private Property and the State*, 1884 (Foreign Languages Press, 1978). See the discussion in Rosalind Coward, *Patriarchal Precedents: Sexuality and Social Relations* (Routledge & Kegan Paul, 1983); and in J. Sayers, M. Evans, N. Redclift, *Engels Revisited: New Feminist Essays* (Tavistock Publications, 1987).

10. E. Evans-Pritchard quoted in S. Collins, 'Categories, Concepts or Predicaments? Remarks on Mauss's Use of Philosophical Terminology' in *The Category of the Person: Anthropology, Philosophy, History*, edited by M. Carrithers, S. Collins, S. Lukes (Cambridge University Press, 1985), p.47.

11. S. Freud's *The Interpretation of Dreams* was published in November 1899, but dated 1900. It remained untranslated and largely ignored until 1913. See James Strachey's introduction to *The Interpretation of Dreams*, 1954 (George Allen & Unwin Ltd, 1982). Note that this edition is a reprint of that included in Volumes IV and V of the *Standard Edition of the Complete Psychological Works of Sigmund Freud*, translated under the general editorship of James Strachey in collaboration with Anna Freud, assisted by Alix Strachey and Alan Tyson (Hogarth Press and Institute of Psycho-Analysis, 1953).

12. E. von Hartmann, *The Philosophy of the Unconscious*, 1868, translated by W. Chatterton Coupland (Trubner, 1884), three volumes. See also F. Nietzsche, *The Birth of Tragedy*, 1871 (J.N. Foulis, 1909); and C. Crawford, *The Beginnings of Nietzsche's Theory of Language* (Walter de Gruyter, 1988).

13. J. Frazer, *The Golden Bough: A Study in Magic and Religion*, two volumes published by Macmillan in 1890; a further two volumes published in 1912 and another eight between 1912 and 1915, abridged edition, 1922 (Macmillan, 1929).

14. E. Durkheim quoted in S. Collins, 'Categories, Concepts or Predicaments?' in M. Carrithers et al., *The Category of the Person*, p.53.

15. M. Mauss, 'A Category of the Human Mind: the Notion of Person; the Notion of Self', 1938, translated by W. Halls, in *The Category of the Person*, p.3.

16. M. Mead, *Sex and Temperament in Three Primitive Societies*, 1935 (New American Library: Mentor, 1950), p.ix. See also R. Benedict, *Patterns of Culture*, 1935 (Routledge & Kegan Paul, 1980).

17. Key examples of this kind of work are M. Bloch, *Feudal Society*, 1938 (Chicago University Press, 1961); G. Casper Homans, *English Villagers of the Thirteenth Century*, 1941 (Russell and Russell, 1960); and G. Duby, *La Société au XIe et XIIe Siècles dans la Région Maconnaise* (Presses Universitaires de France, 1953).

18. See T. Stoianovich, *French Historical Method: The Annales Paradigm* (Cornell University Press, 1976). See review of the same: R. Forster, *Journal of Social History* (Number 4, Summer 1978): 'What is sacrificed [by the *Annales* group] – and I believe consciously – in precise answers to limited problems is fully compensated in a history that, at its best, provides a quasi-sensual experience of having relived the past in all of its nuance, complexity, and – if historians oriented toward the pursuit of the single thesis can bear the phrase – its tragic dimension' (p.591).

19. See E. Fox-Genovese, E. Genovese, 'The Political Crises of Social History: A Marxian Perspective', in *Journal of Social History* (Volume 10, 1976–7), for the sour view: 'Contemporary social history, in its prestigious, not to say pretentious, new forms can be roughly traced from the pioneering works of Lucien Febvre and Marc Bloch during the 1930s' (p.205).

20. The development of the history of *mentalities* and of social history was greatly influenced by the study of historical populations that grew out of renewed European interest in demography following the Second World War. The Institut National des Etudes Demographique was established in Paris in 1945. In 1948 Philippe Aries published his *Histoire des populations françaises et leurs attitudes devant la vie depuis le XVIIIe siècle* (Editions Self, 1948). In 1956 the INED published Michel Fleury and Louis Henry's seminal work: *Des Registres paroissiaux à l'histoire de la population. Manuel de deoillement et d'exploitation de l'état civil ancien.* Demographer Louis Henry and historian Pierre Goubert developed the family reconstitution method (FRM). FRM resulted in the use of aggregate statistics on births, deaths and marriages, and on social differentiation, that raised questions about the nature of the conjugal family in history and of the relationships among its members. See Wheaton, 'Observations', in Hareven and Plakans, *Family History at the Crossroads*, (p.286). For a discussion and critique of the notion of *mentalities* see G. Lloyd, *Demystifying Mentalities* (Cambridge University Press, 1991).

21. See J. Wiener, 'Radical Historians and the Crisis in American History, 1959–1980', *Journal of American History* (Volume 76, Number 2,

September 1989); H. Perkins, 'Social History in Britain', *Journal of Social History* (Volume 10, 1976–7); P. Laslett, 'The Character of Familial History, its Limitations and the Conditions for its Proper Pursuit' in Hareven and Plakans, *Family History at the Crossroads*; A. Ludtke, 'The Historiography of Everyday Life: The Personal and the Political' in R. Samuel, G. Stedman Jones, *Culture, Ideology and Politics* (Routledge & Kegan Paul, 1982).

22. G. Rubin, 'The Traffic in Women: Notes on the "Political Economy" of Sex' in R.R. Reiter, *Towards an Anthropology of Women* (Monthly Review Press, 1975), pp.179–80.

23. M. Foucault, *Power/Knowledge: Selected Interviews and Other Writings, 1972–77*, edited by C. Gordon, translated by C. Gordon et al. (Pantheon Books, 1980), pp.219–20.

24. M. Wittig, 'The Category of Sex' in *Feminist Issues* (Fall, 1982), p.64.

25. G. Bock, 'Women's History and Gender History: Aspects of an International Debate' in *Gender and History* (Volume 1, Number 1, Spring 1989), p.15.

26. M. Wittig, 'The Straight Mind' in *Feminist Issues* (Summer, 1980), p.110.

27. M. Wittig, 'One is not Born a Woman' in *Feminist Issues* (Fall, 1981), p.53.

28. R. Neuman, 'Recent Work on the History of Sexuality' in *Journal of Social History* (Number 3, Spring 1978), p.419.

29. D. Halperin, 'Is There a History of Sexuality' in *History and Theory* (Volume XXVIII, Number 3, 1989), p.257.

30. G. McLennan, *Marxism, Pluralism and Beyond* (Polity Press, 1989): 'Certainly, a sober case has been made out that Derrida, in probing the "unspeakable" condition of philosophical judgement, was in effect taking the classical Kantian investigation of foundations just one necessary step further (Gasche 1986)' (p.175). See R. Gasche, *The Tain of the Mirror: Derrida and the Philosophy of Reflection* (Harvard University Press, 1986).

31. R. Braidotti, 'Envy: Or With Your Brains and My Looks' in *Men in Feminism*, edited by A. Jardine and Paul Smith (Methuen, 1987), p.237.

32. Ibid., p.241.

33. L. Irigaray, *This Sex Which is Not One*, 1977, translated by Catherine Porter and Carolyn Burke (Cornell University Press, 1985), p.164.

34. D. Fuss, *Essentially Speaking: Feminism, Nature and Difference* (Routledge, 1989), p.98.

35. See F. Ankersmit, 'Historiography and Postmodernism' in *History and Theory* (Volume XXVIII, Number 2, 1989), p.138.

36. Ibid., p.149.

37. Ibid., p.150.

38. See J. Lyotard, 'Answering the Question: What is Postmodernism?' (translated by Regis Durand) in *The Postmodern Condition: A Report on*

Knowledge, 1977, translated by Geoff Bennington and Brian Massumi (Manchester University Press, 1989), pp.71–82. See also F. Braudel, 'Personal Testimony' in *Journal of Modern History* (Number 44, 1972).

39. A. Jagger, 'Love and Knowledge: Emotion in Feminist Epistemology' in *Women, Knowledge, and Reality: Explorations in Feminist Philosophy*, edited by A. Garry and M. Pearsall (Unwin Hyman, 1989), p.139.

40. Ibid., p.149.

41. S. Heath, 'Men in Feminism: Men and Feminist Theory' in Jardine and Smith, *Men in Feminism*, pp.45–6.

42. A. Ross, 'Demonstrating Sexual Difference' in Jardine and Smith, *Men in Feminism*, p.47.

43. J. Baudrillard, 'The Ecliptic of Sex', 1979, in *Revenge of the Crystal: Selected Writings on the Modern Object and its Destiny 1968–1983* (Pluto Press, 1990), p.132.

44. A *berdache* was any man who, among the Dakota of the North American plains, 'had voluntarily given up the struggle to conform to the masculine role and who wore female attire and followed the occupations of women'. (Mead, *Sex and Temperament*, p.xiii). Transsexualism can be an option, but it is one that requires some assertion of hermaphrodism, or demands some 'corrective' surgery to bring the body into alignment with the desired social role. See *Herculine Barbin: Being the Recently Discovered Memoirs of a Nineteenth-Century French Hermaphrodite*, 1978, introduced by M. Foucault, translated by R. McDougall (Pantheon Books, 1980); J. Raymond, *The Transsexual Empire*, 1979 (The Women's Press, 1980).

45. Irigaray, *This Sex Which is Not One*, p.28.

46. Another explanation for this 'common ground' may also be found in the considerable institutional manoeuvring and intellectual opportunism employed in the academy to carve a professional space for feminists and gays. However, this must always be a secondary consideration as feminists and gays working on homosexual and women's issues continue to encounter considerable professional difficulties. See J. D'Emilio, 'Not a Simple Matter: Gay History and Gay Historians' in *Journal of American History* (Volume 76, Number 2, September 1989), pp.435–45. For a theoretical engagement with the problems encountered by women entering science and the professions see P. Atkinson, S. Delamont, 'Professions and Powerlessness: Female Marginality in the Learned Occupations' in *The Sociological Review* (Volume 38, Number 1, February 1990).

Chapter 2

1. S. Freud's 'Group Psychology and the Analysis of the Ego', 1921, *Standard Edition* (Volume XVIII, 1955), is a particularly good example of this procedure.

2. S. Freud, 'Beyond the Pleasure Principle', 1920, *Standard Edition* (Volume XVIII, 1955).

3. Moravia became a separate Austrian crownland in 1848 and was integrated into the republic of Czechoslovakia in 1918.

4. H. Ellenberger, *The Discovery of the Unconscious: The History and Evolution of Dynamic Psychiatry* (Allen Lane: the Penguin Press, 1970), pp.419–27.

5. A. Leon, *The Jewish Question: A Marxist Interpretation*, 1946 (Pathfinder Press, 1986), pp.195–256.

6. B. Magee, *Aspects of Wagner*, 1968 (Oxford University Press, 1988), pp.19–28.

7. Ellenberger, *The Discovery of the Unconscious*, p.419.

8. Ibid., p.459.

9. E. Figes, *Patriarchal Attitudes* (Faber & Faber, 1970), p.136. In 1963 Betty Friedan observed: 'Freud, it is generally agreed, was a most perceptive and accurate observer of important problems of the human personality. But in describing and interpreting those problems, he was a prisoner of his own culture.' B. Friedan, *The Feminine Mystique*, 1963 (Penguin Books, 1965), p.93.

10. Max Planck (1858–1947): Quantum Theory propounded in 1900; Albert Einstein (1879–1955): Special Theory of Relativity 1905, and the General Theory of Relativity in 1916; Werner Heisenberg (1901–76) formulated the Uncertainty Principle in 1927.

11. M. Freud, *Glory Reflected, Sigmund Freud: Man and Father* (Angus and Robertson, 1957), pp.108, 121. See also P. Gay, *Freud: A Life for Our Times*, 1988 (Papermac, 1989).

12. E. Jones, *Sigmund Freud: Life and Works*, Volume I, (Hogarth Press, 1953).

13. See 'Anna Freud for Feminists', published by Elizabeth Young-Bruehl in her collection of essays and lectures: E. Young-Bruehl, *Mind and the Body Politic*, 1988 (Routledge, 1989).

14. Between 1876 and 1882 Freud attended the university and also worked under Brucke at the Institute of Physiology in Vienna. He published on anatomy and physiology from 1877, and between 1882 and 1885 he worked at Vienna's General Hospital. This was a perfectly normal record for an ambitious young scientist and physician of the period.

15. S. Freud, 'An Autobiographical Study', 1925, *Standard Edition* (Volume XX, 1959), p.11.

16. Aphasia is a disorder of the central nervous system. The symptoms it produces are a partial or total loss of the ability to communicate, particularly in speech or writing. In 1891 Freud published his monograph *On Aphasia*. John Forrester writes that 'In showing that, even where there is an organic lesion, the explanation of aphasiac phenomena must be understood independently of the location of the lesion, Freud paved the way for the understanding of hysteria as the lesion of an idea.'

J. Forrester, *Language and the Origins of Psychoanalysis* (Macmillan, 1980), pp.29–30.

17. Freud explained 'Talking Cure' very simply: 'Once a picture has emerged from the patient's memory, we may hear him say that it becomes fragmentary and obscure as he proceeds with his description of it. *The patient is, as it were, getting rid of it by turning it into words.*' See 'Studies on Hysteria', 1895, *Standard Edition* (Volume II, 1955), p.280.

18. Ibid., pp.21–40.

19. Ibid., p.160.

20. S. Freud, 'The Interpretation of Dreams', 1900, *Standard Edition* (Volume IV, 1953), p.277.

21. Ibid.

22. S. Freud, 'Revision of the Theory of Dreams', 1933, *Standard Edition* (Volume XXII, 1964), pp.10–11.

23. S. Freud, 'The Interpretation of Dreams', 1900, *Standard Edition* (Volume V, 1953), p.590.

24. Ibid. (Volume IV, 1953), p.310–11.

25. See S. Freud, 'A Note on the Prehistory of the Technique of Analysis', 1920, *Standard Edition* (Volume XVIII, 1955), pp.263–5.

26. However, Freud did not claim to be able to perform cures and wonders. His tentative and modest approach is revealed by a conversation that he had with the German psychiatrist, J.H. Schultz, cited in Ellenberger, *The Discovery of the Unconscious*, p.461, as follows. 'Freud said: "You do not really believe that you are able to cure?" Schultz replied: "In no way, but one can, as a gardener does, remove impediments to growth." Freud responded: "Then we will understand each other."' [From J.H. Schultz, *Psychotherapie, Leben und Werk grosser Aerzte* (Hippokrates-Verlag, 1952).]

27. Havelock Ellis, 'Psycho-Analysis in Relation to Sex', in *The Philosophy of Conflict* (Constable, 1919), pp.206–7.

28. H. Bergson, *Creative Evolution*, 1907 (Macmillan, 1911). See also Bergson's *An Introduction to Metaphysics*, 1903, translated by T. Hulme (Macmillan, 1913).

29. Freud repudiated the kind of idealism that informed *Natur Philosophie*, but it is evident that its outlook permeated the whole of German scientific and literary production during his formative years. He was educated under its influence, and it is certain that in his deployment of intuition, and in the manner in which he constructed hypotheses, Freud was part of the mainstream of German scientific culture. It is easy to detect the influence of Fichte and Schelling in Freud's writings and in his theoretical movement. Johann Gottlieb Fichte (1762–1814) argued that 'through the creative power of reason whatever is posited is made real. Positing, then, is a primordial act, in which the theoretical and the practical coincide, and in which an undivided self is totally

engaged in a single, all-encompassing enterprise.' See J. Fichte, *The Science of Knowledge*, 1794–1802, translated and edited by P. Heath and J. Lachs (Cambridge University Press, 1970), p.xiv. Friedrich Wilhelm Joseph von Schelling (1775–1854) in his *Ideas for a Philosophy of Nature* regarded intuition as 'the primary' or 'the highest' level of knowledge. See F. Schelling, *Ideas for a Philosophy of Nature*, 1797, translated by E. Harris and P. Heath, introduced by R. Stern (Cambridge University Press, 1988), pp.174–7.

30. E. von Hartmann, *Philosophy of the Unconscious*, 1868 (Trubner, 1884), translated by W. Chatterton Coupland, Volume I, p.14.

31. Johann Friedrich Herbart (1776–1841), a philosopher whose ideas concerning the dynamic activity at the 'threshold of perception' exerted a considerable influence upon Freud. See Ellenberger, *The Discovery of the Unconscious*, pp.312, 402, 536.

32. See S. Freud, 'A Project for a Scientific Psychology', written in 1895, first published in 1950, *Standard Edition* (Volume I, 1953). For a discussion of the mythological character of much of the work of Freud's contemporaries (and his immediate predecessors) on cerebral structures, and the assumptions employed, see Ellenberger, *The Discovery of the Unconscious*, pp.477–80.

33. Ibid., p.534.

34. J. Laplanche, J. Pontalis, *The Language of Psycho-Analysis*, 1967, translated by D. Nicholson-Smith, introduced by D. Lagache (Hogarth Press & the Institute of Psycho-Analysis, 1973), pp.128, 249.

35. In 1932 Freud said: 'The theory of instincts is so to say our mythology. Instincts are mythical entities, magnificent in their indefiniteness.' *Standard Edition* (Volume XXII, 1964), p.95. See also S. Freud, 'Three Essays on the Theory of Sexuality', 1905, *Standard Edition* (Volume VII, 1953); and Laplanche, Pontalis, *The Language of Psycho-Analysis*, pp.214–16.

36. For a consideration of idealism and the work of Fechner see G. Stanley Hall, *Founders of Modern Psychology* (Appleton, 1912), pp.125–77; and Ellenberger, *The Discovery of the Unconscious*, p.289.

37. S. Freud, 'Three Essays on the Theory of Sexuality', 1905, *Standard Edition* (Volume VII, 1953), p.148.

38. Laplanche, Pontalis, *The Language of Psycho-Analysis*, p.239.

39. R. Fliess, *Erogeneity and Libido, Addenda to the Theory of Psychosexual Development of the Human* (International Universities Press, 1956), pp.8–9.

40. S. Freud, 'From the History of an Infantile Neurosis', 1918, *Standard Edition* (Volume XVII, 1955), pp.120–1.

41. Ibid., p.97.

42. Laplanche, Pontalis, *The Language of Psycho-Analysis*, p.331.

43. Ibid., p.421.

44. S. Freud, 'Leonardo da Vinci and a Memory of his Childhood', 1910, *Standard Edition* (Volume XI, 1957), p.97.
45. S. Freud, 'Three Essays on the Theory of Sexuality', 1905, *Standard Edition* (Volume VII, 1953), p.172.
46. Ibid., p.166.
47. Ibid., pp.145, 148, 160.
48. Ibid., p.146.
49. Ibid., pp.222–43.
50. J. Lampl-de Groot, 'The Evolution of the Oedipus Complex in Women', 1927, in *The Psycho-Analytic Reader, An Anthology of Essential Papers with Critical Introductions*, edited by R. Fliess (Hogarth Press & the Institute of Psycho-Analysis, 1950), p.181.
51. Laplanche, Pontalis, *The Language of Psycho-Analysis*, p.283.
52. The 'Electra complex' used by Carl Jung (1875–1961) is not employed by Freud because of its tendency to emphasise an analogy between the sexes. See S. Freud, 'Female Sexuality', 1931, *Standard Edition* (Volume XXI, 1961), pp.228–9.
53. H. Deutsch, 'The Psychology of Women in Relation to the Functions of Reproduction', 1925, in Fliess, *The Psycho-Analytic Reader*, p.166.
54. S. Freud, 'Some Psychical Consequences of the Anatomical Distinction Between the Sexes', 1925, *Standard Edition* (Volume XIX, 1961), p.252.
55. See S. Freud, 'Female Sexuality', 1931, *Standard Edition* (Volume XXI, 1961), p.225.
56. J. Mitchell, *Psychoanalysis and Feminism*, 1974 (Penguin Books, 1975), pp.6–7.
57. S. Freud, 'Femininity', 1933, *Standard Edition* (Volume XXII, 1964), p.134.
58. See S. Freud, *Standard Edition* (Volume I, 1953), p.228.
59. S. Freud, 'Femininity', 1933, *Standard Edition* (Volume XXII, 1964), p.116.
60. Ibid.
61. E. Young-Breuhl (introduction and editor), *Freud on Women: A Reader* (Hogarth Press, 1990), p.41.
62. S. de Beauvoir, *The Second Sex*, 1949 (Penguin Books, 1983), p.725.
63. Young-Breuhl, *Freud on Women*, p.41.
64. See S. Freud, 'Analysis Terminable and Interminable', 1937, *Standard Edition* (Volume XXIII, 1964), p.252; and in the 'Outline of Psycho-Analysis', 1938, *Standard Edition* (Volume XXIII, 1964), p.144.
65. S. Freud, 'The Claims of Psycho-Analysis to Scientific Interest', 1913, *Standard Edition* (Volume XIII, 1955), pp.163–90.
66. S. Freud, 'Female Sexuality', 1931, *Standard Edition* (Volume XXI, 1961), p.233.
67. For a discussion of Freud's opponents see the chapter on 'Early Schismatics' in J. Brown's *Freud and the Post-Freudians*, 1961 (Penguin Books,

1987), pp.36–55; E. Fromm, *Sigmund Freud's Mission: An Analysis of His Personality and Influence* (Harper & Brothers, 1959); and C. Jung, 'On Psychic Energy', 1948, translated by R. Hull, *Collected Works*, Volume 8 (Routledge & Kegan Paul, 1972), pp.3–66.

68. The sexual pathologists were those sexologists engaged in establishing an understanding of sexual behaviour and developing a taxonomy of sexual types, most notably, Richard Krafft-Ebing (1840–1902), Albert Moll (1862–1939), and Henry Havelock Ellis (1859–1939).

69. There is no doubt that people have been grinding rhinoceros horn and seeking other aphrodisiacs since time immemorial. They have also consulted priests, fortune tellers and doctors concerning sexual matters for millennia. For example we know in some detail the problems that afflicted Richard Napier's patients. Richard Napier was a physician active in Oxfordshire in England between 1597 and 1634. Existing records indicate that 23.6 per cent of his consultations concerned troubled courtships; 17.6 per cent marital problems; 17.5 per cent bereavements; 12.9 per cent economic problems. These were the most common reasons for presentation. However, it is plain that in this catalogue of distress; of jiltings, seductions, betrayals, premature deaths, heartless parents and truculent friends, we are presented with an antique and vanished world. It is not a world that deploys a scientific or analytical approach toward sexual matters. See M. MacDonald, *Mystical Bedlam: Madness, Anxiety, and Healing in Seventeenth Century England* (Cambridge University Press, 1981), pp.75, 89, 105–9.

70. 'Totem and Taboo', 1913, *Standard Edition* (Volume XIII, 1955); 'The Future of an Illusion', 1927, *Standard Edition* (Volume XX1, 1961); 'Civilisation and its Discontents', 1930, *Standard Edition* (Volume XXI, 1961); 'Moses and Monotheism', 1938, *Standard Edition* (Volume XXIII, 1964).

71. S. Freud, 'Analysis Terminable and Interminable', 1937, *Standard Edition* (Volume XXIII, 1964), p.252.

72. See Skinner on Freud in R. Evans, *Dialogue with B.F. Skinner*, 1968 (Praeger, 1981), p.7.

73. I have taken this phrase from Robert Richardson's 'Biological Reductionism and Gene Selectionism' in *Sociobiology and Epistemology*, edited by J. Fetzer (D. Reidel Publishing Company, 1985), p.133.

Chapter 3

1. *Oedipus* is a figure in Greek myth. He was the son of Laius and Jocasta, the king and queen of Thebes. Unaware that Laius was his father, Oedipus killed him. In a similar state of ignorance he married Jocasta who had four children by him. When the truth dawned he poked out his own eyes, and, Jocasta, his mother-wife, committed suicide. In psy-

choanalytic theory the famous *oedipus complex* manifests itself in infancy as 'a desire for the death of the rival – the parent of the same sex – and a sexual desire for the parent of the opposite sex'. J. Laplanche, J. Pontalis, *The Language of Psycho-Analysis*, 1967, translated by D. Nicholson-Smith, introduced by D. Lagache (Hogarth Press and The Institute of Psycho-Analysis, 1973), p.283.

2. A. Comte, 'Système de Politique Positive', 1851–1854, in *Auguste Comte and Positivism: The Essential Writings*, edited and introduced by Gertrud Lenzer, 1975 (University of Chicago Press, 1983), p.377.

3. See Chapter 3, Book VI, of Comte's, 'Cours de Philosophie Positive', 1830–1842, in Lenzer, *The Essential Writings*, pp.219–21.

4. J.S. Mill, *Auguste Comte and Positivism*, 1865 (George Routledge & Sons, 1908), p.15.

5. Lenzer, *The Essential Writings*, p.xxi.

6. See Chapter 1, Book V, of Comte's 'Cours de Philosophie Positive', 1830–1842, Lenzer, *The Essential Writings*, p.164.

7. Comte's 'Systeme de Politique Positive', 1851–1854, in Lenzer, *The Essential Writings*, pp.411–12.

8. See Chapter 6, Book V, of Comte's 'Cours de Philosophie Positive', Lenzer, *The Essential Writings*, pp.193–4.

9. Comte's 'Systeme de Politique Positive', 1851–1854, in Lenzer, *The Essential Writings*, p.380. For Comte's views on the family see particularly pp.413–14.

10. Ibid., p.373.

11. See C. Darwin, *The Descent of Man*, 1871 (John Murray, 1883), p.564. See also F. Galton, *Hereditary Genius: An Inquiry into its Laws and Consequences*, 1869 (Watts & Co, 1950).

12. Darwin, *The Descent of Man*, p.557.

13. Ibid., p.564.

14. See A. Bebel, *Woman in the Past, Present and Future* introduced by Moira Donald, 1879 (Zwan Publications, 1988), pp.123–30. Originally published as 'Women and Socialism' this book was renamed for its second edition in 1883.

15. I. Berlin, 'Historical Inevitability', in *Four Essays on Liberty*, 1953 (Oxford University Press, 1969), p.43.

16. In the face of biological determinism Bebel boldly asserted: 'The Darwinian Law of the struggle for existence, which finds its expression in nature in the elimination and destruction of lower by stronger and more highly developed organisms, arrives at a different consummation in the human world. Men, as thoughtful and reflecting beings are constantly altering, improving, perfecting their conditions of life, ie, their social arrangements, and everything connected with them, until finally all mankind will exist under equally favourable circumstances.' Bebel, *Woman in the Past*, p.127.

17. For example Alfred Russel Wallace (1823–1913) who, with Charles Darwin was responsible for the theory of natural selection, vigorously opposed materialist conceptions of mental evolution and was an advocate of spiritualism. See A.R. Wallace, 'Dr Carpenter on Spiritualism', and 'Psychological Curiosities of Skepticism', in A.R. Wallace, et al., *The Psycho-Physiological Sciences and Their Assailants* (Colby and Rich, 1878). See also A.R. Wallace's introduction to V.C. Desertis, *Psychic Philosophy*, 1895 (Philip Wellby, 1901). In contrast Charles Darwin was a materialist who early on in his life liked to keep the fact extremely quiet: 'To avoid stating how far, I believe, in Materialism, say only that emotions, instincts degrees of talent, which are hereditary are so because brain of child resembles parent stock – {& phrenologists state that brain alters}/'. This is from page 57 of 'M Notebook', 1838, in *Metaphysics, Materialism and the Evolution of Mind. Early Writings of Charles Darwin*, transcribed and annotated by P. Barrett, 1974 (University of Chicago Press, 1980), p.16. See also George John Romanes, *Mental Evolution in Animals* (Kegan Paul, Trench & Co., 1883: republished by Gregg International Publishers, 1970), p.9. Finally, it is worth noting that the spiritualist A.R. Wallace was an active socialist, and the materialist Darwin a nominal Christian and conservative.

18. Darwin, *Descent of Man*, pp.65–9, 618–19. G.J. Romanes, *Mental Evolution in Man, Origin of Human Faculty* (Kegan Paul, Trench & Co., 1888: republished by Gregg International Publishers, 1970), pp.392, 438–9.

19. C. Darwin, *The Origin of Species by Means of Natural Selection, or, the Preservation of Favoured Races in the Struggle for Life*, 1859 (Penguin Books, 1985), p.459. At this point it should be borne in mind that Darwin's theory of evolution is composed of four specific elements: gradual evolution; common descent; speciation; and the mechanism of natural selection. See E. Mayr, *The Growth of Biological Thought: Diversity, Evolution and Inheritance* (Harvard University Press: Belknap, 1982), p.8.

20. See R. Dunnell, 'The Concept of Progress in Cultural Evolution' in *Evolutionary Progress* edited by M. Nitecki (University of Chicago Press, 1988), pp.169–94.

21. Such florid attacks often end up crudely attributing racism and genocide to the progress of evolutionary theory and the biological sciences. See M. Bressler, 'Biological Determinism and Ideological Indeterminacy', *Sociobiology and Human Politics*, edited by E. White (Gower Publishing: Lexington Books, 1981), p.183. For more useful accounts see J. Harvey, 'Evolutionism Transformed: Positivists and Materialists in the Société d'Anthropologie de Paris from Second Empire to Third Republic; E. Richards, 'Darwin and the Descent of Women'; R. Love, 'Darwinism and Feminism: The "Women Question" in the Life and Work of Olive Schreiner and Charlotte Perkins Gilman'; all in *The Wider*

Domain of Evolutionary Thought, edited by D. Oldroyd, I. Langham (D. Reidal Publishing Company, 1983). pp.289–310, 57–111, 113–31. See also R. Hofstadter's classic work, *Social Darwinism in American Thought: 1860–1915* (University of Pennsylvania Press, 1945).

22. See Bridgewater Treatises on the power, wisdom and Goodness of God as manifested in the Creation. Specifically, *Treatise VII: On the History Habits and Instincts of Animals* by Rev. William Kirby, two volumes (William Pickering, 1835), Volume I, pp.138–44.

23. Darwin, *Origin of Species*, pp.459–60.

24. Romanes, *Mental Evolution in Man*, p.2.

25. S. Patten, *Heredity and Social Progress*, 1903 (Garland Publishing Inc, 1984), p.156.

26. Romanes, *Mental Evolution in Animals*, pp.37–8.

27. Immanuel Kant (1724–1804) replied to the mechanistic views sanctioned by Newtonian physics, the outlook of René Descartes (1596–1650) and the empiricism of David Hume (1711–76). In his critique he set out what he regarded as the limits of reason. He was moved to do this by the desire to 'make room for faith'. See I. Kant, *Critique of Pure Reason*, second edition 1787 (Macmillan, 1986), p.29. Kant's philosophical and scientific activities formed part of a wider intellectual activity concentrated in Germany at the close of the eighteenth century. It ranged from Kant's subjective idealism to the historicism of Hegel (1770–1831). It resulted in the development of the idealist ideology of *Natur Philosophie* by Fichte and Schelling.

28. Mayr, *The Growth of Biological Thought*, p.52.

29. P. Geddes, J. Thomson, *The Evolution of Sex* (Walter Scott, 1890), p.264. 'Nonetheless, Darwin, A.R. Wallace, and Thomas Henry Huxley, the three leading spokesmen of the new view, together supported the theory that nature provided no guide to ethics or social policy – a conclusion Huxley dramatised in his Romanes address at Oxford three decades later.' R. Bannister, *Social Darwinism: Science and Myth in Anglo-American Thought* (Temple University Press, 1979), p.9.

30. For a thorough discussion of these issues see M. Midgley, *Beast & Man: The Roots of Human Nature*, 1978 (Methuen, 1979); C. Darwin, *The Expression of the Emotions in Man and Animals*, 1872 (Chicago University Press, 1965); K. Lorenz, *Evolution and Modification of Behaviour*, 1965 (Methuen, 1966); S. Moscovici, *Society Against Nature*, 1972 (Harvester Press, 1976); S. Walker, *Animal Learning* (Routledge & Kegan Paul, 1987); J. Goodall, *In the Shadow of Man* (Collins, 1971); R. Ardrey, *The Territorial Imperative: A Personal Inquiry into the Animal Origins of Property and Nations* (Collins, 1966).

31. For an account of 'wilful idealism' see the work of Arnold Gehlen. He rejected the conception of evolution and saw man as a wilful creature whose existence demanded determination and order. A. Gehlen, *Man*,

1935–40 (Columbia University Press, 1988). The work of Henri Bergson promoted the concept of the *élan vital*. H. Bergson, *Creative Evolution*, 1907 (Macmillan, 1911).

32. B. Malinowski, *A Scientific Theory of Culture*, 1944 (University of North Carolina Press, 1973), p.75.

33. Ibid., p.77.

34. In this context 'sex appetite' refers to the sexual interest of men: *detumescence* means the subsidence of a swelling, especially the return of a swollen organ, such as a penis, to its flaccid state.

35. Malinowski, *A Scientific Theory of Culture*, p.77.

36. Ibid., p.84.

37. Ibid., p.85.

38. Ibid., p.83.

39. It is evident that the human organism is an animal as distinct from a plant, a chemical reaction, a mineral, a metal, and an artefact. However, insistence upon such an observation leads, spontaneously, to the effacement of that which is most distinctive about human relations and ecology. The most popular advocates of this trend employ the study of animal behaviour to illustrate a conception of men and women as natural creatures whom culture merely 'clothes'. For example, Desmond Morris describes himself as 'a Zoologist viewing man as an animal'. D. Morris, *The Human Zoo* (Jonathan Cape, 1970), p.48. See also D. Morris, *The Naked Ape* (Corgi, 1967). For some balance see S. Barnett, *Biology and Freedom: An Essay on the Implications of Human Ethology* (Cambridge Univerity Press, 1988).

40. M. Midgely in foreword to E. Tomlin, *Psyche, Culture and the New Science: The Role of Psychic Nutrition* (Routledge & Kegan Paul, 1985), p.3. See also D. Holbrook, *Evolution and the Humanities* (Gower, 1987); M. Denton, *Evolution: a Theory in Crisis* (Burnett Books, 1985); R. Goldschmidt, *The Material Basis of Evolution* (Yale University Press, 1940); R. Sheldrake, *The Presence of the Past*, 1988 (Fontana, 1989). Other modern writers have strayed towards the irrational, even the occult, in their attempt to grasp the indeterminacy of living things.

41. S. Rose, R. Lewontin, L. Kamin, 1984, *Not in Our Genes* (Penguin: Pelican, 1985), p.57.

42. See Mayr, *The Growth of Biological Thought*, pp.51–9, for a description of the distinctive features of the process of living. pp.51–9.

43. Ibid., pp.52–3.

44. A. Hodges, *Alan Turing: The Enigma* (Burnett Books, 1983), pp.314–89; Rose, et al., *Not in Our Genes*, p.58; Mayr, *The Growth of Biological Thought*, pp.123–4.

45. Ibid., p.122.

46. R. Sager, F. Ryan, *Cell Heredity*, 1961 (Wiley & Sons, 1963), p.150.

47. Molecular biology can trace its orgins back to the late 1860s. However, it is not until the discovery of the structure of DNA in 1953 that the investigation of life processes at the molecular level was able to proceed effectively. Since that time there has been a general acceleration of discoveries. The behaviour of molecules, and the interaction of cells, have become an increasingly rich focus for study. All cells are able to behave appropriately in relation to other cells and in relation to the circumstances of the whole organism. Indeed, if cells could not sense the general status of the organism, and the functional status of other cells, multicellular organisms could never have evolved. So communication between cells is a necessary condition for the organisation of cells into organisms. 'The nervous and endocrine systems provide the two major modes of intercellular and inter-organ communication within the body, and underpin all homeostatic processes. Until relatively recently, that is until the 1950s, they were regarded as functionally distinct, but it is now clear that there is considerable overlap between them ... In fact, current developments in the identification and localisation of a variety of neural products have shown that peptides are widely used by the nervous system in conveying signals from one area to another, and since peptides possess hormonal activity in addition to their signalling capacity within the nervous system, it becomes increasingly difficult to distinguish between neurotransmitters, neuromodulators (a term introduced to cope with this dilemma), and hormones ... Thus ... the boundaries between neural and endocrine function become increasingly blurred.' B. Donovan, *Hormones and Human Behaviour* (Cambridge University Press, 1985), pp.4–5.

48. N. Morgan, *Cell Signalling* (Open University Press, 1989), pp.4–5.

49. For a consideration of the manner and multiplicity of interactions, their mutability and flexibility, see M. Parker, 'Gene Regulation by Steroid Hormones' in *Hormones and their Actions*, edited by B. Cooke, R. King, H. van der Molen, Part I (Elsevier, 1988), pp.39–48.

50. Morgan, *Cell Signalling*, p.7.

51. For example, hormonal treatments can, in certain circumstances, improve sexual functioning and perhaps predispose the people concerned to increase their sexual activity. This is a tonic effect, improving physical well-being and performance, but having no effect upon orientation or type of behaviour. See A. Mooradian, J. Morley, S. Korenman, 'Biological Actions of Androgens' in *Endocrine Reviews* (Volume 8, Number 1), pp.1–28; C. Carini, A. Scuteri, P. Marrama, J. Bancroft, 'The Effects of Testosterone Administration and Visual Erotic Stimuli on Nocturnal Penile Tumescence in Normal Men', *Hormones and Behaviour* (Volume 24, Number 3, September 1990), pp.435–41; D. Zini, C. Carini, A. Baldini, A. Ghizzani, P. Marrama, 'Sexual Behaviour of Men with Isolated Hypogonadotropic Hypogandism or

Prepubertal Anterior Panhypopituitarism', *Hormones and Behaviour* (Volume 24, Number 2, June 1990), pp.174–85. For an interesting discussion of the problems involved see papers in *Science* (Volume 211, Number 4488, March 1981): A. Eherhardt, H. Meyer-Bahlburg, 'Effects of Prenatal Sex Hormones on Gender-related Behaviour' (pp.1312–18); R. Rubin, J. Reinisch, R. Haskett, 'Postnatal Gonadal Steroid Effects on Human Behaviour' (pp.1318–24); N. MacLusky, F. Naftolin, 'Sexual Differentiation of the Central Nervous System' (pp.1294–303). See also H. Meyer-Bahlburg, 'Hormones and Psychosexual Differentiation: Implications for the Management of Intersexuality, Homosexuality and Transsexuality' in *Clinics in Endocrinology and Metabolism*, 11, 1982, pp.681–701. See J. Money, 'The Genealogical Descent of Sexual Psychoneuroendocrinology from Sex and Health Theory: The Eighteenth to the Twentieth Century' in *Psychoneuroendocrinology*, Volume 8, Number 4, 1983, pp.391–400. However, 'No imprinting of the human brain by androgens or estrogens has been convincingly demonstrated to date. The hypothalamic-pituitary control of LH [luteinizing hormone] and FSH [follicle-stimulating hormone] secretion can be switched from the tonic male pattern in adult male humans to the cyclic female pattern by exposing the males to cyclic administration of ovarian hormones, so that there appears to be no innate maleness in the human hypothalamus or pituitary regarding the regulation of gonads.' L. Crapo, *Hormones, the Messengers of Life* (W.H. Freeman & Co., 1985), p.110.

52. For the extent of the dependence upon animal studies in contemporary work on hormones and behaviour see *Hormones and Behaviour*, Volume 23, Number 4, December 1989 to Volume 24, Number 1, March 1990.

53. B. Donovan, J. Van der Werff ten Bosch, *Physiology of Puberty* (Edward Arnold Ltd, 1965). Most authorities believe in the interaction of biochemical, and social and psychological factors. However, some reject a biochemical role in depression, for example D. Rowe, *The Depression Handbook* (Collins, 1991). In contrast, some authorities argue that mental states, absence of stress, and a positive sense of well-being may all assist in prolonging the life of geriatric patients, and in the case of breast cancer, of suppressing pain: D. Spiegel, 'Can Psychotherapy Prolong Cancer Survival?' in *Psychosomatics* (Volume 31, Number 4, Fall 1990), pp.361–6.

54. C.R. Badcock, *The Problem of Altruism: Freudian-Darwinian Solutions* (Blackwell, 1986), p.25.

55. Ibid., pp.25–6, p.189.

56. Midgley, *Beast & Man*, p.91.

57. There is, however, much skulduggery and even unwitting misrepresentation. For example, Roger Trigg in his book *The Shaping of Man*

attributes to W. Quine the idea that human beings are not much more than 'inputs' and 'outputs' (p.21). But in W. Quine's essay 'Epistemology Naturalised' he clearly opts for a much more interactive approach; see W. Quine, *Ontological Relativity and Other Essays* (Columbia University Press, 1969), pp.69–90. And despite the insights of neural computing and connectionism, mental functions are rarely reduced to neural (that is, physical) laws. In fact, there is a widespread rejection of any law-like connection between mental events and physical science. As Donald Davidson notes, 'We explain a man's free actions, for example, by appeal to his desires, habits, knowledge and perceptions. Such accounts of intentional behaviour operate in a conceptual framework removed from the direct reach of physical law by describing both cause and effect, reason and action, as aspects of a portrait of a human agent.' D. Davidson, *Essays on Actions and Events* (Clarendon Press, 1980), p.225.

58. For a discussion of some of the nastier political consequences of deterministic and sociobiological trends see Rose et al., *Not in Our Genes*. It is also the case that reflex psychology and behaviourism have produced their fair share of unpleasant political spin-off and dystopias. However, we should not allow this to obscure the manner in which these outlooks have informed scientific thinking in ways remote from any political purpose or effect. See J. Watson, *Behaviourism*, 1924 (W.W. Norton & Co, 1970); R. Evans, *Dialogue with B.F. Skinner and Richard Evans*, 1968 (Praeger, 1981); B. Skinner, *Reflections on Behaviourism and Society* (Prentice-Hall, 1978); V. Segerstrale, 'Sociobiology and Conflict and the Conflict about Sociobiology: Science and Morals in the Larger Debate' in *Sociobiology and Conflict* edited by J. van der Dennen, V. Falger (Chapman and Hall, 1990); H. Kaye, *The Social Meaning of Modern Biology: From Social Darwinism to Sociobiology* (Yale University Press, 1986).

59. B. Skinner, *About Behaviourism* (Cape, 1974), cited in R. Trigg, *The Shaping of Man: Philosophical Aspects of Sociobiology* (Blackwell, 1982), p.23.

Chapter 4

1. F. Engels, *The Origin of the Family, Private Property and the State*, 1884 (Foreign Languages Press, 1978), p.96.

2. A. Pannekoek, *Marxism and Darwinism*, translated by N. Weiser (Charles H. Kerr & Company, 1912), p.7. This employment of the Hegelian dialectic and of evolutionary theory permitted a form of speculation, known as the *logical* reconstruction of history, to acquire scientific status. As Engels explains: 'Though this stage may have lasted thousands of years, we have no direct evidence to prove its existence; but once the evolution of man from the animal kingdom is admitted, such a transitional stage must necessarily be assumed.' Engels, *The Origin of the Family*, p.24.

3. This tradition was inextricably enmeshed with the development of Monist ideas. The triumphant development of science, particularly of biology, laid the foundations for a species of materialism that could begin to understand man and nature without the mechanistic limits of the past. As Ernst Haeckel urged: 'It is above all things necessary to make a complete and honest return to Nature and to natural relations. This return, however, will only become possible when man sees and understands his true "place in nature". He will then, as Fritz Ratzel has excellently remarked, "no longer consider himself an exception to natural laws, but begin to seek for what is lawful in his own actions and thoughts, and endeavour to lead a life according to natural laws". He will come to arrange his life with his fellow-creatures – that is, the family and the state – not according to the laws of distant centuries, but according to the rational principles deduced from knowledge of nature.' E. Haeckel, *The History of Creation, or, the development of the earth and its inhabitants by the action of natural causes: A popular exposition of the development of evolution in general, and of that of Darwin, Goethe, and Lamarck in particular*, 1873, translated by E. Lankester (Kegan Paul, Trench, Trubner & Co. Ltd, 1892) Volume II, pp.496–7. See also F. Engels, *Anti-Dühring*, 1878, translated by E. Burns (Lawrence & Wishart, 1943); F. Engels, *The Dialectics of Nature*, 1883, translated by Clemens Dutt (Foreign Languages Publishing House, Moscow, 1954); V.I. Lenin, *Materialism and Empiro-Criticism*, 1908, translated by A. Fineberg (Foreign Languages Publishing House, Moscow, 1947); V.I. Lenin, *Philosophical Notebooks*, 1895–1916, V.I.Lenin, Collected Works, Volume 38 (Progress Publishers: Lawrence & Wishart, 1972).

4. See W. Lecky, *History of European Morals from Augustus to Charlemagne*, 1869 (Longmans, Green & Co., 1911), Volume II, p.294. This was an influential work that went through 18 printings over 4 editions between 1869 and 1911. For a more popular account, from the English working-class movement, of the abominable vice of the Cities of the Plain (Sodom and Gomorrah), see the talk by the Chartist, John Frost, on life at the penal colony at Van Diemen's Land (Tasmania) during the 1840s and 1850s, J. Frost, *The Horrors of Convict Life*, 1856 (Sullivan's Cove, 1973).

5. Engels to Marx, letter 210, 22 June 1869. See also Marx to Engels, letter 275, 17 December 1869, *Marx/Engels, Collected Works*, Volume 43, 1868–70 (Lawrence & Wishart, 1988), pp.295–6, 403–5.

6. Engels, *The Origin of the Family*, p.74. Engels also notes that 'in the course of their migrations the [ancient] Germans had morally much deteriorated, particularly during their south-easterly wanderings among the nomads of the Black Sea steppes, from whom they acquired not only equestrian skill but also gross, unnatural vices ...' (p.80). Krafft-Ebing, the professor of Psychiatry and Neurology at the University of Vienna,

put this view in its more usual urban setting: 'It is shown by the history of Babylon, Nineveh, Rome, and also by the "mysteries" of life in modern capitals, that large cities are the breeding places of nervousness and degenerate sensuality.' R. Von Krafft-Ebing, *Psychopathia Sexualis, with special reference to contrary sexual instinct: a medico-legal study*, 1892, translated by C. Chaddock (Rebman, 1893), p.7. See also 'The Epistle of Paul the Apostle to the Romans', 1:24–7, *The Holy Bible* (Authorised Version, 1611).

7. A. Bebel, *Woman in the Past, Present and Future*, 1879, translated by H. Adams Walter, introduced by Moira Donald (Zwan Publications, 1988), p.104.

8. A. Bebel, *Woman Under Socialism*, a translation by Daniel De Leon in 1917 of the work issued in 1879 as *Woman and Socialism* and in 1883 as *Woman in the Past, Present and Future* (New York Labor News Company, 1917), p.165.

9. Albert Moll chastised the enthusiast of homosexual love, Edward Carpenter (1844–1929), for suggesting that young men and boys often seek out older sexual partners of the same sex. Moll makes the point that even if this were the case, the older man should be able to repulse them – and should do so! See A. Moll, *The Sexual Life of the Child*, translated by E. Paul (George Allen & Co., 1912), pp.226–7. See also E. Carpenter, *Homogenic Love, and its Place in a Free Society*, 1894/1895 (Redundancy Press, undated).

10. See J. Steakley, *The Homosexual Emancipation Movement in Germany* (Arno Press, 1975), pp.2–4; W. Eissler, *Arbeiterparteien und Homosexuellenfrage, zur Sexualpolitik von SPD und KPD in der Weimarer Republik* (Verlag rosa Winkel, 1980); W. Harbutt Dawson, *German Socialism and Ferdinand Lassalle: A Biographical History of German Socialistic Movements during this Century*, 1888 (Swan Sonnenschein & Co., 1899).

11. E. Bernstein, 'On the Occasion of a Sensational Trial' [Oscar Wilde], and 'The Judgement of Abnormal Sexual Intercourse', articles from *Die Neue Zeit*, 1895, translated by Angela Clifford, in *Bernstein on Homosexuality* (Athol Books, 1977), pp.10–27.

12. *Vorwärts*, 15 November 1902, in *Jahrbuch für sexuelle Zwischenstuffen* (1903), pp.1308, 1309, cited by Steakley, *The Homosexual Emancipation Movement*, p.32.

13. Die Zukunft, cited by Steakley, *The Homosexual Emancipation Movement*, p.37.

14. Reichstag, *Protokolle*, Volume 204, p.5829, cited by Steakley, *The Homosexual Emancipation Movement*, p.35. For the views on the natural character of homosexuality current at the time see J.A. Symonds, 'Ulrich's Views' in Havelock Ellis, *Studies in the Psychology of Sex*, Volume I (Sexual Inversion) (Wilson & Macmillan, 1897), pp.258–72. See also M. Dannecker, *Theories of Homosexuality*, 1978, translated by

David Fernbach (Gay Men's Press, 1981). Some writers developed a perspective that dealt with homosexuality as a naturally occurring anomaly: 'Every family runs the risk of producing a boy or a girl whose life will be embittered by inverted sexuality, but who in all other respects will be no worse or better than the normal members of the home. Surely, then, it is our duty and our interest to learn what we can about its nature, and to arrive through comprehension at some rational method of dealing with it.' J.A. Symonds, *A Problem of Modern Ethics. Being an Inquiry into the Phenomenon of Sexual Inversion* (Symonds, 1896), p.4. Only 100 numbered copies of this work, addressed 'Especially to Medical Psychologists and Jurists', were produced.

15. Reichstag, *Protokolle*, Volume 204, p.5838, cited in Steakley, *The Homosexual Emancipation Movement*, p.35.

16. Ibid. Belief in 'sexual moderation' was widespread in the SPD, often going hand in hand with an advocacy of sexual abstinence up to 24 years of age. Until 1900 condemnation of masturbation, and opposition to contraception, was widespread within the party. See R.P. Neuman, 'The Sexual Question and Social Democracy in Imperial Germany', *Journal of Social History*, Volume 7, Number 3, 1974, pp.280–6.

17. Emma Goldman, 'The Traffic in Women', pp.183–200, in E. Goldman, *Anarchism and Other Essays* (Mother Earth Publishing Association, 1911), p.192.

18. Bebel, *Woman*, Zwan edition, p.86.

19. The view that homosexuality was an abnormality produced by the rotten social conditions that prevail under capitalism was in common currency in socialist circles in England until the late 1960s. Here is a typical response from the period: 'As I pointed out before, the possibility of a solution of the problem [of homosexuality] under class society is remote. It is only when there is complete equality between the sexes in all respects, beginning with economic equality and extending throughout all aspects of life; when psychological development will be more balanced through freedom from the struggle for existence we fight today, and people more tolerant; when submission for gain is unnecessary because of the poisoning effect of the money cancer is absent, that homosexuality would disappear naturally. If nature then produced an abnormality which it might do in a small number of cases, medical treatment would take good care of it. *Socialist Review*, Volume 7, Number 2, December 1957. For a similar view from a more libertarian tradition see A.S. Neill, *Summerhill: A Radical Approach to Education*, 1926 (Gollancz, 1962) pp.234–5.

20. P. Lafargue, 'The Woman Question', pp.111–38, in *The Right To Be Lazy, and Other Studies*, translated by C. Kerr (Charles H. Kerr & Co., 1907), p.138.

21. Bebel, *Woman*, Zwan edition, p.86.

22. R. Carlile, *Every Woman's Book, or What is Love,* fourth edition (Carlile, 1826) pp.10, 20, 43. See also *The Republican,* 12 April 1826 in the Francis Place Collection, British Library.

23. Carlile, *Every Woman's Book,* p.37.

24. T.R. Malthus, *An Essay on the Principle of Population,* 1798 (John Murray, 1826), Volume I, pp.23–4.

25. Ibid., Volume II, p.285.

26. W. Godwin, *Of Population, An Enquiry Concerning the Power of Increase in the Numbers of Mankind, Being an Answer to Mr Malthus's Essay on that Subject* (Longman, Hurst, Rees, Orme & Brown, 1820), p.615.

27. F. Place, *Illustrations and Proofs of the Principle of Population Including an Examination of the Proposed Remedies of Mr Malthus, and a Reply to the Objections of Mr Godwin and Others* (Longman, Hurst, Rees, Orme & Brown, 1822), p.165.

28. See N. Himes, *Medical History of Contraception* (George Allen & Unwin Ltd, 1936), p.213.

29. See also A. McLaren, *A History of Contraception from Antiquity to the Present Day* (Basil Blackwell, 1990), p.184.

30. R. Dale Owen, *Moral Physiology, or, a Brief and Plain Treatise on the Population Question,* third edition (Wright & Owen, 1831), p.8.

31. Ibid., pp.16–17.

32. Ibid., p.42.

33. C. Knowlton, *Fruits of Philosophy, An Essay on the Population Question,* 1831 (Freethought Publishing Company, 1877), p.45. This book was originally subtitled: *Or, the Private Companion of Young Married People.* See E. Royle, *Radicals, Secularists and Republicans: Popular Freethought in Britain* (Manchester University Press, 1980), pp.12–19.

34. For example, see Francis Place's evidence presented to a select committee of the British Parliament on the drunkenness of the people: F. Place, *Improvement of the Working People, Drunkenness – Education,* 1829 (Charles Fox, 1834). See also F. Engels, *The Condition of the Working Class in England,* 1844 (Granada Publishing Limited: Panther, 1972).

35. Knowlton, *Fruits of Philosophy,* p.34.

36. Ibid., p.6.

37. Campaigning aimed at elevating the domestic work of women and their role at the heart of family life was heavily promoted in America by Catharine Beecher (1800–78) and Harriet Beecher Stowe (1811–96). This movement was also linked to anti-saloon leagues, the prohibition of alcohol, and the struggle to ensure that young working-class women did not engage in 'irregular' sexual relations, drinking, crime or prostitution. Such campaigns also opposed contraception and women's suffrage. The morality crusade in the USA became very much stronger in 1873. In that year Anthony Comstock (1844–1915) helped to found the New York Society for the Prevention of Vice. He also induced

Congress to pass a law which prohibited the use of the mails to communicate any information about contraception or abortion. Comstock served (unpaid until 1907) as an inspector for the US Post Office department. Pamphlets, books, pills and rubber goods were constantly seized and destroyed; publishers and distributors, agitators and organisers for contraception, and for women's rights, became liable to arrest, fines and imprisonment. See C. Beecher, *A Treatise on Domestic Economy for the Use of Young Ladies at Home and at School* (Marsh, Capen, Lyan, and Webb, 1841); C. Beecher, H. Beecher Stowe, *The American Woman's Home: Or, Principles of Domestic Science. Being a Guide to the Formation and Maintenance of Economical, Healthful, Beautiful, and Christian Homes* (J.B. Ford and Co., 1869); C. Beecher, *Woman's Profession as Mother and Educator with Views in Opposition to Woman Suffrage* (Maclean, Gibson & Co., 1872); N. Hahn Rafter, 'Chastising the Unchaste: Social Control Functions of a Women's Reformatory 1894–1931', in *Social Control and the State*, edited by S. Cohen and A. Scull, 1983 (Basil Blackwell, 1986). In England Social Purity campaigning was very largely concentrated around the age at which girls could consent to sexual intercourse, and to the issues of syphilis and prostitution. Havelock Ellis was bitter in his condemnation of the moral campaigners: 'So gross is the ignorance of the would-be moral legislators – or, some may think, so skilful their duplicity – that the methods by which they process to fight against immorality are the surest methods for enabling immorality not merely to exist – which it would in any case – but to flourish.' Havelock Ellis, *The Task of Social Hygiene* (Constable, 1912), p.299. For a thorough consideration of these issues see F. Mort, *Dangerous Sexualities, Medico-Moral Politics in England Since 1830* (Routledge & Kegan Paul, 1987). See also Josephine Butler, *Social Purity* (Dyer Brothers, 1881); Josephine Butler, *Some Thoughts on the Present Aspect of the Crusade Against the State Regulation of Vice* (W. Llewelyn Esq, 1874); Josephine Butler, *Simple Words for Simple Folk, About the Repeal of the Contagious Diseases Acts (Women) which License Prostitution, and Place Women under the Arbitrary Power of Spy Police* (J.W. Arrowsmith, 1886).

38. E. Westermarck, *The Origin and Development of the Moral Ideas* (Macmillan, 1906), Volume I, p.20. See also K. Kautsky, 'Ethics and the Materialist Conception of History', 1906, in *Karl Kautsky: Selected Political Writings*, edited and translated by Patrick Goode (Macmillan, 1983), pp.33–45.

39. Havelock Ellis, *Studies in the Psychology of Sex*, Volume VI (Sex in Relation to Society) (F.A. Davis, 1911), p.582. See also Walter Arnstein, *The Bradlaugh Case: Atheism, Sex and Politics among the Late Victorians*, 1963 (University of Missouri Press, 1983); Annie Besant, *The Law of Population: its Consequences, and its Bearing upon Human Conduct and Morals*, 1877 (Freethought Publishing Company, 1884), reissued in S. Chan-

drasekhar, *A Dirty Filthy Book* (University of California, 1981); Sheila
Rowbotham, *Hidden From History* (Pluto Press, 1973).

40. Jane Clapperton, *Scientific Meliorism and the Evolution of Happiness* (Kegan
     Paul, Trench & Co., 1885) in *Eugenics Then and Now*, Benchmark Papers
     in Genetics/5, edited by C.J. Bajema (Dowden, Hutchinson & Ross
     Inc., 1976), p.336.

41. Ellis, *Social Hygiene*, p.31. The word 'eugenics' was coined by Sir
     Francis Galton (1822–1911) in 1883. It denotes the range of researches
     and activities that were designed to ensure the production of better
     physical, psychological and moral types. As Galton wrote: 'Eugenics is
     the science which deals with all influences that improve the inborn
     qualities of a race; also with those that develop them to the utmost
     advantage.' He continued: 'The aim of Eugenics is to bring as many
     influences as can be reasonably employed, to cause the useful classes in
     the community to contribute *more* than their proportion to the next
     generation.' F. Galton, 'Eugenics: Its Definition, Scope and Aims', 1904,
     in *Essays In Eugenics*, published by the Eugenics Education Society, 1909
     (Garland Publishing Inc., 1985), pp.35, 38; L.A. Farrell, *The Origins and
     Growth of the English Eugenics Movement 1865–1925*, Doctoral Thesis,
     1969 (Garland Publishing Inc., 1985); S.F. Weiss, *Race Hygiene and
     National Efficiency: The Eugenics of Wilhelm Schallmayer* (University of
     California Press, 1987). For a less apocalyptic (more scientific), 'tran-
     sitional' example of eugenics, as it begins to blend with social hygiene
     and modern population policies, see Raymond Pearl, *The Biology of
     Population Growth* (Alfred Knopf, 1925).

42. Ellis, *Social Hygiene*, p.41. Attitudes of this sort flourished in an envi-
     ronment where the criminology of Cesare Lombroso (1835–1909)
     and Enrico Ferri (1856–1929) was widely accepted by socialists as
     truly scientific and entirely progressive. This school of criminology
     believed that criminality could be innate in *born* 'criminal types', or it
     could be acquired as a result of weakness and immorality, or it could
     be the result of rotten social conditions. E. Ferri, *Criminal Sociology* (T.
     Fisher Unwin, 1895); E. Ferri, *The Positive School of Criminology*, lectures
     delivered at Naples in 1901, published in 1906 (Charles H. Kerr &
     Company, 1913); C. Lombroso, *Crime, Its Causes and Remedies*,
     translated by H. Horton, 1899 (William Heinemann, 1911); C.
     Lombroso, W. Ferrero, *The Female Offender* (T. Fisher Unwin, 1895);
     H. Kurella, *Cesare Lombroso: A Modern Man of Science*, translated by M.
     Eden Paul (Rebman Limited, 1911).

43. Ellis, *Social Hygiene*, pp.30–1.

44. Ibid., p.43.

45. Ibid., p.403. For a subtle and much more forgiving account of Havelock
     Ellis and his milieu see S. Rowbotham, J. Weeks, *Socialism and the New*

Life: The Personal and Sexual Politics of Edward Carpenter and Havelock Ellis (Pluto Press, 1977).

46. Bebel, *Woman*, Zwan edition, p.256.

47. M. Stopes, *Contraception (Birth Control)* (John Bale, Sons & Danielsson Ltd, 1923), p.9.

48. M. Sanger, *The Pivot of Civilization* (Jonathan Cape, 1923), pp.219–20.

49. Her most explicitly anti-Marxist and anti-communist book was introduced by the British Fabian socialist, H.G. Wells (1866–1946): *The Pivot of Civilization*, pp.9–16.

50. Marie Stopes was bold and explicit in her discussion of the physical aspects of sex and the need for thoroughgoing sex education. She was also very tough in her battle for the equality of women: 'Marriage can never reach its full stature until women possess as much intellectual freedom and freedom of opportunity within it as do their partners. 'That at present the majority of women neither desire freedom for creative work, nor would know how to use it, is only a sign that we are still living in the shadow of the coercive and dwarfing influences of the past.' M. Stopes, *Married Love, Or, Love in Marriage* (Critic & Guide Company, 1918), pp.156–7.

51. R. Hall, *Marie Stopes*, 1977 (Virago, 1978) p.326.

52. A. Kollontai, *Communism and the Family*, 1918 (SWP/ISO, 1984), p.16.

53. Ibid.

54. Ibid., p.14.

55. A. Kollontai, *Sexual Relations and the Class Struggle*, 1919, translated by Alix Holt (SWP/ISO, 1984), p.16.

56. V.I. Lenin, *The Tasks of the Youth Leagues*, 1920, a speech delivered at the Third All-Russia Congress of the Russian Young Communist League (Progress Publishers, 1985), p.16.

57. On 31 March 1804 (30 Ventose, Year XII) the *Code civil des français* became law. This code had widespread influence, informing the practice of many states attempting to modernise or rationalise legal systems encrusted with monarchical, religious and noble privilege. 'It cemented the ideas of freedom of person and of contract (including the right to enter any occupation), equality of all Frenchmen, and freedom of civil society from ecclesiastical control. As the first truly modern code of laws, the *Code Napoléon* for the first time in modern history gave a nation a unified system of law applicable to all citizens without distinction.' R. Holtman, *The Napoleonic Revolution*, 1967 (Louisiana State University Press, 1978), p.98. The code's penal provisions, promulgated in 1810, said very little about sexuality, as if the state did not regard sexuality to be the business of the law.

58. The Social Democratic intellectual milieu existed in a broader climate in Germany during the Weimar years. The influential weekly *Die*

Weltbuhne (published April 1918 to March 1933) reflected the opinion of the non-party republican intelligentsia. As Willem Melching has argued: 'We can conclude that from 1918 onwards the change in views on sexuality accelerated. The left-wing intellectuals of the *Weltbuhne* considered this great progress compared to the cultural climate of Wilhelminian Germany. The underlying assumption in the *Weltbuhne* articles was that the state had to retreat in questions of sexual taste, in order to secure optimal individual freedom, but at the same time, the government should take steps if the citizen's health was endangered. According to the *Weltbuhne*, the existing legislation [in Germany] was not only aimed at forcing morality on the population, but also supported the conservation of outdated and aggressive conceptions of economic and military force.' W. Melching, '"A New Morality": Left-wing Intellectuals on Sexuality in Weimar Germany', *Journal of Contemporary History*, Volume 25, Number 1, January 1990. p.82.

59. G. Batkis, *Die Sexualrevolution in Russland*, 1923 (Fritz Kater, 1925), cited in J. Lauritsen, D. Thorstad, *The Early Homosexual Rights Movement 1864–1935* (Times Change Press, 1974), p.64.

60. Ibid.

61. Ibid., p.65.

62. In 1922 Kollontai was sent abroad to engage in diplomatic work by the acting party secretary, Joseph Stalin. As Cathy Parter writes: 'by 1923 her liberating vision of happier and freer relationships between men and women was denounced as "bourgeois" and "decadent", and yet more slanderous epithets were invoked in the years to come.' See C. Parter's introduction to her translation of A. Kollontai, *A Great Love*, 1923, (Virago, 1981), pp.7–8. See also Wilhelm Reich, *The Sexual Revolution*, fourth edition 1949 (Vision Press, 1972), pp.208–11.

63. Batkis, cited by Reich in *The Sexual Revolution*, p.183.

64. See Lenin in conversation with Clara Zetkin, cited by Reich in *The Sexual Revolution*, pp.187–8.

65. In 1934 Ernst Roehm, leader of the Nazi Party's SA (the 'Brownshirts') was assassinated on Hitler's orders. Ernst Roehm was homosexual and the life of the upper echelons of the SA were subsequently presented, by left and right alike, as a gross example of homosexual decadence. In Leon Trotsky's (1879–1940) opinion: 'In Nazi "socialism" the psychological survivals of the "class reconciliation" of the trenches are still very important. "Barracks socialism", the expression that Martov and other Mensheviks used to apply to Bolshevism – without the slightest foundation – is fully applicable to the Nazis, at least to their recent past. In the figure of Roehm himself this barrack- room 'brotherhood' is very organically connected with pederasty.' L. Trotsky, *Trotsky's Diary in Exile, 1935*, translated by Elena Zarudnaya (Harvard University Press, 1958), February 11, 1935, p.24. During the same period the leading

Soviet writer, Maxim Gorky, wrote: 'In the fascist countries, homo-sexuality, which ruins youth, flourishes without punishment; in the country where the proletariat has audaciously achieved social power, homosexuality has been declared a social crime and is heavily punished. There is already a slogan in Germany, "Eradicate the homosexual and fascism will disappear."' Cited in Reich, *The Sexual Revolution*, p.210.

66. See discussion of objective psychology, reflex psychology and Freudo-Marxism in Elizabeth Roudinesco's *Jacques Lacan & Co*, 1986, translated by Jeffrey Mehlman (Free Association Books, 1990), pp.35–47; L.S. Vygotskii, *Mind in Society* (Harvard University Press, 1978); N. Bruss, 'V.N. Volosinov and the Structure of Language in Freudianism', Appendix II, in V.N. Volosinov, *Freudianism, A Marxist Critique*, 1927, translated by I.R. Titunik (Academic Press, 1976); L. Attwood, *The New Soviet Man and Woman* (Macmillan in association with the Centre for Russian and East European Studies at the University of Birmingham, 1990), pp.32–66.

67. Volosinov, *Freudianism*, p.90.

68. Ibid., pp.11, 91.

69. '... amid the welter of innumerable changes taking place in nature, the same dialectical laws of motion are in operation as those which in history govern the apparent fortuitousness of events; the same laws as those which similarly form the thread running through the history of devel-opment of human thought and gradually rise to consciousness in the mind of man; the laws which Hegel first developed in all-embracing but mystical form, and which we made it our aim to strip of this mystic form and to bring clearly before the mind in their complete simplicity and universality.' Engels, *Anti-Dühring*, pp.15–16. See also G.V. Plekhanov, *In Defence of Materialism, The Development of the Monist view of History*, 1895, translated by Andrew Rothstein (Lawrence & Wishart, 1947).

70. K. Kautsky, *Die Materialistische Geschichtsauffassung* (Verlag J.H.W. Dietz, 1927). For extracts in English, K. Kautsky, *The Materialist Conception of History*, abridged and annotated by J.H. Kautsky, translated by Raymond Meyer (Yale University Press, 1988), p.92.

71. Apart from Carl Gustav Jung (1875–1961), Wilhelm Reich was the most influential of Freud's colleagues to desert the psychoanalytic camp. Reich's 'treachery' was two-fold. He became politically involved, joining the Communist Party in 1928 (expelled 1933). More impor-tantly, he set out on a trajectory that led him to challenge the Freudian distinction between biology and the psychical apparatus. Reich spent more than 20 years attempting to prove the objective physical basis of his cosmic energy theory. His claims that he could measure the 'blue haze', and his subsequent 'collection' of energy in the Orgone Accu-mulator eventually raised fears for his sanity. Whether he became mad

or not, his belief in the biological basis of instincts and his desire to release them had widespread appeal. See I. Ollendorff Reich, *Wilhelm Reich* (Elek, 1969); W. Reich, *The Function of the Orgasm*, 1940 edition (Souvenir Press, 1983); W. Reich, *Sex-Pol Essays 1929–1934*, edited by L. Baxandall, (Vintage Books, 1972); W. Reich, *The Invasion of Compulsory Sex-Morality* 1931 (Souvenir Press, 1971); W.Reich, *Listen Little Man*, 1948 (Souvenir Press, 1972). See also B. Ollman, 'Social and Sexual Revolution', and, 'The Marxism of Wilhelm Reich: The Social Function of Sexual Repression' in B. Ollman, *Social and Sexual Revolution: Essays on Marx and Reich* (Pluto Press, 1979), pp.159–75, 176–203.

72.   H. Marcuse, *Eros and Civilisation*, 1955 (Sphere Books: Abacus, 1973), p.149.

73.   Ibid., pp. 142–3. See also E. Fromm, *The Sane Society*, 1955 (Routledge & Kegan Paul, 1963); E. Fromm, *The Anatomy of Human Destructiveness*, 1973 (Penguin Books, 1977); E. Fromm, 'Psychoanalysis – Science or Party Line?' in *The Dogma of Christ and Other Essays on Religion, Psychology and Culture* (Routledge & Kegan Paul, 1963); J.A.C. Brown, *Freud and the Post-Freudians*, 1961 (Penguin, 1987).

74.   See Mort, *Dangerous Sexualities*, pp.153–200.

Chapter 5

1.   Oedipal Triangle is a reference to an effect of the oedipus complex. In the work of Jacques Lacan the triangle implicit in the oedipus complex is a symbolic device. Its participants are never people but symbols brought together in the idea of *triangulation*. Lacan criticises biologism in psychoanalysis and that which might inhere in oedipus. However, in the collaboration of Gilles Deleuze and Felix Guattari (1930–92), *Anti-Oedipus*, any employment of the oedipal triangle suggests a restriction on the unconscious which should be open and unfettered. See G. Deleuze, F. Guattari, *Anti-Oedipus*, 1972 (Athlone Press, 1983).

2.   J. Lacan, 'Guiding Remarks for a Congress on Feminine Sexuality', 1964, in *Feminine Sexuality: Jacques Lacan and the Ecole Freudienne*, edited by J. Mitchell, J. Rose (Macmillan, 1982), p.92.

3.   André Breton (1896–1966); Georges Bataille (1897–1962); Roman Jakobson (1896–1982); Jacques Lacan (1901–81); Claude Lévi-Strauss.

4.   J. Lacan, *The Four Fundamental Concepts of Psycho-Analysis*, 1973 (Hogarth Press and the Institute of Psycho-Analysis, 1977), p.37.

5.   Ibid., pp.53, 60.

6.   André Breton, 'First Surrealist Manifesto', 1925, in A. Breton, *Manifestos of Surrealism*, translated by R. Seaner and H. Lane, (University of Michigan Press, 1974).

7. Dada was an anti-rationalist and iconoclastic artistic movement founded in Zurich in 1916. According to some accounts it was named *Dada* quite arbitrarily, from a French children's word for hobbyhorse. Dada's leading light, Tristan Tzara (1896–1963) wrote: 'Psychoanalysis is a dangerous idea; it deadens men's anti-real tendencies and systematizes the bourgeosie.' Cited in E. Roudinesco, *Jacques Lacan & Co: A History of Psychoanalysis in France 1925–1985*, 1986 (Free Association Books, 1990 [an abridged translation]), p.3.

8. Ibid., p.8.

9. Ibid., p.12.

10. Ibid., p.5.

11. S. Freud, 'Dr Reik and the Problem of Quackery', 1926 *Standard Edition* (Volume XXI, 1961), p.248. See also S. Freud, 'The Question of Lay Analysis', 1926, *Standard Edition* (Volume XX, 1959), pp.177–250.

12. See Sherry Turkle, 'French Anti-psychiatry', in *Critical Psychiatry: The Politics of Mental Health*, edited by D. Ingleby (Penguin, 1981).

13. Roudinesco, *Jacques Lacan*, p.5.

14. Ibid., pp.16–17.

15. A. Breton, *Nadja*, 1928, translated by R. Howard (Grove Press, 1960); G. Bataille, *Story of the Eye*, 1928, translated by J. Neugroschal (Penguin, 1982).

16. Breton, *Nadja*, p.160.

17. See discussion in R. Barthes, 'The Metaphor of the Eye', 1963, in Bataille, *Story of the Eye*, pp.119–27.

18. G. Bataille, 'Eye', 1929, in *Georges Bataille, Visions of Excess: Selected Writings 1927–1939*, edited by A. Stoekel (Manchester University Press, 1983), p.17.

19. André Breton, 'Second Surrealist Manifesto', 1930, in Breton, *Manifestoes*, p.184.

20. Ibid., p.128.

21. Ibid., pp.151–2.

22. Ibid., p.180.

23. G. Bataille, 'The "Old Mole" and the Prefix *Sur* in the Words *Surhomme* [Superman] and *Surrealist'*, written 1930 (first published 1968); see Stoekel, *Visions of Excess*, p.32.

24. Ibid., p.43.

25. It must be remembered that at this time the most powerful conception of the operation of 'the dialectic' was expressed in the mechanistic ideas of the Soviet dictatorship: '[The] Marxist materialist philosophy holds that matter, nature, being, is an objective reality existing outside and independent of the mind; that matter is primary, since it is the source of sensations, ideas, mind, and that mind is secondary, derivative, since it is a reflection of matter, a reflection of being; that thought is a product of matter which in its development has reached a high degree

of perfection, namely of the brain, and the brain is the organ of thought; and that therefore one cannot separate thought from matter without committing a grave error.' J. Stalin, *Dialectical and Historical Materialism*, 1938 (Lawrence & Wishart, 1941), p.12. For a feel of how these ideas were deployed see J. Stalin, *Anarchism or Socialism?*, 1905–6 (Foreign Languages Publishing House, 1950).

26. Roudinesco, *Jacques Lacan*, p.32.
27. G. Bataille, 'The Critique of the Foundations of the Hegelian Dialectic', 1932, in Stoekel, *Visions of Excess*, p.108.
28. Alexander Kojeve (1902–68). His original name was Kojevnikov and he left Russia in 1919 in order to study philosophy at Heidelberg. Unable to return home, he settled in Paris in 1928. In the early 1930s he was invited by Alexandre Koyre to teach Hegel at the Ecole practique des hautes études. His seminars on Hegel's *Phenomenology of Mind* took place between 1933 and 1939. They were published in A. Kojeve, *Introduction to the Reading of Hegel*, 1949, translated by J. Nicholls (Basic Books, 1969).
29. G.W.F. Hegel, *Phenomenology of Mind*, 1807, translated by J. Baille (Allen & Unwin, 1931).
30. Kojeve, *Introduction*, p.4.
31. Ibid.
32. Ibid.
33. Ibid., p.5.
34. See J. Fichte, *The Science of Knowledge*, 1794–1802 (Cambridge University Press, 1970). For the development of this idea of man as the creature of action, see A. Gehlen, *Man*, 1935–40 (Columbia University Press, 1988).
35. Kojeve, *Introduction*, p.6. This sort of reasoning – the Desire of Desire for Desire – grew out of the dialectic of the Master and Slave (Lordship and Bondage). Master and Slave are two definite forms of existence described in classic fashion by Hegel: 'The one is independent, and its essential nature is to be for itself; the other is dependent, and its essence is life or existence for another. The former is the Master, or Lord, the latter the Bondsman.' (Hegel, *Phenomenology of Mind*, p.234.) The slave is forced to work for the master. His being is a giving-away, a spending for another. In this way he gives the master recognition without receiving recognition in return. As a result the Master is faced with the problem that he is recognised by one whom he does not recognise. Consequently, his recognition is never what it should be. He is alienated from the recognition he receives and thus never recognises his own recognition.
36. Roudinesco, *Jacques Lacan*, p.104.

37. See R. Jakobson, 'Two Aspects of Language and Two Types of Aphasic Disturbance' in R. Jakobson, M. Halle, *Fundamentals of Language* (Mouton and Co., 1956).

38. Martin Heidegger (1889–1976). See M. Heidegger, *Being and Time*, 1927, translated by J. Macquarrie, E. Robinson (Basil Blackwell, 1967).

39. Lacan, *The Four Fundamental Concepts*, p.20.

40. Ibid. Lacan is informed here by the relationship between nature and culture proposed by Lévi-Strauss: 'Culture is not merely juxtaposed to life nor superimposed upon it, but in one way serves as a substitute for life, and in the other, uses and transforms it, to bring about the synthesis of a new order.' Lévi-Strauss is led to conclude that 'No empirical analysis ... can determine the point of transition between natural and cultural facts, nor how they are connected.' C. Lévi-Strauss, *The Elementary Structures of Kinship*, 1949, translated by J. Bell, J. Von Sturmer, R. Needham (Eyre & Spottiswood, 1968), pp.3–4, 8.

41. Lacan, *The Four Fundamental Concepts*, p.20.

42. Ibid., p.10.

43. Ibid., p.21.

44. Ibid., p.22.

45. Metapsychology: there has been a tendency to adopt a more or less topographical approach to discussions on the structure of the mind that lend rather too much firmness, clarity and definition to Freud's ideas. See S. Freud, 'The Ego and the Id', 1923, *Standard Edition* (Volume XIX, 1962).

46. Lacan, *The Four Fundamental Concepts*, p.149.

47. Ibid., p.154.

48. See G. Bataille, 'The Use Value of D.A.F. De Sade: An Open Letter to My Current Comrades' (first published in 1970), in Stoekel, *Visions of Excess*.

49. G. Bataille, *Inner Experience*, 1943 (University of New York, 1988).

50. G. Bataille, *Eroticism*, 1957 (Marion Boyars, 1987).

51. Ibid., p.23.

52. Ibid., p.39.

53. This refers to a great swathe of writings. In order to get a grip, or fix a gaze, on postmodernist writing it is important to read F. Nietzsche, *On the Genealogy of Morals*, 1887, translated by W. Kaufmann (Vintage Books, 1969); S. Freud, 'Beyond the Pleasure Principle', 1920, *Standard Edition* (Volume XVIII, 1961); J. Derrida, *Writing and Difference*, 1967 (Routledge & Kegan Paul, 1978); J. Derrida, *Spurs: Nietzsche's Styles*, 1978, translated by B. Harlow (Chicago University Press, 1979).

54. M. Foucault, *The Order of Things: An Archaeology of the Human Sciences* (Tavistock Publications, 1970) p.xxiii.

55. Ibid., p.387.

56. Ibid., pp.340–3.

57. G. Deleuze, *Foucault*, 1986, translated by S. Hand (Athlone Press, 1988), p.51. For the disruptive view see J. Baudrillard, *Forget Foucault*, 1977 (Semiotext(e), 1987).

58. M. Foucault, *The History of Sexuality (Volume 2): The Use of Pleasure*, 1984 (Penguin, 1988), p.4.

59. Ibid., p.6. See also M. Foucault 'The History of Sexuality: Interview', 1977, translated by G. Bennington, in *The Oxford Literary Review*, Volume 4, Number 2, 1980.

60. M. Foucault in 'Truth, Power, Self' an interview conducted by R. Martin, 25 October 1982, in *Technologies of the Self: A Seminar with Michel Foucault*, edited by L. Martin, H. Gutman, P. Hutton (University of Massachusetts Press, 1988), p.10.

Chapter 6

1. J. Derrida, *The Ear of the Other*, 1982 (University of Nebraska Press, 1988), p.86.

2. For discussion of the 'sworn virgins' of the Balkans see the essay by René Gremaux in *From Sappho to De Sade: Moments in the History of Sexuality*, edited by J. Bremmer (Routledge, 1990). For Masoch (1836–95) see his 'Venus in Furs', 1870, and the contribution by Gilles Deleuze, 'Coldness and Cruelty', 1969, in G. Deleuze, *Masochism* (Zone Books, 1989). For the development of the homosexual bar see Nancy Achilles, 'The Development of the Homosexual Bar as an Institution' in J. Gagnon, W. Simon, assisted by D. Carns, *Sexual Deviance* (Harper & Row, 1967).

3. M. Foucault, *The History of Sexuality, Volume One: An Introduction*, 1976 (Penguin, 1981), p.69.

4. Ibid., p.70.

5. Ibid., p.90.

6. J. Weeks, 'Discourse, Desire and Sexual Deviance: Some Problems in a History of Homosexuality' in *The Making of the Modern Homosexual*, edited by K. Plummer (Hutchinson, 1981) pp.76–111.

7. K. Plummer, 'Homosexual Categories: Some Research Problems in the Labelling Perspective of Homosexuality' in Plummer, *The Making of the Modern Homosexual*, p.75.

8. J. Weeks, 'The Development of Sexual Theory and Sexual Politics' in *Human Sexual Relations: A Reader. Towards a Redefinition of Sexual Politics*, edited by M. Brake (Penguin, Harmondsworth, 1982), pp.293–309.

9. Weeks, 'Discourse, Desire, Sexual Deviance' in Plummer, *The Making of the Modern Homosexual*, p.111.

10. Ethnomethodology is the study that focuses upon the way men and women construct a recognisable social world through everyday utterances

and actions. See H. Garfinkel, *Studies in Ethnomethodology*, 1967 (Polity Press, 1984); E. Goffman, *Frame Analysis: An Essay on the Organisation of Experience*, 1974 (Penguin Books, 1975).

11. 'Symbolic interactionism, evolved out of pragmatism and formalism, was named in 1937 when Herbert Blumer called it a "barbarous neologism"', and came into its own in the 1940s, 1950s, and 1960s.' P. Rock, 'Symbolic Interaction and Labelling Theory', 1990, in *Symbolic Interactionism*, Volume 1, edited by K. Plummer (Edward Elgar Publishing Ltd, 1991), p.240. See also E. Goffman, *Strategic Interaction*, 1969 (Ballantine Books, 1972).

12. P. Berger, T. Luckman, *The Social Construction of Reality*, 1966 (Penguin Books, 1979), pp.13, 15.

13. K. Erikson, 'Notes on the Sociology of Deviance' in *The Other Side: Perspectives on Deviance*, edited by H. Becker (The Free Press, 1964), p.11. See also E. Goffman, *Stigma: Notes on the Management of Spoiled Identity* (Prentice-Hall, 1964).

14. H. Becker, 'Introduction' in Becker, *The Other Side*, p.3.

15. J. Gagnon, W. Simon, *Sexual Conduct: The Social Sources of Human Sexuality*, 1973 (Hutchinson, 1974), p.9.

16. K. Plummer, *Sexual Stigma: An Interactionist Account* (Routledge & Kegan Paul, 1975), pp.12–13.

17. Ibid., p.13.

18. Rock, 'Symbolic Interaction and Labelling Theory' in Plummer, *Symbolic Interactionism*, Volume 1, p.228.

19. Ibid., p.230.

20. Ibid.

21. Ibid., p.235.

22. Ibid., p.236. It is evident that the existence of the I/Self in some kind of noumenal realm is assumed. We cannot ever really know this I/Self so the interactionist infers its existence.

23. M. Brake, 'Sexuality as Praxis: a Consideration of the Contribution of Sexual Theory to the Process of Sexual Being' in Brake, *Human Sexual Relations*, p.30.

24. E. Laclau, C. Mouffe, *Hegemony & Socialist Strategy: Towards a Radical Democratic Politics*, 1985 (Verso, 1989), p.127.

25. Ibid., pp.140–1.

26. Ibid., p.144.

27. J. Weeks, *Coming Out: Homosexual Politics in Britain from the Nineteenth Century to the Present*, 1977 (Quartet Books, 1990), p.xi.

28. 'Repressive hypothesis'. Discussed most perceptively by Michel Foucault in the first volume of his *History of Sexuality*, the repressive hypothesis refers to the view that modern industrial societies ushered in an age of increased sexual repression. In another sense it also refers to the belief that sexual repression is a principal means of social control orchestrated

by the state through family policy, moral panics, and the management of 'deviancy'.

29. E.P. Thompson, an interview conducted by Mike Merrill in New York City, March 1976, in *Visions of History*, edited by H. Abelove, et al. (Manchester University Press, 1983), p.7.

30. E.P. Thompson, *The Making of the English Working Class*, 1963 (Penguin Books, 1980), p.14.

31. E.P. Thompson, *The Poverty of Theory and Other Essays* (Merlin Press, 1978).

32. R. Scruton, *Thinkers of the New Left* (Longman, 1985), p.15.

33. Ibid., p.11.

34. L. Althusser, 'Reply to John Lewis', 1973, in L. Althusser, *Essays in Self-Criticism*, translated by G. Lock (NLB, 1976), p.95.

35. Ibid. For a rearguard defence of 'essentialism' see Scott Meikle, *Essentialism in the Thought of Karl Marx* (Duckworth, 1985). For a much broader discussion of these issues see R. Johnson, 'Histories of Culture/Theories of Ideology: Notes on an Impasse' in *Ideology and Cultural Production*, edited by M. Barrett, P. Corrigan, A. Kuhn, J. Wolff (Croom Helm, 1979), pp.49–77. See also A. Schmidt, *History and Structure: An Essay on Hegalian-Marxist and Structuralist Theories of History*, 1971, translated by J. Herf (MIT Press, 1981).

36. Weeks, *Coming Out*, pxi.

37. J. Weeks, *Sexuality* (Ellis Horwood and Tavistock Publications, 1986), pp.119, 25.

38. Rock, 'Symbolic Interaction and Labelling Theory' in Plummer, *Symbolic Interactionism*, p.236.

39. 'Internal standards allow only a limited situational objectivity; external standards allow for a broader transitional objectivity ... The problem of 'external standards' is the most serious epistemological problem that can be encountered. Without holding one, all knowledge becomes trivialized.' Plummer, *Sexual Stigma*, p.13.

40. Berger, Luckman, *The Social Construction of Reality*, p.65.

41. A. Gehlen, *Man: His Nature and Place in the World*, 1950 (Columbia University Press, 1988).

42. Berger, Luckman, *The Social Construction of Reality*, p.69. See also M. Bloch, *Marxism and Anthropology: The History of a Relationship* (Clarendon Press, 1983); M. Godelier, *Perspectives in Marxist Anthropology* (Cambridge University Press, 1977).

43. I. Kant, *Anthropology from a Pragmatic Point of View*, 1797, translated by M. Gregor (Martinus Nijhoff, 1974), p.183.

44. K. Soper, *Humanism and Anti-Humanism* (Hutchinson, 1986), p.147.

45. F. Mort, *Dangerous Sexualities: Medico-Moral Politics in England since 1830* (Routledge & Kegan Paul, 1987), p.220. For a discussion of some of the problems inherent in social construction theory, see Carole S.

Vance, 'Social Construction Theory: Problems in the History of Sexuality', and Saskia Wieringa, 'An Anthropological Critique of Constructionism: Berdaches and Butches'. Both essays are in D. Altman et al., *Homosexuality, Which Homosexuality?* (GMP Publishers/Uitgeverij An Dekker/Schorer, 1989).

46. J. Weeks, *Sexuality and Its Discontents: Meanings, Myths & Modern Sexualities*, 1985 (Routledge & Kegan Paul, 1986), p.260.

47. Ibid.

Chapter 7

1. Within the range of the repressive hypothesis, encouragement of family formation is not conceived simply as an instrument of state policy aimed at maintaining and enhancing social discipline. On the contrary, family life is understood as vital to the organisation and performance of the unpaid work of women in the form of home-based child rearing, care for the elderly and infirm, and in the provision (without cost to the state or the employers) of essential domestic services to the paid labour force. See K. Marshall, *Real Freedom* (Junius Publications, 1982). See also O. Adamson, C. Brown, J. Harrison, J. Price, 'The Material Basis of Women's Oppression' in *Revolutionary Communist*, Number 5, October 1976. For a more wide-ranging discussion of these issues see *The Politics of Housework*, edited by E. Malos, 1980 (Allison & Busby, 1982). See also N. Folbre, 'The Unproductive Housewife: Her Evolution in Nineteenth-Century Economic Thought' in *Signs*, Volume 16, Number 3, Spring 1991. For further consideration of the family see J. Donzelot, *The Policing of Families: Welfare versus the State*, 1977, translated by R. Hurley (Hutchinson, 1980); and for a criticism of the same, see M. Barrett, M. McIntosh, *The Anti-social Family*, 1982 (Verso, 1987).

2. See D. Milligan, *The Politics of Homosexuality* (Pluto Press, 1973). See also M. Fitzpatrick, D. Milligan, *The Truth About the Aids Panic* (Junius Publications, 1987). I do not wish to disown the basic arguments I have put forward (since 1986) concerning the distribution of HIV infection (and the onset of Aids) in Britain. However, both pamphlets are flawed by their employment of the repressive hypothesis.

3. On occasions this belief is reinforced by the pronouncements of right-wing politicians. A fine example was given by the British prime minister in 1983: 'I was brought up by a Victorian grandmother. We were taught to work jolly hard. We were taught to prove yourself; we were taught self-reliance; we were taught to live within our income. You were taught that cleanliness was next to Godliness. You were taught self-respect. You were taught always to give a hand to your neighbour. You were taught tremendous pride in your country. All of these things are Victorian

values. They are also perennial values.' Margaret Thatcher, 'Those Good Old Days by Maggie', *Standard* (London), 15 April 1983.

4. T.H. Van de Velde, *Ideal Marriage*, 1926, translated by Stella Browne (Heinemann, 1928), p.54.

5. Ibid., pp.169–71.

6. E. Brecher, *The Sex Researchers* (Andre Deutsch, 1970), p.83.

7. In 1891 Pope Leo XIII had pronounced: 'As we have said, the family is a true society equally with the state and, like the state, it possesses its own source of government, the authority of the father.' Leo XIII, *Rerum Novarum: Encyclical Letter of Pope Leo XIII on the Condition of the Working Classes*, 1891, translated by J. Kirwan, (Catholic Truth Society, 1983), paragraph 10, p.7. See also Pius XI, *Casti Conubii: Encyclical Letter of His Holiness Pope Pius XI*, 1931 (Sheed & Ward, 1933), pp.33–6.

8. Ibid., p.27. It should be borne in mind that while it was radical for a modern Pope to express this outlook it was not novel within the church. In times past even *coitus interruptus* had been advocated by priests as a means of birth control. See J. Dunbabin, *A Hound of God: Pierre de la Palud and the Fourteenth Century Church* (Clarendon Press, 1991). For discussion of the continuing struggle within the Roman Catholic Communion see R. Kaiser, *The Encyclical That Never Was: The Story of the Pontifical Commission on Population, Family and Birth, 1964–66*, 1985 (Sheed & Ward, 1987).

9. N. Himes, *Medical History of Contraception* (George Allen & Unwin Ltd, 1936), p.202. See also, S. Rowbotham, *A New World for Women: Stella Browne – Socialist Feminist*, 1977, (Pluto Press, 1978).

10. Ibid., pp.202–6. It should be noted that the vulcanised rubber condom had been exhibited in Philadelphia at the Centennial Exposition in 1876.

11. A. Kinsey, W. Pomeroy, C. Martin, *Sexual Behaviour in the Human Male* (W.B. Saunders, 1948), pp.11–12.

12. Ibid., pp.651–2. Kinsey was unhappy with the total size of his sample (12,000). He considered a survey covering a 100,000 people would have been more reliable. However, of his 12,000 total 6300 were male, of whom 5300 were white. Consequently, 'The story for the Negro male cannot be told now, because the Negro sample, while of some size, is not yet sufficient for making analyses comparable to those made here for the white male.' Kinsey, *Human Male*, pp.6–7. For further insight into the work of the Kinsey team see W. Pomeroy, *Dr Kinsey and the Institute for Sex Research* (Yale University Press, 1982).

13. Kinsey, *Human Male*, p.656.

14. J. D'Emilio, *Sexual Politics, Sexual Communities* (University of Chicago Press, 1983), p.34.

15. As John D'Emilio has noted: 'Kinsey's work gave an added push at a crucial time to the emergence of a gay subculture. Kinsey also provided

ideological ammunition that lesbians and homosexuals might use once they began to fight for equality.' D'Emilio, *Sexual Politics*, p.37.

16. A. Kinsey, W. Pomeroy, C. Martin, P. Gebhard, *Sexual Behaviour in the Human Female* (W.B. Saunders, 1953), p.475.

17. A. Montagu, 'A Most Important Book, But...' in *An Analysis of the Kinsey Report on Sexual Behaviour in the Male and Female*, edited by D. Geddes (Frederick Muller, 1954), p.123. See also Lionel Trilling's critical assessment of Kinsey in L. Trilling, *The Liberal Imagination*, 1951 (Mercury Books, 1961).

18. G. Westwood, *Society and the Homosexual* (Victor Gollancz, 1952), p.31.

19. Ibid.

20. Leo Abse, MP, 'Speech for the 2nd Reading of the Sexual Offences Bill', 1966, in *Law and Morality* edited by L. Blom-Cooper, QC, G. Drewry (Duckworth, 1976), pp.108–9.

21. Sir John Wolfenden, *Report of the Committee on Homosexual Offences and Prostitution* (HMSO, 1957).

22. W. Masters, V. Johnson, *Human Sexual Response* (Little, Brown & Co, 1966), p.45. For interesting criticism of this work see P. Robinson, *The Modernization of Sex* (Paul Flew, 1976). For further discussion of vaginal orgasm, see A. Ladas, B. Whipple, J. Perry, *The G Spot* (Corgi Books, 1983).

23. W. Masters, V. Johnson, *Homosexuality in Perspective*, 1979 (Bantam Books, 1982), p.308.

24. T. Szaz, *Sex: Facts, Frauds and Follies* (Basil Blackwell, 1980), p.39.

25. A. Bloom, *The Closing of the American Mind*, 1987 (Penguin Books, 1988), pp.97–8.

26. Ibid., p.101.

27. Kinsey, *Human Male*, p.4.

28. Wolfenden, *Report*, p.11.

29. Ibid., p.22.

30. Ibid., p.24. In 1955 Derrick Sherwin Bailey published his authoritative book on the origins and development of Christian hostility towards homosexuality. In a long exegetical discussion of biblical passages concerning Sodom and Gomorrah Bailey challenged the textual authority for the condemnation of homosexuality and masturbation. The book had a liberalising effect on discussion within the Church of England and it greatly assisted the work of Sir John Wolfenden's committee. See D. Bailey, *Homosexuality and the Western Christian Tradition* (Longman Green and Co., 1955).

31. Sir Patrick Devlin, *The Enforcement of Morals* (Oxford University Press, 1959), p.6.

32. Ibid., p.15.

33. Ibid., pp.17–18.

34. H.L.A. Hart, *Law, Liberty and Morality* (Oxford University Press, 1963), p.26.

35. Ibid., pp.50–1.

36. Ibid., p.51.

37. T.E. Utley, 'A Nation Sad to be Bad', *The Times* (London), 18 January 1988.

38. S. Hall, 'Reformism and the Legislation of Consent' in *Permissiveness and Control*, edited by National Deviancy Conference (Macmillan, 1980), p.1.

39. Hart, *Law, Liberty and Morality*, p.15.

40. For example see 'Report of the Committee on Obscenity and Pornography', 1970, and a discussion of its fate in *The Pornography Controversy*, edited by R. Rist (Transaction Books, 1975). For an example of legislative thinking and change in the USA see D. Drucker, *Abortion Decisions of the Supreme Court, 1973 through 1989: A Comprehensive Review with Historical Commentary* (McFarland & Co. Inc., 1990); E. Rubin, editor, *Abortion Politics and the Courts: Roe v Wade and its Aftermath*, 1982 (Greenwood, 1987).

41. M. Whitehouse, *Whatever Happened to Sex?* (Hodder and Stoughton, 1977), p.82. For the thinking of purity campaigners in Britain during the years spanning the 1960s and 1970s see *Pornography: The Longford Report*, the report of the committee chaired by the Earl of Longford (Coronet Books, 1972). For insight into the more celebratory attitude of the opposition, see Alex Comfort, *The Joy of Sex: A Gourmet Guide to Lovemaking*, 1972 (Mitchell Beasley, 1989). For a more sustained and sophisticated argument from the right see F. Mount, *The Subversive Family: An Alternative History of Love and Marriage* (Cape, 1982). For a more recent study see M. Durham, *Sex and Politics: The Family and Morality in the Thatcher Years* (Macmillan, 1991).

42. V. Riches, 'The Politics of Responsible Parenthood' in *Families Matter*, edited by R. Whitfield, cited in J. Phillips, *Policing the Family: Social Control in Thatcher's Britain* (Junius Publications, 1988), p.24.

43. In Britain battles have been waged throughout the 1980s and into the 1990s against abortion rights, against the rights of people who are HIV positive and of those with Aids, against the civil rights of gays and lesbians, against scientific research on human embryos, and for the intensification of censorship. In all these struggles the leaders within many different state institutions, local authorities, political parties and churches have played a contradictory role. At no time has the state coalesced around a resolutely reactionary position, nor has it fought for a forthright liberal outlook. At every stage, it has attempted to persuade the most panic stricken elements of society that it is doing something to halt the spread of perversion, disorder and disease. Simultaneously, political leaders and prominent public officials have gone to considerable lengths to

ensure that the framing and implementation of public policy remains as rational, and as practical, as the public mood and political circumstances will permit. The upshot has been greater restrictions on abortion, and new restrictions on what local authorities may do to fund lesbian and gay services. At the same time the state has felt compelled to support the struggles of many gays and lesbians for the establishment of a network of services designed to meet the needs of people with Aids and people who are HIV positive, and to promote Aids awareness and safer sex.

These struggles have produced a vast contemporary literature of their own. A useful start can be made in developing an understanding of this period by reading the Williams' Report: *Report of the Committee on Obscenity and Film Censorship* (HMSO, 1979); D. Morgan and R. Lee, *Blackstone's Guide to the Human Fertilisation and Embryology Act 1990* (Blackstone Press, 1991); V. Gillick, *Dear Mrs Gillick: The Public Respond* (Marshalls, 1985); J. Guillebaud, *The Pill,* 1980 (Oxford University Press, 1984); J. Keown, *Abortion, Doctors and the Law: Some Aspects of the Legal Regulation of Abortion in England from 1803–1982* (Cambridge University Press, 1988). On lesbian and gay issues a start might be made with P. Crane, *Gays and the Law* (Pluto, 1982); S. Shepherd, Mick Wallis, editors, *Coming on Strong: Gay Politics and Culture* (Unwin Hyman, 1989); M. Colvin, J. Hawksley, *Section 28: A Practical Guide to the Law and its Implications* (NCCL, 1989); Rights of Women, *Lesbian Mothers on Trial: A Report on Lesbian Mothers and Child Custody* (Rights of Women, 1984); Hall Carpenter Archives Oral History Group, *Inventing Ourselves: Lesbian Life Stories* (Routledge, 1989). For an introduction on the impact of Aids and HIV infection on Britain see P. Aggleton, P. Davies, G. Hart, editors, *Aids: Individual, Cultural and Policy Dimensions* (Falmer, 1990); E. Carter, S. Watney, editors, *Taking Liberties: Aids and Cultural Politics* (Serpent's Tail/ICA, 1989); Advisory Committee on Dangerous Pathogens, *LAV/HTLV III: The Causative Agent of Aids and Related Conditions* (ACDP, June 1986). Monthly and quarterly reports on HIV/Aids for the United Kingdom and Northern Ireland are available from the Press Office, Department of Health, Whitehall, London WC1. See also D.Milligan, 'Fighting the Epidemic' in *Rouge,* Issue 2, Spring 1990.

Bibliography

Abelove, H., et al., editors, *Visions of History* (Manchester University Press, 1983).

Achebe, C., *Things Fall Apart*, 1958 (Heinemann Educational Books, 1988).

Aggleton, et al., editors, *Aids: Individual, Cultural and Policy Dimensions* (Falmer, 1990).

Althusser, L., *Essays in Self-Criticism* (NLB, 1976).

Altman, D., et al., *Homosexuality, Which Homosexuality?* (GMP Publishers/Uitgeverij An Dekker/Schorer, 1989).

Ardrey, R., *The Territorial Imperative* (Collins, 1966).

Arnstein, W., *The Bradlaugh Case*, 1963 (University of Missouri Press, 1983).

Attwood, L., *The New Soviet Man and Woman* (Macmillan & CREES [Birmingham], 1990).

Badcock, C., *The Problem of Altruism: Freudian-Darwinian Solutions* (Blackwell, 1986).

Bailey, D., *Homosexuality and the Western Christian Tradition* (Longman Green and Co., 1955).

Bajema, C. (editor), *Eugenics Then and Now* (Dowden, Hutchinson & Ross Inc., 1976).

Bannister, R., *Social Darwinism* (Temple University Press, 1979).

Barbin, H., *Herculine Barbin*, 1978, introduced by M. Foucault (Pantheon Books, 1980).

Barnett, S., *Biology and Freedom: An Essay on the Implications of Human Ethology* (Cambridge University Press, 1988).

Barrett, M., et al., editors, *Ideology and Cultural Production* (Croom Helm, 1979).

Barrett, M., McIntosh, M., *The Anti-social Family*, 1982 (Verso, 1987).

Barthes, R., *Barthes: Selected Writings*, 1982 (Collins: Fontana, 1983).

Bataille, G., *Story of the Eye*, 1928 (Penguin, 1982).

——, *Inner Experience*, 1943 (University of New York, 1988).

——, *Eroticism*, 1957 (Marion Boyers, 1987). See A. Stoekel.

Baudrillard, J., *Revenge of the Crystal* (Pluto Press, 1990).

——, *Forget Foucault*, 1977 (Semiotext[e], 1987).

Bebel, A., *Woman in the Past, Present and Future*, 1879 (Zwan Publications, 1988),

——, *Woman Under Socialism*, 1879 (New York Labor News Company, 1917).

Becker, H., editor, *The Other Side* (Free Press, 1964).

Beecher, C., *A Treatise on Domestic Economy* (Marsh, Capen, Lyan, and Webb, 1841).

———, *Woman's Profession as Mother and Educator* (Maclean, Gibson & Co., 1872).

Beecher, C., Beecher Stowe, H., *The American Woman's Home* (J.B. Ford and Co., 1869).

Benedict, R., *Patterns of Culture*, 1935 (Routledge & Kegan Paul, 1980).

Berger, P., Luckman, T., *The Social Construction of Reality*, 1966 (Penguin Books, 1979).

Bergson, H., *An Introduction to Metaphysics*, 1903 (Macmillan, 1913).

———, *Creative Evolution*, 1907 (Macmillan, 1911).

Berlin, I., *Four Essays on Liberty*, 1953 (Oxford University Press, 1969).

Bernstein, E., *Bernstein on Homosexuality*, 1895, newspaper articles translated by Angela Clifford (Athol Books, 1977).

Besant, A., *The Law of Population*, 1877 (Freethought Publishing Company, 1884), reissued in S. Chandrasekhar, *A Dirty Filthy Book* (University of California, 1981).

Bloc, M., *Feudal Society*, 1938 (Chicago University Press, 1961).

Bloch, M., *Marxism and Anthropology* (Clarendon Press, 1983).

Blom-Cooper, QC, L., Drewry, G., *Law and Morality* (Duckworth, 1976).

Bloom, A., *The Closing of the American Mind*, 1987 (Penguin Books, 1988).

Brake, M., editor, *Human Sexual Relations* (Penguin, Harmondsworth, 1982).

Brecher, *The Sex Researchers* (Andre Deutsch, 1970).

Bremmer, J., editor, *From Sappho to De Sade* (Routledge, 1990).

Breton, A., *Manifestoes of Surrealism*, 1925–1930 (University of Michigan Press, 1974).

——— *Nadja*, 1928 (Grove Press, 1960).

Brown, J., *Freud and the Post-Freudians*, 1961 (Penguin Books, 1987).

Butler, J., *Some Thoughts* (on state regulation of vice) (W. Llewelyn Esq, 1874).

———, *Social Purity* (Dyer Brothers, 1881).

———, *Simple Words for Simple Folk* (J.W.Arrowsmith, 1886).

Carlile, R., *Every Woman's Book* (Carlile, 1826).

Carpenter, E., *Homogenic Love*, 1894/95 (Redundancy Press, undated).

Carrithers, M., Collins, S., Lukes, S., editors, *The Category of the Person* (Cambridge University Press, 1985).

Carter, E., Watney, S. editors, *Taking Liberties: Aids and Cultural Politics* (Serpent's Tail/ICA, 1989).

Cohen, S., Scull, A., editors, *Social Control and the State*, 1983 (Basil Blackwell, 1986).

Colvin, M., Hawksley, J., *Section 28: A Practical Guide* (NCCL, 1989).

Comfort, A., *The Joy of Sex*, 1972 (Mitchell Beasley, 1989).

Comte, A., *Auguste Comte and Positivism: The Essential Writings*, 1975 (University of Chicago Press, 1983).

Cook, B., et al., editors, *Hormones and their Actions* (Elsevier, 1988).

Coward, R., *Patriarchal Precedents* (Routledge & Kegan Paul, 1983).

Crane, P., *Gays and the Law*, (Pluto, 1982).

Crapo, L., *Hormones, the Messengers of Life* (W.H. Freeman & Co., 1985).

Crawford, C., *The Beginnings of Nietzsche's Theory of Language* (Walter de Gruyter, 1988).

Dannecker, M., *Theories of Homosexuality*, 1978 (Gay Men's Press, 1981).

Darwin, C., *The Origin of Species by Means of Natural Selection, or, the Preservation of Favoured Races in the Struggle for Life*, 1859 (Penguin Books, 1985).

——, *The Expression of the Emotions in Man and Animals*, 1872 (Chicago University Press, 1965).

——, *The Descent of Man*, 1871 (John Murray, 1883).

——, *Metaphysics, Materialism and the Evolution of Mind, Early Writings of Charles Darwin*, annotated by P. Barrett, 1974 (University of Chicago Press, 1980).

Davidson, D., *Essays on Actions and Events* (Clarendon Press, 1980).

Dawson, W., *German Socialism and Ferdinand Lassalle*, 1888 (Swan Sonnenschen & Co., 1899).

de Beauvoir, S., *The Second Sex*, 1949 (Penguin Books, 1983).

Deleuze, G., *Foucault*, 1986 (Athlone Press, 1988).

——, *Masochism* (Zone Books, 1989).

Deleuze, G., Guattari, F., *Anti-Oedipus*, 1972 (Athlone Press, 1983);

D'Emilio, J., *Sexual Politics, Sexual Communities* (University of Chicago Press, 1983).

Denton, M., *Evolution: a Theory in Crisis* (Burnett Books, 1985).

Derrida, J., *Writing and Difference*, 1967 (Routledge & Kegan Paul, 1978.

——, *Spurs: Nietzsche's Styles*, 1978 (Chicago University Press, 1979).

——, *The Ear of the Other*, 1982 (University of Nebraska Press, 1988).

Desertis, V.C., *Psychic Philosophy*, 1895 (Philip Wellby, 1901).

Devlin, Sir P., *The Enforcement of Morals* (Oxford University Press, 1959).

Donovan, B., *Hormones and Human Behaviour* (Cambridge University Press, 1985).

Donovan B., J. Van der Werff ten Bosch, *Physiology of Puberty* (Edward Arnold, 1965).

Donzelot, J., *The Policing of Families: Welfare versus the State*, 1977 (Hutchinson, 1980).

Druker, D., *Abortion Decisions of the Supreme Court* (McFarland & Co. Inc., 1990).

Duby, G., *La Société au XIe et XIIe siècles dans le région maconnaise* (Presses Universitaires de France, 1953).

Dunbabin, J., *A Hound of God* (Clarendon Press, 1991).

Durham, M., *Sex and Politics: The Family and Morality in the Thatcher Years* (Macmillan, 1991).

Eissler, W., *Arbeiterparteien und Homosexuellenfrage* (Verlag Rosa Winkel, 1980).

Ellenberger, H., *The Discovery of the Unconscious* (Allen Lane, the Penguin Press, 1970).

Ellis, H., *Studies in the Psychology of Sex*, Volume I (Sexual Inversion) (Wilson & Macmillan, 1897); Volume VI (Sex in Relation to Society) (F.A. Davis, 1911).

——, *The Philosophy of Conflict* (Constable, 1919).

——, *The Task of Social Hygiene* (Constable, 1912).

Engels, F., *The Condition of the Working Class in England*, 1844 (Panther, 1972).

——, *Anti-Dühring*, 1878 (Lawrence & Wishart, 1943).

——, *The Dialectics of Nature*, 1883 (Foreign Languages Publishing House, Moscow, 1954).

——, *The Origin of the Family, Private Property and the State*, 1884 (Foreign Languages Press, Peking, 1978).

Evans, R., *Dialogue with B.F. Skinner*, 1968 (Praeger, 1981).

Evans-Pritchard, E., *A History of Anthropological Thought* (Faber & Faber, 1981).

Falger, V., Dennen, J. Van der, editors, *Sociobiology and Conflict* (Chapman and Hall, 1990).

Farrell, L., *The Origins and Growth of the English Eugenics Movement* (Garland Publishing Inc., 1985).

Ferri, E., *Criminal Sociology* (T. Fisher Unwin, 1895).

——, *The Positive School of Criminology*, 1906 (Charles H. Kerr & Company, 1913).

Fetzer, J., editor, *Sociobiology and Epistemology* (D. Reidel Publishing Company, 1985).

Fichte, J., *The Science of Knowledge*, 1794–1802 (Cambridge University Press, 1970).

Figes, E., *Patriarchal Attitudes* (Faber & Faber, 1970).

Fitzpatrick, M., Milligan, D., *The Truth About the Aids Panic* (Junius Publications, 1987).

Fliess, R., (editor) *The Psycho-Analytic Reader* (Hogarth Press & Institute of Psycho-Analysis, 1950).

——, *Erogeneity and Libido* (International University Press, 1956).

Forrester, J., *Language and the Origins of Psychoanalysis* (Macmillan, 1980).

Fortes, M., *Kinship and the Social Order: the Legacy of Lewis Henry Morgan*, 1969 (Routledge & Kegan Paul, 1970).

Foucault, M., *The Order of Things*, 1966 (Tavistock Publications, 1970).

——, *Power/Knowledge: Selected Interviews and Other Writings, 1972–77*, edited by C. Gordon (Pantheon Books, 1980)

——, *An Introduction*, 1976, Volume 1 of 'The History of Sexuality' (Penguin, 1981).

——, *The Use of Pleasure*, 1984, Volume 2 of 'The History of Sexuality' (Penguin, 1984).

——, *Technologies of the Self: A Seminar with Michel Foucault* (University of Massachusetts Press, 1988).

Frazer, J., *The Golden Bough: a Study in Magic and Religion*, (Macmillan, 1890–1915), abridged edition, 1922 (Macmillan, 1929).

Freud, M., *Glory Reflected, Sigmund Freud - Man and Father* (Angus and Robertson, 1957).

Freud, S., *Standard Edition of the Complete Psychological Works of Sigmund Freud* (Hogarth Press and the Institute of Psycho-Analysis, 1953–1964).

Friedan, B., *The Feminine Mystique*, 1963 (Penguin Books, 1965).

Fromm, E., *Sigmund Freud's Mission: An Analysis of His Personality and Influence* (Harper & Brothers, 1959).

——, *The Sane Society*, 1955 (Routledge & Kegan Paul, 1963).

——, *The Dogma of Christ* (Routledge & Kegan Paul, 1963).

——, *The Anatomy of Human Destructiveness*, 1973 (Penguin Books, 1977).

Frost, J., *The Horrors of Convict Life*, 1856 (Sullivan's Cove, 1973).

Fuss, D., *Essentially Speaking: Feminism, Nature and Difference* (Routledge, 1989).

Gagnon, J., Simon. W., assisted by Carns, D., *Sexual Deviance* (Harper & Row, 1967.

——, *Sexual Conduct*, 1973 (Hutchinson, 1974).

Galton, F., *Hereditary Genius: An Inquiry into its Laws and Consequences*, 1869 (Watts & Co., 1950).

Galton, F., et al., *Essays in Eugenics*, published by the Eugenics Education Society, 1909 (Garland Publishing Inc., 1985).

Garfinkel, H., *Studies in Ethnomethodology*, 1967 (Polity Press, 1984).

Garry, A., Pearsall, M., editors, *Women, Knowledge, and Reality: Explorations in Feminist Philosophy* (Unwin Hyman, 1989).

Gasche, R., *The Tain of the Mirror* (Cambridge, Mass: University Press, 1986).

Gay, P., *Freud: A Life for Our Times*, 1988 (Papermac, 1989).

Geddes, D., editor, *An Analysis of the Kinsey Report* (Frederick Muller, 1954).

Geddes, P., Thompson, J. *The Evolution of Sex* (Walter Scott, 1890).

Gehlen, A., *Man*, 1950 (Columbia University Press, 1988).

Gillick, V., *Dear Mrs Gillick* (Marshalls, 1985).

Godelier, M., *Perspectives in Marxist Anthropology* (Cambridge University Press, 1977).

Godwin, W., *Of Population* (Longman, Hurst, Rees, Orme & Brown, 1820).

Goffman, E., *Stigma* (Prentice-Hall, 1964).

——, *Strategic Interaction*, 1969 (Ballantine Books, 1972).

——, *Frame Analysis*, 1974 (Penguin Books, 1975).

Goldman, E., *Anarchism and Other Essays* (Mother Earth Publishing Association, 1911).

Goldschmidt, R., *The Material Basis of Evolution* (Yale University Press, 1940).

Goodall, J., *In the Shadow of Man* (Collins, 1971).

Guillebaud, J., *The Pill*, 1980 (Oxford University Press, 1984).

Haeckel, E., *The History of Creation*, 1873 (Kegan Paul, Trench, Trubner & Co. Ltd, 1892).

Hall, R., *Marie Stopes*, 1977 (Virago, 1978).

Hall Carpenter Archives Oral History Group, *Inventing Ourselves: Lesbian Life Stories* (Routledge, 1989).

Hart, H.L.A., *Law, Liberty and Morality* (Oxford University Press, 1963).

Hegel, G.W.F., *Phenomenology of Mind*, 1807 (Allen & Unwin, 1931).

Heidegger, M., *Being and Time*, 1927 (Basil Blackwell, 1967).

Hereven, T., Plakans, A., editors, *Family History and the Crossroads* (Princeton University Press, 1987).

Himes, N., *Medical History of Contraception* (George Allen & Unwin Ltd, 1936).

Hite, S., *The Hite Report on Male Sexuality*, 1981 (Ballantine Books, 1982).

Hodges, A., *Alan Turing: The Enigma* (Burnett Books, 1983).

Hofstadter, R., *Social Darwinism in American Thought: 1860–1915* (University of Pennsylvania Press, 1945).

Holbrook, D., *Evolution and the Humanities* (Gower, 1987).

Holtman, R., *The Napoleonic Revolution*, 1967 (Lousiana State University Press, 1978).

Homans, G. Casper, *English Villagers of the Thirteenth Century*, 1941 (Russell and Russell, 1960).

Ingleby, D., editor, *Critical Psychiatry: The Politics of Mental Health* (Penguin, 1981).

Irigaray, L., *This Sex Which is Not One*, 1977 (Cornell University Press, 1985).

Jakobson, R., Halle, M., *Fundamentals of Language* (Mouton & Co., 1956).

Jardine, A., Smith, P., editors, *Men in Feminism* (Methuen, 1987).

Jones, E., *Sigmund Freud: Life and Works* (Hogarth Press, 1953).

Jung, C., *Collected Works* (Routledge and Kegan Paul, 1957-79).

Kaiser, R., *The Encyclical That Never Was*, 1985 (Sheed & Ward, 1987).

Kant, I., *Critique of Pure Reason*, second edition 1787 (Macmillan, 1986).

——, *Anthropology*, 1797 (Martinus Nijhoff, 1974).

Kautsky, K., *Karl Kautsky: Selected Political Writings* (Macmillan, 1983).

——, *The Materialist Conception of History*, 1927, abridged by J.H. Kautsky (Yale University Press, 1988).

Kaye, H., *The Social Meaning of Modern Biology* (Yale University Press, 1986).

Keown, J., *Abortion, Doctors and the Law* (Cambridge University Press, 1988).

Kinsey, A., et al., *Sexual Behavior in the Human Male* (W.B. Saunders, 1948).

——, *Sexual Behavior in the Human Female* (W.B. Saunders, 1953).

Kirby, Rev W., *Treatise VII: On the History, Habits and Instincts of Animals* (in two volumes), being part of the *Bridgewater Treatises* (William Pickering, 1835).

Knowlton, C., *Fruits of Philosophy*, 1831 (Freethought Publishing Company, 1877).

Kojeve, A., *Introduction to the Reading of Hegel*, 1949 (Basic Books, 1969).

Kollontai, A., *Communism and the Family*, 1918 (SWP/ISO, 1984).

——, *Sexual Relations and the Class Struggle*, 1919 (SWP/ISO, 1984).

——, *A Great Love*, 1923 (Virago, 1981).

Kroeber, A., *The Nature of Culture* (University of Chicago Press, 1952).

Kurella, H., *Cesare Lombroso* (Rebman Limited, 1911).

Lacan, J., *The Four Fundamental Concepts of Psycho-Analysis*, 1973 (Hogarth Press and The Institute of Psycho-Analysis, 1977). See also Mitchell and Rose.

Laclau, E., Mouffe, C., *Hegemony & Socialist Strategy*, 1985 (Verso, 1989).

Ladas, A., et al., *The G Spot* (Corgi Books, 1983).

Lafargue, P., *The Right to be Lazy, and Other Studies* (Charles H. Kerr & Co., 1907).

Laplanche, J., Pontalis, J., *The Language of Psycho-Analysis*, 1967 (Hogarth Press & Institute of Psycho-Analysis, 1973).

Lauritsen, J., Thorstad., D, *The Early Homosexual Rights Movement*, (Times Change Press, 1974).

Lecky, W., *History of European Morals from Augustus to Charlemagne*, 1869 (Longmans, Green & Co., 1911).

Leo XIII, *Rerum Novarum*, 1891 (Catholic Truth Society, 1983).

Leon, A., *The Jewish Question, A Marxist Interpretation*, 1946 (Pathfinder Press, 1986).

Lenin, V.I., *Materialism and Empiro-Criticism*, 1908 (Foreign Languages Publishing House, Moscow, 1947).

——, *Philosophical Notebooks*, 1895–1916, *Collected Works*, Volume 38 (Lawrence & Wishart, 1972).

——, *The Tasks of the Youth Leagues*, 1920 (Progress Publishers, 1985).

Lévi-Strauss, C., *The Elementary Structures of Kinship*, 1949 (Eyre & Spottiswood, 1968).

Lloyd, G., *Demystifying Mentalities* (Cambridge University Press, 1991).

Lombroso, C., *Crime, Its Causes and Remedies*, 1899 (William Heinemann, 1911).

Lombroso, C., Ferrero, W., *The Female Offender* (T. Fisher Unwin, 1895).

Longford, Earl of, *Pornography: The Longford Report* (Coronet Books, 1972).

Lorenz, K., *Evolution and Modification of Behaviour*, 1965 (Methuen, 1966).

Lyotard, J., *The Postmodern Condition: A Report on Knowledge*, 1977 (Manchester University Press, 1989).

MacDonald, M., *Mystical Bedlam: Madness, Anxiety, and Healing in Seventeenth Century England* (Cambridge University Press, 1981).

McLaren, A., *A History of Contraception* (Basil Blackwell, 1990).

McLennan, G., *Marxism, Pluralism and Beyond* (Polity Press, 1989).

Magee, B., *Aspects of Wagner*, 1968 (Oxford University Press, 1988).

Malinowski, B., *A Scientific Theory of Culture*, 1944 (University of North Carolina Press, 1973).

Malos, E., editor, *The Politics of Housework*, 1980 (Allison & Busby, 1982).

Malthus, T., *An Essay on the Principle of Population*, 1798 (John Murray, 1826).

Marcuse, H., *Eros and Civilisation*, 1955 (Sphere Books: Abacus, 1973).

Marshall, K., *Real Freedom* (Junius Publications, 1982).

Marx, K. and Engels, F., *Marx/Engels, Collected Works*, Volume 43, 1868–70 (Lawrence & Wishart, 1988).

Masters, E., Johnson, V., *Human Sexual Response* (Little, Brown & Co., 1966).

——, *Homosexuality in Perspective*, 1979 (Bantam Books, 1982).

Mayr, E., *The Growth of Biological Thought* (Harvard University Press: Belknap, 1982).

Mead, M., *Sex and Temperament in Three Primitive Societies*, 1935 (New American Library: Mentor, 1950).

Meikle, S., *Essentialism in the Thought of Karl Marx* (Duckworth, 1985).

Midgley, M., *Beast & Man: The Roots of Human Nature*, 1978 (Methuen, 1979).

Mill, J.S., *Auguste Comte and Positivism*, 1865 (George Routledge & Sons, 1908).

Milligan, D., *The Politics of Homosexuality* (Pluto Press, 1973).

Mitchell, J., *Psychoanalysis and Feminism*, 1974 (Penguin Books, 1975).

Mitchell, J., Rose., J., editors, *Feminine Sexuality: Jacques Lacan and the Ecole Freudienne* (Macmillan, 1982).

Moll, A., *The Sexual Life of the Child* (George Allen & Co., 1912).

Morgan, D., Lee, R., *Blackstone's Guide to the Human Fertilisation and Embryology Act 1990* (Blackstone Press, 1991).

Morgan, L.H., *Ancient Society* (Henry Holt & Co., 1877).

Morgan, N., *Cell Signalling* (Open University Press, 1989).

Morris, D., *The Naked Ape* (Corgi, 1967).

——, *The Human Zoo* (Jonathan Cape, 1970)

Mort, F., *Dangerous Sexualities* (Routledge & Kegan Paul, 1987).

Moscovici, S., *Society Against Nature*, 1972 (Harvester Press, 1976).

Mount, F., *The Subversive Family* (Cape, 1982).

National Deviancy Conference, editors, *Permissiveness and Control* (Macmillan, 1980).

Neill, A.S., *Summerhill*, 1926 (Gollancz, 1962).

Nietzsche, F., *The Birth of Tragedy*, 1871 (J.N. Foulis, 1909).

——, *On the Genealogy of Morals*, 1887 (Vintage Books, 1969).

Nitecki, M., *Evolutionary Progress* (University of Chicago Press, 1988).

Oldroyd, D., Langham, I., editors, *The Wider Domain of Evolutionary Thought* (D. Reidel Publishing Company, 1983).

Ollendorff Reich, I., *Wilhelm Reich* (Elek, 1969).

Ollman, B., *Social and Sexual Revolution* (Pluto Press, 1979).

Owen, R. Dale, *Moral Physiology* (Wright & Owen, 1831).

Pannekoek, A., *Marxism and Darwinism* (Charles H. Kerr & Company, 1912).

Patten, S., *Heredity and Social Progress*, 1903 (Garland Publishing, 1984)

Pearl, R., *The Biology of Population Growth* (Alfred Knopf, 1925).

Phillips, J., *Policing the Family* (Junius Publications, 1988).

Pius XI, *Casti Conubii* (Sheed & Ward, 1933).

Place, F., *Illustrations and Proofs of the Principle of Population* (Longman, Hurst, Rees, Orme & Brown, 1822).

——, *Improvement of the Working People*, 1829 (Charles Fox, 1834).

Plummer, K., editor, *Sexual Stigma* (Routledge & Kegan Paul, 1975).

——, *The Making of the Modern Homosexual* (Hutchinson, 1981).

——, *Symbolic Interactionism* (Edward Elgar Publishing Ltd, 1991).

Pomeroy, W., *Dr Kinsey and the Institute for Sex Research* (Yale University Press, 1982).

Quine, W., *Ontological Relativity and Other Essays* (Columbia University Press, 1969).

Raymond, J., *The Transsexual Empire*, 1979 (The Women's Press, 1980).

Reich, W., *Sex-Pol Essays 1929–1934* (Vintage Books, 1972).

——, *The Invasion of Compulsory Sex-Morality*, 1931 (Souvenir Press, 1971).

——, *The Function of the Orgasm*, 1940 edition (Souvenir Press, 1983).

——, *Listen Little Man*, 1948 (Souvenir Press, 1972).

——, *The Sexual Revolution*, fourth edition, 1949 (Vision Press, 1972).

Reiter, R., editor, *Towards an Anthropology of Women* (Monthly Review Press, 1975).

Rights of Women, *Lesbian Mothers on Trial* (Rights of Women, 1984).

Rist, R., editor, *The Pornography Controversy* (Transaction Books, 1975).

Robinson, P., *The Modernisation of Sex* (Paul Flew, 1976).

Romanes, G.J., *Mental Evolution in Animals* (Kegan Paul, Trench & Co., 1883: republished by Gregg International Publishers, 1970).

——, *Mental Evolution in Man, Origin of Human Faculty* (Kegan Paul, Trench & Co., 1888: republished by Gregg International Publishers, 1970).

Rose, S., Lewontin, L., Kamin L., *Not in our Genes*, 1984 (Penguin: Pelican, 1985).

Roudinesco, E., *Jacques Lacan & Co*, 1986 (Free Association Books, 1990).

Rowe, D., *The Depression Handbook* (Collins, 1991).

Rowbotham, S., *Hidden From History* (Pluto Press, 1973).

——, *A New World for Women*, 1977 (Pluto Press, 1978).

Rowbotham, S. and Weeks, J., *Socialism and the New Life* (Pluto Press, 1977).

Royle, E., *Radicals, Secularists and Republicans* (Manchester University Press, 1980).

Rubin, E., editor, *Abortion Politics and the Courts*, 1982 (Greenwood, 1987).

Sager, R., Ryan, F., *Cell Heredity*, 1961 (Wiley & Sons, 1963).

Samuel, R., Stedman Jones, G., editors, *Culture, Ideology, and Politics* (Routledge & Kegan Paul, 1982).

Sanger, M., *The Pivot of Civilization* (Jonathan Cape, 1923).

Schmidt, A., *History and Structure*, 1971 (MIT Press, 1981).

Scruton, R., *Sexual Desire* (Weidenfeld and Nicolson, 1986); *Thinkers of the New Left*, (Longman, 1985).

Seward, A., editor, *Science and the Nation* (Cambridge University Press, 1917).

Sheldrake, R., *The Presence of the Past*, 1988 (Fontana, 1989).

Shepherd, S., Wallis, M., editors, *Coming on Strong: Gay Politics and Culture* (Unwin Hyman, 1989).

Skinner, B., *Reflections on Behaviourism and Society* (Prentice-Hall, 1978).

Soper, K., *Humanism and Anti-Humanism* (Hutchinson, 1986).

Stalin, J., *Anarchism or Socialism?*, 1905–1906 (Foreign Languages Publishing House, 1950).

——, *Dialectical and Historical Materialism*, 1938 (Lawrence & Wishart, 1941).

Stanley Hall, G., *Founders of Modern Psychology* (Appleton, 1912).

Steakley, J., *The Homosexual Emancipation Movement in Germany* (Arno Press, 1975).

Stoianovich, T., *French Historical Method: The Annales Paradigm* (Cornell University Press, 1976).

Stoekel, A., editor, *Georges Bataille, Visions of Excess: Selected Writings 1927–1939* (Manchester University Press, 1983).

Stopes, M., *Married Love* (Critic & Guide Company, 1918).

——, *Contraception (Birth Control)* (John Bale, Sons & Danielsson Ltd, 1923).

Symonds, J.A., *A Problem of Modern Ethics*, private publication (J.S. Symonds, 1896).

Szaz, T., *Sex: Facts, Frauds and Follies* (Basil Blackwell, 1980).

Thompson, E.P., *The Making of the English Working Class*, 1963 (Penguin Books, 1980).

——, *The Poverty of Theory* (Merlin Press, 1978).

Tomkins, S., *The Origins of Mankind* (Cambridge University Press, 1984).

Tomlin, E., *Psyche, Culture and the New Science: The Role of Psychic Nutrition* (Routledge & Kegan Paul, 1985).

Trigg, R., *The Shaping of Man: Philosophical Aspects of Sociobiology* (Blackwell, 1982).

Trilling, L., *The Liberal Imagination*, 1951 (Mercury Books, 1961).

Trotsky, L., *Trotsky's Diary in Exile, 1935* (Harvard University Press, 1958).

Tylor, E., *Primitive Culture*, 1871. Published as *Origins of Culture* (Harper & Row, 1958).

Van de Velde, T.H., *Ideal Marriage* (Heinemann, 1928).

Van der Dennen, J., Falger, V., editors, *Sociobiology and Conflict* (Chapman and Hall, 1990).

Volosinov, V.N., *Freudianism*, 1927 (Academic Press, 1976).

Von Hartmann, E., *The Philosophy of the Unconscious*, 1868 (Trubner, 1884).

Von Krafft-Ebing, R., *Psychopathia Sexualis*, 1892 (Rebman, 1893).

Von Schelling, F.W.J., *Ideas for a Philosophy of Nature*, 1797 (Cambridge University Press, 1988).

Vygotskii, L.S., *Mind in Society*, (Harvard University Press, 1978).

Walker, S., *Animal Learning* (Routledge & Kegan Paul, 1987)

Wallace, A.R., et al., *The Psycho-Physiological Sciences and Their Assailants* (Colby and Rich, 1878).

Watson, J., *Behaviourism*, 1924 (W. W. Norton & Co, 1970).

Weeks, J., *Coming Out*, 1977 (Quartet, 1990).

——, *Sexuality and Its Discontents*, 1985 (Routledge & Kegan Paul, 1986).

——, *Sexuality* (Ellis Horwood and Tavistock Publications, 1986).

Weiss, S., *Race Hygiene and National Efficiency* (University of California Press, 1987).

Westermarck, E., *The Origin and Development of the Moral Ideas* (Macmillan, 1906).

——, *Sociology as a University Study* (John Murray, 1908).

Westwood, G., *Society and the Homosexual* (Victor Gollancz, 1952).

White, E., editor, *Sociobiology and Human Politics* (Gower Publishing: Lexington Books, 1981).

Whitehouse, M., *Whatever Happened to Sex?* (Hodder and Stoughton, 1977).

Williams, B., *Report of the Committee on Obscenity and Film Censorship* (HMSO, 1979).

Williams, R., *Culture and Society 1780–1950*, 1958 (Penguin Books, 1961).

Wolfenden, Sir J., *Report of the Committee on Homosexual Offences and Prostitution* (HMSO, 1957).

Young-Bruehl, E., *Mind and the Body Politic*, 1988 (Routledge, 1989).

——, *Freud on Women: A Reader* (Hogarth Press, 1990).

Periodicals

Archives of Sexual Behaviour
Clinics in Endocrinology and Metabolism
Endocrine Reviews
Feminist Issues
Gender and History
History and Theory
Hormones and Behaviour
Journal of American History
Journal of Contemporary History
Journal of Modern History
Journal of Social History
Oxford Literary Review
Psychoneuroendocrinology
Psychosomatics
Revolutionary Communist
Rouge
Signs
Science
Socialist Review
Sociological Review

Index